The Marriage Scam

The
Marriage Scam

E.S. Williams

Belmont House Publishing

London

The Marriage Scam
is published by Belmont House Publishing

ISBN 0 9548493 5 3

Published by Belmont House Publishing
36 The Crescent
Belmont
SUTTON
Surrey SM2 6BJ

Website www.belmonthouse.co.uk

A Catalogue record for this book is available from the British Library.

This book was first published in September 2013 as:

Seductive Theories of Marriage Education (ISBN 0 9548493 4 5)

Sincere thanks to the Christian brothers and sisters who commented on the text and helped with proof-reading.

The Marrriage Scam

Table of contents:

Preface

To most people it is self-evident that marriage education must be a good thing. And this is especially so in view of the large number of marriages that end in divorce, and the large number of children who are born outside of marriage. Surely marriage education, which aims to help couples achieve happy, long-lasting relationships, must be beneficial for all? But a word of caution: I believe that before we give marriage education our wholehearted approval, we need to understand the actual view of marriage that is being promoted by the marriage educators.

The Marriage Scam sets out to understand what marriage education actually teaches about marriage. As I studied the claims of the marriage education movement, it soon became as clear as day that its proponents are deeply hostile to the biblical concept of marriage as taught in Scripture. Virtually all marriage educators are vehemently opposed to the idea that the wife should submit to her husband. The marriage education movement is quite open about its intention of creating a new marriage culture which is fundamentally opposed to the biblical view. The new way is called 'equal-regard' marriage, in which husband and wife practise mutual submission, and the 'new husband' is taught to accept that the idea of male headship is a thing of the past.

At the heart of marriage education is the notion that for a couple to achieve a happy, long-lasting relationship they need to be taught the skills and techniques of humanistic positive psychology, such as the skill of communicating their deepest feelings, the power of positive affirmation and conflict resolution, hence my term *marriage psycho-education*.

I was surprised to find that the Christian version of marriage education eagerly follows the same agenda as the secular marriage educators, teaching that psychological skills and techniques, combined with some biblical texts, is the pathway to marital happiness. And so, in the name of marriage education, the ideas of humanistic psychology, which have always sought to undermine the Christian faith, are flooding into the Church, thereby diluting the truth of God's Word with the folly of men's ideas.

It was only after I had spent a considerable amount of time studying the influence of psychology on the Christian faith, that I came to understand that the greatest conduit through which godless psychological thinking enters the Church is via the burgeoning Christian marriage education movement. *The Marriage Scam* is a book which explains how the theories of the marriage education movement are misleading many in the Church. *The Marriage Scam* forms a trilogy with my other two books on psychology in the Church, namely, *The Dark Side of Christian Counselling* (2009) and *Christ or Therapy?* (2010).

E.S. Williams

1

Marriage education movement

This book is about the marriage education movement, a movement that has gained much prominence in both the secular and the Christian worlds. No less a figure than US President Barack Obama, setting out his political philosophy in *The Audacity of Hope* (2006), makes the case for marriage education. He asserts that 'research shows that marriage education workshops can make a real difference in helping married couples stay together and in encouraging unmarried couples who are living together to form a more lasting bond'. He believes that policies to strengthen marriage and marriage education are common sense approaches to a large social problem.[1]

Marriage and family issues are firmly on the agenda of the Church on both sides of the Atlantic. In the USA marriage and relationships conferences are now held in towns and cities across the country, featuring popular Christian speakers and entertainers in an atmosphere that combines teaching, entertainment and excitement.

An example is the nationwide marriage enrichment weekend seminar, 'Renewing Your Love', held at the Mel Tillis theatre in Branson, Missouri, that was hosted by Dr Gary Smalley, widely regarded as America's relationship doctor, and James Dobson, who founded Focus on the Family. Over three hundred sites in America, Canada, and the Bahamas were linked via simulcast, reaching an estimated eighty thousand people. Speakers included James and Shirley Dobson and Gary Smalley. Couples were motivated to renew their love through six dynamic sessions. Gary Smalley, a leading exponent of Christian marriage education and prolific author (discussed in chapter 12) was jubilant: 'I've spent over 30 years inspiring couples to increase their marital satisfaction. This event is the culmination of those 30 years of experience, I couldn't be more excited!' He said couples would gain encouragement by learning how to ensure lasting commitment, by discovering the motives behind their personalities and by effectively resolving their biggest conflicts.[2] The cost for a couple attending the two-day seminar was $40.

Another example is 'The Marriage You've Always Wanted' conference, sponsored by Moody Bible Institute. 'Led by Dr Gary Chapman, author of the best-selling *Five Love Languages*, this conference is not a dry, formal marriage seminar—it's a time of fun and discovery that can help you build the love relationship of your dreams. Whether you're getting married in six months—or have been married 60 years—you'll get solutions you can use. With biblical advice and a healthy dose of laughter, Dr Chapman gives valuable tips on breaking unhealthy patterns and choosing to develop a God-honoring, happy marriage. Couples both married and engaged will benefit from practical sessions addressing topics like communication differences, dealing with criticism, understanding love languages, and making sex mutually fulfilling. Join us for a day that will be a highlight for your marriage!' Similar marriage and family life conferences, seminars and road shows are common across the landscape of the USA.

In the UK, 'The Marriage Course' from Holy Trinity Brompton, London, is popular among churches across the doctrinal spectrum. Such is the enthusiasm for marriage seminars that Valentine's Day has been used as a marketing opportunity. An advertising blurb declared that thousands of couples around the world have discovered tools to help them build a strong, lasting and fulfilling relationship. The Marriage Course launched the first national Valentine's Day invitation: 'It's a great opportunity to make a real difference in your local community. Just imagine the impact that strengthened relationships could have in your area.' A romantic Valentine's dinner is used as the platform to give couples a 'taste' of The Marriage Course.[3]

The secular world also has developed a real interest in marriage and relationship education. In California the four-day annual conference of The National Association for Relationship and Marriage Education invites us to 'Come and experience relevant workshops from the experts in relationship education, go home ready with new approaches to strengthen families and marriages, network with your peers from across the nation, and enjoy all that Southern California has to offer including beautiful beaches, Disneyland and lots more!' Plenary speakers include national experts in the field of marriage education, and even the prolific Christian author Gary Smalley and his two sons, Greg and Michael.

In the USA marriage and relationship education programmes are new in the social services arena. The goal is to enhance current relationships and prevent future problems by teaching couples and individuals—generally in a group setting—the skills, attitudes, and behaviours needed to help them form and sustain healthy relationships and marriages. Marriage education differs from marriage therapy in that it is provided to a group of people, whereas marriage therapy is provided one-on-one to a couple by a licensed therapist, who focuses on their particular, deep-seated relationship problems.

So marriage and relationship education is skill-based, educational, and delivered in a group setting.[4] Couples learn listening and problem-solving skills and how to manage their emotions. Programmes help couples discuss and resolve different expectations about their relationship, how to deal with conflict, and some also emphasise the importance of marital virtues such as commitment, loyalty, fairness, and forgiveness.

The Smart Marriages website of the Coalition for Marriage, Family and Couple Education (discussed in chapter 3) has an extensive directory of marriage education programmes and seminars. 'We can all learn how to have successful relationships, and happy families... all the courses listed in this directory will help you become smarter about your marriage or relationship. All the courses teach the basic marriage skills in one format or another.' We are reassured: 'The programs listed work for any couple at any stage – dating, engaged, newlywed, cohabiting, remarried, or on the brink of divorce. Take a class and dramatically improve your odds of success. And, it turns out, an old dog can learn new tricks – you can fall back in love even when your love is on the rocks.'[5] The directory contains literally hundreds of programmes and courses, including Active Relationships, Adventure In Intimacy, Better Marriages, Laugh Your Way to a Better Marriage Seminars, Prevention and Relationship Enhancement Program (PREP), Couple Communication and Practical Application of Intimate Relationship Skills (PAIRS). The agenda of some of these programmes is discussed in later chapters.

The 'marriage' word

At the start of our study we need to recognise that the word 'marriage' is now deeply contentious, for there is no longer a consensus on the meaning of the word. In the 1960s a dictionary defined 'marriage' as 'the social institution under which a man and a woman establish their decision to live as husband and wife by legal commitments, religious ceremonies, etc.'[6] This definition is consistent with biblical truth, namely, that the essential feature of marriage is a union between one man and one woman who become husband and wife. This is the meaning contained in the word 'marriage'.

By the 1990s the Oxford Dictionary was defining marriage as 'the legal union of a man and a woman in order to live together and often to have children', omitting reference to husband and wife.

In our study we shall see that the word 'marriage' is not popular in some quarters. As a consequence the marriage education movement accommodates itself to modern views by using alternative terms, such as 'couples education' or 'relationship education', thus indicating its reluctance to use the word 'marriage', which conveys a large body of traditional and biblical meaning. The term 'marriage and relationship education' is an interesting compromise, for while it uses that word 'marriage' the term carries with it the implication that there is little difference between marriage and a cohabiting relationship. The problem is that when marriage is used in this way it is divested of its essential meaning. Therefore when we hear the word 'marriage' we must carefully discern what the writer or speaker actually means.

Same-sex marriage

Adding confusion to the meaning and purpose of marriage is the issue of same-sex marriages. In the battle for same-sex marriage in the UK, the deputy British Prime Minister, Nick Clegg, in a speech leaked to the press, intended to denounce opponents of gay marriage as 'bigots'. The campaign group, 'Coalition for Marriage', which opposes any change to the law, described Clegg's remarks as intolerant. The chastened deputy Prime Minister, realising that he was in danger of offending many decent people, when he opened an 'equal marriage' reception in London (attended by celebrity campaigners and religious figures who back the legalising of gay marriage) said that the leaked speech was released in error and did not reflect his views.[7]

British Prime Minister, David Cameron, however, made no secret of his intention to introduce legislation to legalise the marriage of same-sex couples. He achieved his wish when The Marriage (same-sex couples) Act was passed by Parliament in early 2013.

The Heritage Foundation in the USA says the arguments for same-sex marriage, 'although often couched in terms of tolerance and inclusion, are based fundamentally on the idea that preserving marriage as unions of husband and wife is a form of bigotry, irrational prejudice, and even hatred against homosexual persons who want the state to license their relationships. As increasing numbers of individuals and institutions, including public officials and governmental bodies, embrace this ideology, belief in marriage as a relationship between a man and a woman likely will come to be viewed as an unacceptable form of discrimination that should be purged from public life through legal, cultural, and economic pressure.'[8]

The homosexual lobby in the USA is not content with the idea of a civil partnership, for they want the union of two men or two women to be recognised as a marriage. As the editors of *National Review* state, 'The campaign for same-sex marriage is primarily motivated by one specific benefit: the symbolic statement by government that committed same-sex relationships are equivalent to marriage'.[9] What same-sex 'marriage' advocates seek is to divest marriage of its essential meaning as a union between one man (husband) and one woman (wife). Indeed, to call same-sex partnerships marriage would be to change the meaning of the word, for same-sex 'marriage' would dispense with the concept of husband and wife. In effect, the same-sex lobby would have usurped the word 'marriage'.

Marriage education

The marriage education movement really started in earnest in 1997 with the creation of the Coalition for Marriage, Family and Couples Education in the USA, and a few years later the Coalition for Relationship Education in the UK. During the last decade there has been a massive growth in marriage education on both sides of the Atlantic, with literally hundreds of organisations, both Christian and secular, delivering marriage education courses, seminars and conferences.

To most people it seems self-evident that marriage education ought to be a good thing, for it is supposed to help couples stay together. This book challenges this assumption, and sets out to show that marriage education, which claims to help couples achieve successful, happy marriages, is, in fact, undermining the traditional, biblical view of marriage that has been at the foundation of family life for centuries in all Western nations. Many readers will be incredulous at this statement. But I ask the reader to bear with me as we carefully examine the ideology that gives rise to and drives the marriage education movement.

Marriage wars

Ever since the permissive 1960s marriage has been a deeply divisive issue in the UK and the USA. On one side of the divide are those who have raised a serious ideological challenge to marriage. A growing body of literature, both academic and popular, has questioned the relevance of marriage in a modern world. Some voices have even sought to persuade us that the 'old-fashioned' institution of marriage should be reinvented.[10] As this way of thinking has gained currency, many people now casually shrug their shoulders and decide that if they aren't happy in marriage they will just walk away.

Marriage has been portrayed as the foundation of the patriarchal society, in which men have power over women. Many have claimed that marriage is a relationship based on sexual inequality that oppresses women and inhibits their psychological growth. Some professionals who write about marriage – counsellors, therapists, academics, and popular authors – appear to have an innate hostility, depicting marriage as archaic and inherently oppressive. Others give it tepid support as just one of many acceptable couple arrangements. The report 'Closed Hearts, Closed Minds', from the Council on Families, under the auspices of the Institute for American Values, analysed twenty textbooks that are used in eight thousand college courses around the USA to teach about marriage and family. The report concluded that these books are a national embarrassment, offering a determinedly bleak view of marriage as more of a problem than a solution.[11] According to columnist John Leo, 'Marriage is depicted more as a convenience than as a commitment. As a result, children appear in the books as almost incidental to marriage and authors expend great energy to show that they don't need two parents and aren't really harmed by divorce.'[12]

In the UK ideological opposition to marriage has been led by feminists and humanists. And among the political and academic establishments there has also been intense hostility to marriage. The terms of reference for a government Committee on Family Policy to oversee the welfare of the family did not even mention marriage. A feature article in the *Daily Telegraph* commented, 'The status to be given to marriage in government policy is turning into one of the great hidden debates of our time... Among ministers and civil servants, the use of the m-word has become contentious.'[13] Ideological considerations have made many politicians fear 'that if they accept that marriage is a good thing, they will be locked into that most forbidden of modern heresies, intolerance of alternative lifestyles'.[14] Few political leaders are prepared to make the link between the family and marriage, for it is no longer politically safe to do so. Opposition to marriage among the political establishment is such that the words 'husband' and 'wife' have been replaced with the word 'partner' in official government reports. The 2010 coalition government in its policy statement says that it 'believes that strong and stable families of all kinds are the bedrock of a strong and stable society'. While claiming to support families, the policy statement does not use the word marriage.[15]

On the other side of the marriage divide are socially conservative thinkers who have always believed that marriage is the foundation of the good society. Others support marriage because of the latest sociological research that shows that marriage is the sensible, healthy choice and good for children. For example, the editors of *National Review* recently stated, 'The reason marriage exists is that the sexual intercourse of men and women regularly produce children... it takes one of each type in our species to perform the act that produces children'. They continue, 'What a healthy marriage culture does is encourage adults to arrange their lives so that as many children as possible are raised and nurtured by their biologic parents in a common household'.[16] A small remnant supports the traditional view that marriage, as taught by Holy Scripture, is an honourable estate ordained by God. In this traditional view of marriage, husband and wife make vows in the presence of God and before witnesses 'to have and to hold, from this day forward, for better, for worse, for richer, for poorer, in sickness and in health, to love and to cherish, as long as we both shall live, according to God's holy ordinance; and thereto I pledge you my trust.' The biblical view of marriage is discussed in chapter 5.

The war over marriage has had major consequences for society. The past four decades have been characterised by a sharp fall in first marriage rates in both the UK and the USA, with a corresponding rise in couples living together who are not married. As a consequence there has been a large increase in the number of children that are born outside wedlock. In both the UK and the USA just under half of all births are to unmarried mothers, half of which are born to women in a cohabiting relationship. These profound social trends have led to changes in family structure characterised by a collapse in the traditional family. A report issued by the National Marriage Project at Rutgers University, USA, in 2005 said that only 63% of American children grow up with both biological parents – the lowest figure in the Western world. As first marriage rates have declined there has been a large increase in the divorce rate. In the 1970s, when more and more states in the USA were adopting no-fault divorce laws, the annual number of divorces increased sharply. It is estimated that at current rates around four out of ten marriages will end in divorce. Divorce rates in the UK, which started from a much lower base, have reached the levels of their American cousins.

While the divorce revolution was gathering momentum the Church stood by uncertain how it should react. Many of the mainline churches even sought an accommodation with the divorce mentality of the time. In 1976 the United Methodist Church, one of the largest mainline Protestant denominations in America at the time, issued a statement which read in part:

> In marriages where the partners are, even after thoughtful reconsideration and counsel, estranged beyond reconciliation, we recognize divorce and the right of divorced persons to remarry, and express our concern for the needs of the children of such unions. To this end we encourage an active, accepting, and enabling commitment of the Church and our society to minister to the needs of divorced persons.'[17]

The Church of England, which for centuries accepted that marriage was an indissoluble lifelong union of one man with one woman until they were parted by death, in 1981 passed a General Synod motion to say 'that there are circumstances in which a divorced person may be married [this means remarried, but they did not want to use the word] in church during the lifetime of a former spouse'.[18] However, such was the uncertainty around the issue of remarriage, that the Synod was unable to define the circumstances in which remarriage in church could take place until 2002.

The Marriage Movement

After four decades of mass divorce, the social consequences are plain for all to see. The idea of the good divorce proved to be an illusion. Divorce did not lead to the psychological growth promised by the marriage therapists, but to economic hardship and unhappy children. There is no longer any doubt that marriage breakdown is bad for men, women and children. A large body of research shows that children of divorce do far worse in every measure of social and educational status.

In the year 2000 a remarkable event occurred in the USA. Because of deep concern about the social consequences of widespread divorce, a group of eminent Americans from all walks of life met together to form a grass roots movement to protect and strengthen marriage and to publish a document entitled 'The Marriage Movement: A Statement of Principles'. Academics and civic and Christian leaders who supported the Marriage Movement, pledged that 'in this decade we will turn the tide on marriage and reduce divorce and unmarried childbearing, so that each year more children will grow up protected by their own two happily married parents and more adults' marriage dreams will come true.' Behind the Movement are three influential organisations, namely, The Coalition for Marriage, Family and Couples Education; the Religion, Culture, and Family Project of the University of Chicago Divinity School; and the Institute for American Values. They explained their grand design in these words:

> WE COME TOGETHER AS SUPPORTERS OF SOMETHING NEW: a grass roots movement to strengthen marriage. We come together to give public voice and direction to this new movement—to

9

explain our intentions, specify our goals, and seek the support of our fellow citizens.

We are teachers and scholars, marriage counselors and marriage educators. We are judges, divorce lawyers, and legal reformers. We are clinicians, service providers, policy analysts, social workers, women's leaders, religious leaders, and advocates for responsible fatherhood. We are people of faith, asking God's blessing in the great task before us. We are agnostics and humanists, committed to moral and spiritual progress. We are women and men, liberals and conservatives, of different races and ethnic groups. We come together to pursue a common goal. We come together for a marriage movement.[19]

The document argues that a large body of research has shown that current rates of divorce, family conflict, and unwed childbearing are not good for children, for adults, or for society.

New research from pioneering marriage educators and therapists are laying out exciting new paths to marital success. Innovative leaders—in state and local government, civic organizations, faith communities, academia, education, child welfare, psychology, marriage education, and therapy—are beginning to focus on the vital new question: What can we do to strengthen marriage? Support for marriage, we emphasize, does not require turning back the clock on desirable social change, promoting male tyranny, or tolerating domestic violence...[20]

We come together to enlarge and energize this emerging effort to renew the marriage vow and the marriage vision. We come together to help more men and women achieve a caring, collaborative, and committed bond, *rooted in equal regard* between spouses.[21] [emphasis mine]

Coalition for Marriage, Family and Couples Education

The Coalition was set up in 1997 by marriage and family therapist Diane Sollee and is dedicated to making marriage education widely available. The goal is to make available in user-friendly, affordable and accessible format research information on what makes marriage work. According to Diane Sollee: 'It's the idea that marriage is skill-based, like football. The way we have it set up now a couple gets married and we send them out there to win based on "love and commitment." That's like asking a football team to win on team spirit... The basis for the smart marriage concept is exciting new research that finds that what is different about the marriages that make it – that go the distance and stay happy – are behaviours or skills. And even more exciting they are simple skills that anyone can learn.'[22]

Religion, Culture, and Family Project of the University of Chicago

This project is directed by Don S. Browning, Professor Emeritus of Ethics and the Social Sciences, Chicago University Divinity School, and funded by a grant from the Lilly Endowment. 'Don Browning has interests in the relation of religious thought to the social sciences, specifically in the way theological ethics may employ sociology, psychology, and the social scientific study of religion. A student of psychology, he has special interests in psychoanalysis, self-psychology, object-relations theory, and evolutionary psychology.'[23] In the book, *Does Christianity teach male headship? The equal-regard marriage and its critics* (2004), edited by David Blakenhorn and Mary Stewart Van Leeuwen, Don Browning makes it clear that he disagrees with the concept of male headship in marriage. He supports what he calls 'equal-regard marriage'.

Institute of American Values

The Institute of American Values, founded in 1987 by David Blankenhorn, is a non-profit, non-partisan think tank in New York City that believes in the importance of marriage for a civilised society. The Institute brings together approximately 100 leading scholars—from across the human sciences and across the political spectrum. The Center for Marriage and Families is a part of the Institute that seeks to study and strengthen marriage as an institution. It holds that marriage opens social opportunity, nurtures bonds between parents and children, enabling the whole person to thrive. The Center's tools are rigorous research, writing based on strong scholarship, engaging ideas in the public square, and contributing intellectually to innovations in public and social policy.[24]

The report, 'Why Marriage Matters', sponsored by the Institute and written by a team of family scholars and sociologists, comments that 'the changes that have swept over American families in the last two generations have inspired a large body of social scientific research and a growing number of marriage education programs aimed at better preparing couples for marriage and better equipping couples with the knowledge, values, and skills required for successful marriage in today's world'.[25] The report says that 'despite its inherent limitations, good social science is a better guide to social policy than uninformed opinion or prejudice'.[26] The main conclusion is that marriage is an important social and public good, associated with a broad array of positive outcomes for children and adults alike that extend to the poor and minority communities.

Relationship education in the UK

Because of the intense political and ideological opposition to traditional marriage in the UK, a movement that uses the word marriage was not likely to receive widespread popular support. To overcome this obstacle the term Couple Relationship Education (CRE) has been coined. The annual National Relationships Education Conference, which met for the first time in 2002, brings together organisations that share an interest in relationship education. It provides an opportunity for both Christian and secular organisations to share ideas and plans for improving their relationship education programmes. Secular participants include Relate, the largest provider of relationship support services in the UK, and the family and parenting support organisations Parenting UK and Positive Parenting. Christian participants include Care for the Family, Marriage Care, and The Marriage Course of Holy Trinity Brompton.

What makes the marriage/relationship education movement in the USA and UK a remarkable achievement is that despite the bitter ideological war over marriage, a large group of people with widely differing beliefs and views on marriage have been able to meet together and agree a common approach. Because the marriage/relationship education agenda is held to be so important liberals and conservatives, Christians and humanists, agnostics and religious leaders have been able to set aside their differences. Because the cause is so important, people and organisations with widely differing worldviews and religious beliefs have become of one mind, and are working together to strengthen marriage and relationships. To achieve common purpose around marriage education they have had to put to one side their religious and ideological differences. Many Christians are now content to join together with unbelievers in the great cause of marriage education.

The thesis of this book

It is not difficult to see that the marriage education movement is founded on a spirit of compromise, whereby Christians, with a biblical view of marriage, and secular humanists, with a psychological view of relationships, have agreed to work together. The marriage movement has stressed that 'people of faith', together with agnostics and humanists, are now engaged in the great task to improve society's understanding of marriage. But what understanding of marriage is it that they are seeking to improve? Our task is to explain the ideas behind the marriage movement and to explore how it is that Christians, whose view of marriage should be based on Scripture, have been able to work together with humanists and agnostics who have a very different view of marriage. The thesis of this book is that marriage education and its cousin, couple relationship education, are a subtle but hugely damaging attack on the biblical view of marriage.

(Endnotes)

1 Cited from: The Relationships Foundation, 'Building Strong Foundations - The Case for Couple Relationship Education' (2009), Report by Michael Clark, Rose Lynas and David Percival, p3
2 Smart Marriages website, Gary Smalley National Retreat/to the village/apology - 4/10/02
3 Website, relationshipcentral.org/valentines
4 What Works in Marriage and Relationship Education? A Review of Lessons Learned with a Focus on Low-Income Couples, http://www.healthymarriageinfo.org/educators/marriage-relationship-resources/index.aspx
5 Smart Marriages website, http://www.smartmarriages.com/directory_browse.html#type_12
6 The Random House Dictionary of the English Language, editor Laurence Urdang, 1968, p819
7 *The Guardian*, 'Nick Clegg's office withdraws "bigots" email about same-sex marriage', 11 September 2012
8 The Heritage Foundation, 'The Price of Prop 8', Published on October 22, 2009 by Thomas Messner

13

9 *National Review*, 'The Case for Marriage', September 20, 2010, p20

10 Heritage Foundation, 'Change Views on Marriage', Published on June 30, 2009 by Rebecca Hagelin

11 'Marriage bashing a la mode' by John Leo, cited from *US News*, September 1997

12 Ibid.

13 Clifford Longley. 'What exactly do we mean by a family?' *Daily Telegraph*, 30 January 1998

14 Janet Daley. 'Why are they afraid of using the M-word?' *Daily Telegraph*, 20 January 1998

15 'The Coalition: our programme for government', signed by David Cameron and Nick Clegg, issued by the Cabinet Office, Publication date: May 2010

16 *National Review*, September 20, 2010, 'The Case for Marriage', pp16-20

17 Cited in The National Marriage Project, 'The Evolution of Divorce', W. Bradford Wilcox, p 82

18 Norman Doe, *The Legal Framework of the Church of England*, London, Oxford University Press, 1996, pp377-8

19 The Marriage Movement, 'A Statement of Principles', 2000, Coalition for Marriage, Family and Couples Education: Institute for American Values: Religion, Culture, and Family Project, University of Chicago Divinity School, p3

20 Ibid. p4

21 Ibid. p4

22 Smart Marriages website, Diane Sollee, Jon Galuckie interviews Diane Sollee, founder of the Coalition for Marriage, Family and Couples Education, LLC (CMFCE)

23 The Marriage Institute website, Don S. Browning, Alexander Campbell Professor Emeritus of Ethics and the Social Sciences, the Divinity School. http://www.marriageinstitute.ca/IM/presenters.html

24 Center for Marriage and Families website, http://www.centerformarriageandfamilies.org/

25 *Why Marriage Matters* (2nd edition), 'Twenty-Six Conclusions from the Social Sciences', Institute for American Values, second edition 2005, Executive summary, p1

26 Ibid. p4

2

Divorce culture

In the first chapter we saw that the sponsors of the marriage education movement have based their hope for improving marriage on sociological research. The three organisations behind the marriage movement are all committed to the latest research findings from sociology and psychology. Their pledge to strengthen marriage and reduce divorce is based on the belief that sociological research has shown how we can improve our relationships. We are told by the Marriage Movement that 'new research from pioneering marriage educators and therapists are laying out exciting new paths to marital success'.[1] Even the clergy are encouraged to improve their faith-based marriage preparation programmes by incorporating the latest research.[2]

But here we must pause for a moment, for not so long ago sociological research was telling us that marriage was an oppressive institution and that divorce was a useful device that provided a way out for unhappy women. Yet we are now being asked to believe that the findings of sociological research can improve our marriage relationships. What has brought about such a change of heart among those who have been so ideologically opposed to marriage? To come to terms with the marriage education movement, and the thinking behind it, we need to understand the anti-marriage ideology that led to mass divorce in the second half of the twentieth century. So the starting point of our study must be to examine the ideological link between the divorce culture and the marriage education movement.

Stay together for the sake of the children

During the first half of the twentieth century it was self-evident to all that children were better off being brought up in a family by their own mother and father. Common sense shouted from the rooftops that a broken home was bad for children, and most parents readily accepted they had a duty towards their children to maintain the family home. Divorce was regarded as shameful because of the hurt and suffering caused to children. This meant that divorce was seen as the last resort, for the family was simply too important to be broken up on the whim of an unhappy husband or wife. It was expected that father and mother would resolve their differences and stay together for the sake of the children. Anyone who suggested otherwise would have been regarded as perverse and blind to the most basic facts of life. That is how things were in the 1950s, before the ideology of mass divorce had taken root in Western society.

Following the Second World War there was a gradual increase in divorce in both the UK and the USA as changes in the divorce law made it easier for a marriage to be dissolved. But the increase in divorce presented a moral dilemma, for it was still widely believed that the break-up of the home was deeply damaging to children. In the 1950s there was still a strong taboo against divorce, and those parents who followed the divorce path felt guilty for betraying their children.

Sociological research – marriage is a patriarchal institution

However, within little more than a decade this common-sense view had been overturned, for in the 1960s the so-called sociological experts produced research 'evidence' to show that children were actually *better off* out of a family in which the parents were unhappy. In the 1970s and 80s it became increasingly common for sociologists to condemn marriage as an oppressive institution, and a vast literature declared that divorce was a legitimate response to an unhappy marriage and the oppression of the patriarchal family.

Two examples demonstrate the deep antagonism that mainstream sociology felt towards marriage and the traditional family. The eminent sociologist, Jessie Bernard, published *The Future of Marriage* in 1972. This book was immediately acclaimed as a seminal contribution to the literature of marriage and sex roles. Bernard writes: 'Some of the shocks that marriage may produce have to do with the lowering of status that it brings to women. For, despite all the clichés about the high status of marriage, it is for women a downward status step.'[3] She insists that the psychological and emotional cost of becoming a wife shows up in the increasing unhappiness of wives with the passage of time and in their increasingly negative and passive outlook on life.[4] Bernard informs her readers that at marriage a woman moves from the status of female to that of neuter being. The decline in sexual attractiveness of women is attributable to their role as wife; when they become mothers this 'neutralization' is carried even further. These changes contribute to the sad picture of the mental health of married women.[5] This book was little more than a tirade against marriage in the name of sociology.

In her book, *Housewife* (1974), Ann Oakley, a mainline British sociologist, whose books and papers are widely used in British universities and colleges, calls for an outright ideological rejection of marriage and the family. She disparages the role of the housewife, whom she sees as subordinate to men,[6] for housework is demeaning, pathogenic, and directly opposed to the possibility of human self-actualisation. Any woman who expresses contentment with her role as a housewife is guilty of anti-feminism.[7] Oakley is also opposed to the family. She writes that the family's gift to women is a direct apprenticeship in the housewife's role. 'For this reason, the abolition of the housewife role requires the abolition of the family, and the substitution of more open and variable relationships.' She acknowledges that, 'if the family goes, so, of course does marriage'.[8] Oakley believes that the only way for women to achieve the ideological revolution that they desire is to abolish the housewife's role, and therefore, abolish marriage and the family. But even that is not enough. Women must also teach their daughters not to be housewives.

So the dominant trend in sociological thinking was increasingly to view divorce as the solution for the social problems caused by the 'oppressive' model of the patriarchal family. It is not surprising that in this climate sociological research set about producing 'evidence' to show that children benefited from divorce. A review of a large body of sociological research concluded that discord and conflict in the home can be more detrimental than the father's absence; therefore, the reviewers concluded, 'one is forced to prefer a "good" one-parent home for a child'.[9] This 'evidence' spread the message that parents in an unhappy marriage should divorce for the sake of their children. Thus the instinctive common-sense consensus of previous generations was overturned by the 'scientific findings' of modern sociology.

The result was that parents were told that it was better for their children to be removed from family conflict by means of divorce, than to remain in a family with their unhappy father and mother. The experts claimed that following the divorce children rapidly adjust to their new family circumstances and therefore the effects would be short-lived. Some social commentators asserted that divorce did not harm children, even suggesting that it might help their development.

The message was clear—marriage is simply one lifestyle choice that, while it suits some people, is potentially dangerous in that it often leads to male domination and exploitation. Divorce is a useful resource for liberating women and children from unsuitable family arrangements. On the basis of its research findings, sociology successfully removed divorce from the moral arena by presenting it as a pragmatic solution to a social problem. Sociologists derided the idea that divorce had a moral dimension as old-fashioned, superstitious nonsense. Moreover, those who held such views had no right to impose their moral beliefs on other people. They should keep their views to themselves, and not disturb the consciences of others with their outdated morality. It never occurred to these experts that they were imposing *their* beliefs on an entire society.

The sociological views described above can be read in any standard textbook, and were widely taught to students in schools, colleges and universities. They also received wide coverage in the popular news media, so that most people were aware of the 'evidence' that disparaged marriage. Sadly, many Christians modified their views on marriage and divorce to take account of the 'evidence' provided by sociological research. As a consequence much of what goes for Christian teaching today is an accretion of sociological theory with some biblical texts. Politically correct sociological theories have become the new orthodoxy on family and marriage, replacing the biblical view that held sway until the middle of the last century.

Psychological research – divorce for the sake of your children

Psychological research published in the 1960s claimed that children did not experience divorce as a negative event. In 1971 a review of ten years of psychological research concluded that while a child's separation from his family caused short-term distress, it was of little direct importance as a cause of long-term disorder. The message was that the break-up of the family caused by divorce was only a minor influence.[10]

The experts claimed that, on the basis of their research, children, while feeling initially upset and downcast, on the whole do not have negative feelings towards their parents' divorce, and sometimes found that it facilitated their development. Indeed, it could be the beginning of the child's emotional recovery, as a significant proportion of children thought divorce was best for all concerned. Antisocial behaviour that occurred at the time of the family break-up was due not to the divorce but to the discord that preceded it. The claim was that many children from unhappy homes felt greater security and happiness after the divorce of their parents.

Much of the research showed what most academics wanted to believe—that it was all right to divorce and that the children did not really mind if their parents did so. Once the research papers were published the findings were soon regarded as 'scientific' evidence, and as such, had an enormous influence on society's thinking. And so it was that psychological research made the amazing claim that children do not really mind the divorce of their parents.

An article on the women's page of *The Times* provides a typical example of the message that was spread by the popular media in the late 1960s. It addressed the question of whether the children of divorce are worse off. The journalist was incredulous that many parents of their own free will preferred to perpetuate their 'negative relationship in order to carry out what they consider to be their inescapable responsibility – that of rearing their young in the accepted home-plus-mother-plus-father syndrome. Why do they think that this almost inevitably strained state of affairs is better for the children? There is no proof that a child of one marriage, later brought up in another, fares better or worse than a child whose parents, though at odds with each other, keep their marriage going.'[11] Feature articles in newspapers and women's magazines made sure that the 'evidence' from psychological research received wide publicity. As a consequence the idea that divorce did not harm children became common currency.

The Courage to Divorce (1974), written by two social workers, gives the basic message that divorce could liberate children and bring them psychological benefits. The authors claimed that if a divorce was handled well, 'it is more likely to be a potentially liberating experience which restructures family life in a healthier way and provides potential emotional gratification for all family members'.[12] The authors insist that because of the very nature of their life experience, children of divorce have particular advantages and opportunities that their peers may not have. A properly handled divorce is a relatively non-traumatic event for children, and children of divorce have a unique opportunity of experiencing a variety of family styles.[13] The authors say that divorce is also likely to improve the relationship between non-resident fathers and their children, as they are liable to pay more attention to their children than unhappily married fathers do.[14]

In their book, *Marriage and How to Survive It* (1983), psychologists Dougal Mackay and Jill Frankham claimed that marriage experts are unanimous in rejecting the idea that a marriage should be preserved for the sake of the children. 'Divorce may cause them [children] distress but a bad marriage will have an even worse effect on them psychologically.'[15] Therefore the argument that parents should stay together for the sake of the children does not really hold up, for a bad marriage can do more harm than a broken home. The authors claim that research findings indicate clearly that the children whose parents have divorced are much better adjusted in many key aspects than those from unhappy homes. 'This suggests that if you do what is right for you [get a divorce], you will be doing right by the rest of your family.'[16]

All these claims, which are based on research findings, are wildly wide of the mark, as marriage educators now admit. The reason that these claims are so wide of the mark is because they are based on ideological research that sets out to prove what it already believes. The damage that divorce causes to children is well documented, and described in some detail in my book, *The Great Divorce Controversy* (2000).[17]

In *Divorce: The American Experience* (1975), Joseph Epstein observed how ready society was to receive the new wisdom. 'Once upon a time – and not so very long ago at that – people who had a bad marriage often stayed together "for the sake of the children". Today people who have a bad marriage could well as often bust up their marriage "for the sake of the children". Psychologists, marriage counselors, clergymen (excluding Roman Catholics), lay people, everyone in fact seems to have fallen in step with the new conventional wisdom on the subject of divorce and children. This wisdom holds that a divorce is preferable to bringing up children in a loveless home; that, in other words, a broken home is psychologically healthier for children than a damaged one.'[18]

By the 1980s there was a large body of research findings that delivered a clear message. Parents had a responsibility towards their children to terminate their unhappy marriages, for divorce was a means of rescuing children from conflict and allowing them a second chance of finding a happy home—divorcing parents were actually doing their children a good turn and should no longer feel guilty. This message was spread far and wide by experts who were ideologically opposed to marriage. In *Must Divorce Hurt Children?* (1982), Ruth Inglis commented that 'the don't stay together for the sake of the children' lobby was vociferous and campaigning.[19] The media took up the call to correct the false view that parents should stay together for the sake of their children.

Psychotherapeutic divorce

In the eyes of society mass divorce ceased to be a problem and became, instead, a valuable resource, which offered people freedom from unhappy and restrictive marriages. Psychological theory introduced the idea that marriage, divorce and remarriage might be a better way of life than the traditional Christian ideal of marriage until death. A 'good' divorce was portrayed as offering opportunities for inner renewal and self-expression. Parents were invited to open their minds to the possibility that divorce may be a creative rather than a destructive act, and that it could be a better choice for all concerned, including the children.

Writing in *Divorce as a Developmental Process* (1988), Judith Gold said that divorce could result in positive growth for the individual. Indeed, further personal development may not occur if the marriage remained intact. 'For men, women and children involved, divorce, so common today—indeed so familiar, can be used to catalyze constructive individual psychological development.'[20]

21

A consequence of the emphasis on psychological wellbeing was that people started to believe that they should feel good all the time, and when they did not then someone, often their spouse, was to blame for stunting their psychological growth. The effect of this view on commitment to marriage was catastrophic; couples were led to believe that they should feel committed to their marriage only so long as it provided the 'feel good' factor, with ample scope for psychological growth. Failure to achieve psychological growth meant that the marriage was to blame and should be brought to an end.

Ministers of religion, who were uncertain how to advise those who were seeking divorce, were captivated by the psychological approach. According to the analysis of Barbara Whitehead in *The Divorce Culture* (1997), 'Mainline religious denominations led the procession into psychotherapy... Unlike the mainliners, evangelicals tended to use psychology to support traditional religious teaching on marriage and the family, although over time they too came to view marital dissolution in more psychological terms.'[21]

Increasingly the Christian view of marriage became submerged in psychological theory. The 'old-fashioned' biblical view of marriage was almost embarrassing, and certainly no longer relevant in a contemporary society that had access to the wisdom that comes from sociological research and the latest offerings of psychotherapy. Moreover, the evangelical mind had for long been favourably disposed to the idea that the essence of marriage was psychological compatibility. Many argued for a form of marriage that met the emotional needs of husband and wife. When the emotional relationship breaks down then there is no true marriage and divorce is the remedy. Psychotherapists were supposed to be the experts in identifying psychological incompatibility, for they knew when a marriage had ceased to fulfil emotional needs. Their task was to help the couple separate with the least trauma and even to achieve a good divorce.

Many Christian denominations felt comfortable with the values of psychotherapy and were happy to go along with its supposed expertise. Pastors would do their best for couples who were psychologically incompatible, but having no clear biblical advice to offer, they were relieved to be able to rely on psychotherapy for help. Christian pastors became careful not to give judgemental advice that might cause psychological damage to unhappy couples. The counselling advice offered by marriage therapists was characterised by a non-judgemental approach that claimed to take a morally neutral stand, although many therapists were ideologically in favour of easy divorce, and many therapists were themselves divorcees. Unhappy individuals would be told of the potential benefits of being freed from a restrictive, stifling marriage. They would also be reassured that divorce was not harmful to their children.

It followed that those seeking the psychological benefits of divorce should be aided in their effort to make the break. Trying to save crumbling marriages at all costs was seen as an archaic belief that had no place in a modern world. 'Marriage counselors and psychotherapists,' wrote Morton Hunt in the *New York Times* as early as 1967, 'have been adopting the view that where a marriage seems unlikely ever to become satisfying and reasonably free of conflicts, it is proper to help the client get out of it... Divorce counselors would be the surgeons of marriage, wielding the knife when necessary, but managing the operation so as to minimise the damage, speed the convalescence, and maximize the chance of the patient's full health.'[22]

Morton Hunt went on to remind his readers that those who believe that they should 'stay together for the sake of the children' are mistaken, because the evidence gathered by social psychologists pointed in exactly the opposite direction. According to the evidence, children, however distressed they may be at the time of the break-up of the home, are in the long run less damaged by the divorce than they would have been if their parents had remained together. In Hunt's opinion, divorce counselling would 'avoid much of the misery involved in the actual break-up, shorten the interregnum between the old love and the new, and maximize the chances of success in the second marriage'.[23]

Mass divorce led to the belief that psychotherapists were the experts who could offer advice to those in unhappy marriages. The psychotherapeutic industry was not slow in seeing the enormous commercial opportunity that was opening up, for there was money to be made in counselling those in unhappy marriages. In 1966 there were only about 1,800 experts practising in the field of marital therapy, according to the Department of Health and Human Services in the USA. In 2001 the

American Association for Marriage and Family Therapy listed forty-seven thousand marriage and family therapists.

Ideological hostility to marriage

By the 1990s the profession of marriage and family therapy was dominated by liberally-minded therapists, with many feminists and divorcees among their number, who were so ideologically opposed to traditional marriage that they could hardly bear to use the word. Professor William Doherty, Director of the Marriage and Family Therapy Program at the University of Minnesota, explains how therapists sought to justify their opposition to marriage: 'The critique is that "marriage" marginalizes cohabiting couples and especially gay and lesbian couples. Most marital therapists, when giving professional presentations, use the term "couples therapy" or "couples counselling." The list of presentations at national conferences of marriage and family therapists contains multiple references to "couples" and scant references to "marriage".'[24] Professional family and marital therapists were so hostile to marriage, as we shall see in chapter 3, they actually encouraged divorce on the spurious grounds that by doing so they were helping children.

Professor Doherty reported that over 60 percent of marriage and family therapists are 'neutral' on the subject of marriage or divorce in providing therapy.[25] Doherty has also provided us with a real-life example of the type of counselling that was being delivered by marital therapists. He describes the experience of Marsha, a newly-married young wife, who felt something was wrong with her marriage and so decided to consult a marriage therapist. The counsellor starts by telling Marsha that she must learn to trust her feelings. 'Following is how Marsha later recounted the conversation with the counselor: Marsha: "What do you mean, trust my feelings?" Counselor: "You know you are not happy in your marriage." Marsha: "Yes, that's true." Counselor: "Perhaps you need a separation in order to figure out whether you really want this marriage." Marsha: "But I love Paul and I am committed to him." Counselor: "The choice is yours, but I doubt that you will begin to feel better until you start to trust your feelings and pay attention to your unhappiness." Marsha: "Are you saying I should get a divorce?" Counselor: "I'm just urging you to trust your feelings of unhappiness." A stunned Marsha decided not to return to that counsellor, a decision the counsellor no doubt perceived as reflecting Marsha's unwillingness to take responsibility for her own happiness.'[26]

In his article, 'The Marriage Problem', David Blankenhorn makes the point that in the early 1990s 'few scholars, and even fewer academic professional associations, dared even to address the topic of marriage, much less suggest that marriage might be a beneficial institution worthy of societal support. In fact, two of the most relevant professional associations, the National Council on Family Relations and the American Association of Marriage and Family Therapy, consistently refused to address this subject.' He is incredulous that 'an organization with the word marriage in its name had by the mid-1990s long since abandoned any commitment to, or even interest in, marriage.'[27] It is vital for us to recognise that the ethos of the marriage and family industry was intensely hostile towards marriage.

Conclusion

The first point to emerge from our review of the divorce culture is the intense antagonism to marriage felt by sociologists, psychologists, and marriage and family therapists. Many psychotherapists have such an aversion to traditional marriage that they can barely bring themselves to use the word. As we investigate the marriage education movement we will see that this hostility is directed in particular against the biblical view of marriage described in chapter 5. But the advent of the marriage education movement has been characterised by a remarkable turnaround regarding 'marriage' in general, as the hostility once directed towards traditional marriage has been transformed into enthusiasm for a new sociological version of marriage.

The growth of the psychotherapy industry, and in particular the profession of marriage and family therapy, in the second half of the twentieth century has had a major impact on the way people view their marriages. The notion that the purpose of marriage is to meet our emotional needs and make us feel good about ourselves was widely taught and readily accepted by a society fast becoming more permissive in its thinking. The therapeutic industry presented divorce as a resource that both protected women from oppressive marriages and offered them opportunities for psychological growth.

The second point to emerge from our study of the divorce culture is the unreliable nature of sociological research. We have seen how the research findings of sociology and psychology were used to convince parents that divorce was the preferred option for their marriage difficulties. Sociological research gave rise to the false belief that divorce does not really harm children, a false belief that had a massive impact on legitimising the divorce culture.

Why was the research so wrong? It is vitally important for us to understand the answer to this question—the reason is because it was not authentic scientific research, but rather pseudo-scientific research based upon ideology. The presupposed ideology behind the research was that traditional marriage is, by its very nature, an oppressive institution that harms women, and the researchers simply set out to confirm this belief. Additionally, the research findings were based upon subjective rather than objective data, on feelings and personal impressions rather than observable and measurable facts that could be reliably counted and measured. The crucial point for us to understand is that ideological research sets out to prove what it already believes. So we must understand that ideological research is not *scientific* research, and its findings are inherently unreliable and totally predictable. It follows that research by sociologists who are deeply hostile to marriage is bound to prove that divorce is a good thing and that children don't suffer from divorce.

We need to bear in mind this inherent flaw in ideological research as we examine the marriage education movement. If previous sociological research on divorce has now been proved to be so wide of the mark, (as we shall see in chapter 3), how can we naively accept the claims of sociological research produced by marriage educators who are using it to promote a particular view of marriage? Much of the so-called research in the field of marriage education is done by people who are opposed to the biblical view of marriage. Therefore, in order to find the truth about marriage and divorce we must always start with Scripture, not with the dubious findings of sociological research. And Scripture tells us that God hates divorce (Malachi 2.16), so how can it be good for children?

Christians need to know and remember that authentic science has never and will never contradict anything in Scripture. Thus, to avoid being deceived by the claims of ideologically based 'science', Christians must always examine the ideological position of those behind the research, and most importantly, examine the claims made by research in the light of what Scripture teaches on the subject.

(Endnotes)

1 The Marriage Movement, 'A Statement of Principles', 2000, Coalition for Marriage, Family and Couples Education: Institute for American Values: Religion, Culture, and Family Project, University of Chicago Divinity School, p4

2 Ibid. p21

3 Jessie Bernard, *The Future of Marriage*, Yale University Press, 1972, p38

4 Ibid. p41

5 Ibid. pp41-42

6 Ann Oakley, *Housewife*, Allen Lane, 1974, p237

7 Ibid. pp222, 224

8 Ibid. p236

9 Elizabeth Herzog and Cecilia E. Sudia, 'Children in Fatherless Families', in *Review of Child Development Research.* vol. 3, University of Chicago Press, 1973, p220.

10 Michael Rutter. 'Parent-child separation: psychological effects on the children', *Journal of Child Psychology and Psychiatry*, 12, 1971, pp233-60.

11 Diana Kareh. 'The shaky state of the union', *The Times*, London, 16 January 1968.

12 Susan Gettleman and Janet Markowitz, *The Courage to Divorce*, New York, Simon & Schuster, 1974, p83

13 Ibid. p86

14 Ibid. p94

15 Dougal Mackay and Jill Frankham, *Marriage and How to Survive It*, Loughton, Essex, Judy Piatkus Publishers, 1983, p139

16 Ibid. p141

17 ES Williams, *The Great Divorce Controversy*, Belmont House Publishing, 2000.

18 Joseph Epstein, *Divorce: The American Experience*, London, Cape, 1975, p178

19 Ruth Inglis, *Must Divorce Hurt Children?* London, Temple Smith, 1982, p37

20 Judith H. Gold (ed.), *Divorce as a Developmental Process*, Washington D.C., American Psychiatric Press, 1988, introduction, p xi and p xiv

21 Barbara Dafoe Whitehead, *The Divorce Culture*, New York, Alfred A. Knopf, 1997, p49

22 Morton Hunt, 'Help wanted: Divorce Counselor', *New York Times*, 1 January 1967

23 Ibid.

24 'How Therapists Threaten Marriages', William J. Doherty, (The Responsive Community, 7, 31-42), cited from Smart Marriages website

25 'Rethinking Divorce Laws – Fault or No Fault?' by Muller Davis. (This article appeared in *The Christian Century*, June 5-12, 2002, pp28-31)

26 'How Therapists Threaten Marriages', William J. Doherty, (The Responsive Community, 7, 31-42), cited from Smart Marriages website

27 'The Marriage Problem' by David Blankenhorn, *American Experiment Quarterly*, vol. 6, no1, Spring 2003

3

Diane Sollee and Smart Marriages

The counselling offered by marriage and family therapists during the second half of the twentieth century did not lead to the promised land of psychological growth and happiness. On the contrary, the misery caused by widespread divorce was obvious to all, and forced the psychotherapeutic world to rethink its approach. The disgraceful advice offered by psychotherapists registered with the Association of American Marriage and Family Therapists was gaining notoriety, as more and more people became aware that they were not helping couples in marital distress, but were, in effect, *agents provocateurs* actually fomenting martial dissent and divorce among their clientele.

Marriage therapy promotes the good divorce

By the 1990s it was undeniable that mass divorce was causing real suffering among children and even among men and women, who often regretted their decision to divorce. And many people in society were becoming increasingly alarmed at the role of therapists and counsellors in encouraging families to break up.

The Good Divorce (1994), written by the former Director of the Marriage and Family Therapy Training Program at the University of Southern California, illustrates the mindset that was common among marriage and family therapists. The author, psychologist Constance Ahrons, starts by telling us of her acrimonious first divorce in 1965 that affected her two daughters. (For the record, she has been divorced twice.) 'I was the one who left, and for two years my husband and I battled constantly over custody, visitation and child support. There were private detectives, a kidnapping, several lawyers, and two years of legal fees that took me ten years to pay off. That painful time of my life was over thirty years ago and even now it is hard to write about.'

But her painful experience did not stop her from declaring that 'the good divorce' is not a contradiction in terms. 'A good divorce is one in which both adults and children emerge at least as emotionally well as they were before the divorce. Because we have been inundated with negative stories about divorce, divorce immediately carries with it a negative association. Even though we have difficulty conjuring up positive images of divorce, the reality is that most people feel their lives improved after divorce.'[1] Her campaign to promote the good divorce was based on the false claim that divorce improves most people's lives.

She pronounces her advice: 'If people are going to divorce and remarry (and even re-divorce) in droves, as by all predictions they are, then structuring a good divorce process, family by family, has become absolutely essential. Our sanctioning process must be processed into our dreams of the good life, not treated as the root cause of all our social nightmares.'[2] She asserts that families of divorce should be legitimised in order to shatter the deeply ingrained myth 'that only in a nuclear family can we raise healthy children'. She argues that the myth that the only normal family is the nuclear family causes immeasurable harm to the children of divorce and can break kinship ties.[3]

Ahrons challenges her readers' basic beliefs about marriage. 'Your old belief may have been that you'd stay married "till death do us part". In order to work toward a good divorce, you must first challenge your fundamental beliefs about marriage.'[4] She says that 'if we could change our basic belief about the "shoulds" of marriage being "till death us do part" we might be in a better position to acknowledge which problems are relationship-breakers... Your new assumptions will provide the foundation for making positive family changes and implementing a good divorce.'[5] So Ahrons, a trainer of marriage and family therapists, with her self-centred logic, wants to change the traditional belief that marriage is a lifelong union in order to legitimise divorce.

The claim of Ahrons that divorce does not harm children is misleading. An article by American family lawyer Muller Davis presents a more realistic picture. He writes, 'Divorce is a disruption of the collective interests of the family by the self-interest of one or both of the spouses. Divorce is selfish. In 35 years of practicing family law, I have seldom encountered a spouse who obtained a divorce out of concern for his or her partner or for the sake of their children.' He quotes the well-known facts about divorce. An absent father is likely to spend less money on his children's education and to leave them less protected and more vulnerable to abuse, and his daughters are more likely to become pregnant as teenagers. 'Children of divorce perform less well in school, are less likely to graduate and less likely to matriculate into college. The prevalence of delinquency in broken homes is 10 to 15 percent higher than in intact homes. Current findings indicate that children may suffer long-term negative effects from divorce. For example, significant numbers experience moderate to severe depression and difficulty in establishing love relationships. Children of divorced parents are two to three times more likely to dissolve their own marriages than are children of intact marriages. The divorce process itself has a decidedly adverse effect on children. Almost no child wants his parents to divorce.'[6]

The Good Divorce is little more than an attempt of the twice-divorced marital therapist to justify her actions. The book demonstrates the deep aversion that many marriage therapists feel towards the traditional family of father, mother and children. It is no surprise that many people do not agree with the sentiments of the author. A reviewer on Amazon writes: 'I totally agree with some other readers that the book offers nothing except relief from guilt for breaking up a marriage and family; and that the author's purpose for writing the book was to justify her own actions in leaving her husband and hurting her daughter in the process… You know, if my wife (now ex-wife) had not been able to surround herself with two or three so-called friends who were divorce proponents, and this lousy book, we might have had a fighting chance of reconciling our marriage. And my children, our extended families (both sides), and I wouldn't be hurting so terribly now. I can't blame everything on this book, obviously, but it was certainly not helpful, and probably harmful.'[7]

And another: 'As a very successful child of a "good divorce," I cannot think of a more destructive book published in the last 15 years. Despite the fact that a divorce is sometimes necessary (in the case of abusive marriages, for example), the phrase "good divorce" is an oxymoron! This book is not written with the well-being of children in mind, but rather with the well-being of the parents. The very idea that there is ideally no one to blame in the break-up of a marriage is ludicrous.'[8] This book certainly reveals the attitude of many in the marriage and family therapy profession. There is no doubt that the underlying philosophy is to justify and even encourage divorce.

Diane Sollee – mother of marriage education

Diane Sollee, when she was a Director of the Association of American Marriage and Family Counseling during the late 1980s, became aware that her profession was in deep trouble, as more and more people – having read books like *The Good Divorce* – were becoming highly critical of the role of marriage therapists. She attempted to defend her profession: 'The experts used to be saying – and I was one of them – that women do better single than married and that marriage doesn't really matter for kids. Now the research is coming in, and it says whoops, we weren't right. Married women do better on everything you can measure: children's well-being, sexual satisfaction, financial well-being.'[9] And here is Sollee's rather weak excuse, 'When we were saying it doesn't matter in the '60s and '70s and '80s, we didn't have the experience of enough kids in a culture when families were breaking down. It was just our best guess.'[10]

So on the basis of their 'best guess', marriage therapists had blithely advised hundreds of thousands of men and women to seek a divorce! They had been instrumental in the break-up of hundreds of thousands of families. They had caused untold suffering and misery to millions of children. And to quote Sollee, 'whoops, we weren't right'. No change of heart here, then; no remorse for the broken families and hurting children. Instead, Sollee astutely recognised the danger of her profession being exposed as the charlatans that they were. The concern was to rescue their professional careers, not to make amends for the appalling injustice and suffering that they had perpetrated by their outrageous advice. If they had not been so ideologically blind, not so given over to their hatred of marriage, then it would have been obvious to them that children were better off within the family created by the marriage of their parents. Moreover, the advice of marriage therapists was not in reality based on 'a best guess', but on the flawed ideological research that had come from the mindset of psychology and sociology.

A perceptive journalist, clearly disturbed by the role played by marriage therapy, asked Diane Sollee in 1989 why, with so many marriage therapists being trained and registered, the divorce rate was not going down. Sollee was unable to answer the question, for she knew that when it came to helping couples to find ways to stay together, marriage and family therapists were highly ineffective. She realised that her profession was in deep trouble. She knew that marriage therapy was not the answer, and was smart enough to realise that things could not go on the way they were. As she thought around the issue she slowly became aware of a number of marriage education programmes that were being developed by members of her profession. She recognised the close link between marital therapy and marriage enrichment programmes, for both were founded on the same psychotherapeutic principles.

And then she saw an opportunity—the answer was *psycho-education* not *psychotherapy*. So Sollee made the decision to immerse herself in the new field of marriage-skills training.[11] An article in the *Psychotherapeutic Networker* comments: 'What pulled her out of the crisis over her professional direction was learning about a new wave of educational and skills-training programs that took direct aim at the high divorce rate by teaching couples strategies for dealing with marital conflict before they landed in a therapist's office or in divorce court. Soon Sollee was a convert, and even gave the new movement a name: marriage education.'[12] Her ambition was to expand the visibility of these programmes around the country.

Start of the marriage education movement

In a speech at the Conference on Communitarian Pro-Family Policies in Washington, DC, Diane Sollee spoke about increasing access to marital therapy. She explained, 'I am a marriage and family therapist who has spent the past twenty years at the national level doing just that – working hard to increase access to therapy and counseling. I concentrated on increasing the numbers of practitioners, persuading insurers to reimburse for marital therapy, and convincing the public of its effectiveness. Until recently, I believed this was the best way to strengthen marriages and prevent divorce. However, in twenty years, while the numbers of therapists and access have increased dramatically, the divorce rate hasn't budged – it's held steady at 50 per cent'[13]

She said her work at the American Association for Marriage and Family Therapy (AAMFT) involved travelling across the country and around the world checking out the best and brightest the profession had to offer. 'Over the past ten years I became convinced that it is the pioneering work focused on skills-based education that offers the solution.' She related the parable of 'the dedicated marital therapist working the river bank. Day after day he pulls drowning couples from the river. He is only able to save about 20%, and can bear it no longer. He decides to walk upstream to see if there is any way to keep couples from falling in. Thirty years ago, a handful of therapists, discouraged at how tough it was to revive the marriages which made it in for marital therapy, set out to find an approach that made better sense. One they could live with. These marriage education pioneers (Mace, Guerney, Miller, Olson, Gordon, etc) decided they had to teach couples how to keep from falling in the river.'[14]

Her parable is an attempt to justify the work of a profession which has no basis in reality. We have seen that marriage therapists were not pulling drowning couples from the river of marriage difficulty, but were removing their lifebelts. Now these same people, with their same ideological hostility to traditional marriage, are going upstream to carry out their activities on even more couples, even before they fall into the river. The hope is that if couples can be trained in the skills and tools offered by marriage psycho-education then there will be fewer drowning couples. The profession that caused so much unnecessary suffering has cleverly reinvented itself as a preventative against divorce—having formerly been advocates of divorce.

Sollee believes that divorce is about something very simple—a misunderstanding about what makes marriages work or fail. Women leave because they don't have basic knowledge about the nature of marriage and the skills to keep their marriages satisfying. 'My confidence in believing we can celebrate where we are, build on our areas of progress and move forward has to do with my conviction that we have new answers – research, tools, and know-how – at the ready and simply are not putting them to work. We're not getting the new information to the couples that need it. Actually, that's an understatement. It's worse than that. It's not just that we're not putting what we know to work, the new information about what makes marriage work is actually one of America's best kept secrets.'[15]

In January 1996, seven years after her concerns about the effectiveness of marriage therapy in preventing divorce, Diane Sollee was joined by martial therapists, counsellors, researchers, clergy and policy advocates who were passionate about the marriage psycho-education approach and its potential, to organise the Coalition for Marriage, Family and Couples Education (CMFCE) and Smart Marriages. The latter is a web-based organisation which provides a comprehensive marriage education clearinghouse, plus an annual conference that brings together the 'best and the brightest' in the field of marriage psycho-education.

So the modern marriage psycho-education movement emerged from a mindset that had been cultivated by the American Association of Marriage and Family Therapy. A feature article in the *New York* Magazine, shortly before the first Smart Marriages Conference in 1997, referred to Diane Sollee as a 53-year-old aerobicised divorcee who looked and sounded like the head cheerleader. 'She has enlisted more than 100 radical feminists, right-wing Christians, academics, lawyers, and New York shrinks to attend in the hopes of developing a psycho-educational divorce vaccine: "marital-skills training" for the masses, without the messy, soul-baring ordeal of traditional therapy.'[16]

While those attending the first Smart Marriages Conference had wildly different agendas for the future of the American family, most of them insisted that the marriage psycho-education movement is apolitical and that they were willing to make compromises to keep it that way. A feminist scholar and family therapist at the Ackerman Institute, Peggy Papp, argued the need to revise ideas about marriage and the roles of men and women so that people don't want to get divorced. She said: 'If there was a kind of marriage that didn't oppress women, then we wouldn't have as many divorces.'[17] Sollee was optimistically upbeat before the first conference: 'Everybody needs this training! Gay people, cohabiting couples, people in second marriages, it doesn't make any difference. Listen, the fact is 90 percent of the population still gets married, so whether marriage is the answer isn't the point! This is what people do.'[18]

The first Smart Marriages and Happy Families National Conference (1997) featured more than a hundred workshops and seminars. Presentations were made by John Gottman, who had spent twenty-five years studying the difference between couples who stay married and happy and those who don't. David Olson from the University of Minnesota presented his 195 item questionnaire, PREPARE (which claims to predict marital satisfaction with great accuracy) and the ENRICH inventory (which assesses the relationship strengths of those who are already married). Howard Markman, Scott Stanley, and Susan Blumberg from the University of Denver, presented PREP – the Prevention and Relationship Enhancement Program – a 12-hour course on skills and rules for speaking clearly, listening accurately, building commitment, expressing appreciation, and developing a 'team-marriage' orientation.

The mission of marriage psycho-education, according Patty Howell, Vice-President of the California Healthy Marriages Coalition, is nothing less than a cultural change in the way marriage is viewed by society. 'Marriage Education seeks to accomplish—to create full public awareness that "marriage is basically a skills-based relationship", that these skills can be learned, and to have the learning of them become part of everyone's development as a human being. Even with the enormity of this challenge, the unacceptable level of breakdown of American family life calls for us to take action.'[19]

American Association for Marriage and Family Therapy (AAMFT)

Here it is important for us to understand that the thinking of Diane Sollee and others committed to the aims of the Coalition for Marriage, Family and Couples Education has been shaped by the profession of marriage and family therapy. The AAMFT official position on marriage states:

> 'AAMFT believes that all couples who willingly commit themselves to each other, and their children, have a right to expect equal support and benefits in civil society... As opportunities arise, AAMFT will support public policy initiatives that strengthen marriages, couples, civil unions, and families through the provision of technical assistance... We assert the value and positive impact of stable, long-term, emotionally

enriching relationships… We recognize that all family forms have inherent strengths and challenges. As marriage and family therapists we focus our study and skills on how individuals in our society couple – choosing partners and establishing households – and form family groups. We study and intervene to assist in these relationships whether that means a marriage has occurred in the legal sense, whether there is co-habitation, or other forms of family. We invite members of heterosexual, same-sex, culturally similar, intercultural/interracial and other forms of family composition to engage with marriage and family therapists for relational development and problem solving within their cultural contexts.'[20]

What is clear from this statement is that the Association does not recognise the special significance of marriage above any other type of 'stable long-term relationship'. There is no distinction between legal marriage and cohabitation or any other form of relationship—all are of equal value. And all 'family' groups, such as single parent, cohabiting and same-sex families, are of equal validity, deserving equal support and benefits. In the eyes of the AAMFT there is no link between marriage and the traditional family. And this is the profession that is behind marriage psycho-education.

The Association informs us that premarital and marital education comes in many formats. Some courses last only a few hours or a day or two and are lecture-based. Others last longer and provide more skills practice and interaction between couples. The Association mentions several programmes that have been developed by its members, such as Couple Communication, developed by Sherod Miller; Relationship Enhancement, developed by Bernard Guerney; PREP, created by Scott Stanley and Howard Markman; PREPARE/ENRICH, designed by David Olson; and PAIRS, created by Lori Gordon.

Equal-regard marriage

One of the key aims of marriage education is to promote the concept of equal-regard marriage. Don Browning, a prominent intellectual in the marriage education movement, explains why he opposes male headship. He writes that 'the equal-regard marriage gives a couple equal freedom to define their respective responsibilities and privileges in both the private sphere of domestic life and the public sphere of politics and paid employment. A marriage based on equal regard does not give up parental authority; equal regard functions as an ideal that guides parenting so that children grow into adults capable of equal regard themselves.'[21]

He says that 'many marriage education programs assume the moral validity of the equal-regard marriage and actually help couples to learn the skills needed to talk the talk and walk the walk.' He argues that for society to achieve equal-regard marriage and implement a critical marriage culture, it cannot be left to individual couples. 'It requires a revolution in our cultural symbols and values, religious institutions, patterns of work, governmental supports, and systems of education. A love ethic of equal regard is not just a sentiment tucked away in the psyches of good men and women. It is that, but it is also a public ethic that should guide the organization of our public resources.'[22]

Ideology of marriage education

We have seen that the marriage psycho-education movement has developed out of the thinking and practice of the profession of marital and family therapists, a profession that is ideologically opposed to traditional marriage. So when the proponents of marriage psycho-education claim to support marriage, it is not traditional biblical marriage they support, but their own psychological version of marriage. This is why Diane Sollee has made it clear that the aim of the Coalition for Marriage, Family and Couples Education is to change the culture of marriage. A press release promoting the 2003 Smart Marriage conference speaks of a new way of thinking about marriage: 'We are now entering a new era – a Marriage Renaissance – fuelled by powerful new research and understanding about how to make marriage work.'[23] This cultural change involves a rejection of the traditional biblical view of marriage in favour of the psychological view promoted by the Coalition for Marriage.

We shall see throughout this book that the profession of marriage and family therapy opposes the biblical view of marriage. The concept of the husband as the head of the family and the wife as a homemaker, who willingly submits to the headship of her husband, is anathema to the secular, feminist mindset that is so popular among marriage therapists.

However, the marriage psycho-education movement that is so bitterly opposed to traditional marriage is content to accept, and even to support, a secular version of marriage based on sexual equality. And so the Coalition for Marriage, Family and Couples Education has established its ideological ground—secular, equal-regard marriage is a useful relationship, while biblical marriage is beyond the pale, totally unacceptable. The large variety of marriage education programmes that are now available in the USA and the UK are based on this ideological position.

(Endnotes)

1 Constance Ahrons, *The Good Divorce*, HarperCollins, 1994, p2

2 Ibid. p3

3 Ibid. p4

4 Ibid. p247

5 Ibid. pp248-249

6 'Rethinking Divorce Laws – Fault or No Fault?' by Muller Davis. (This article appeared in *The Christian Century*, June 5-12, 2002, pp. 28-31)

7 Amazon review of *The Good Divorce*, 'This book is destructive to families', 2 June 2003, by A Customer, http://www.amazon.ca/product-reviews/0060926341

8 Bethany Book review of *The Good Divorce*, 'One of the Most Toxic Books of the Last Two Decades', 17 April 2006, http://www.shopbethany.com/item/constance-ahrons/the-good-divorce/161339.html

9 Diane Sollee cited in, 'Some States Act to Save Marriages Before the "I Dos"', by Pam Belluck, *The New York Times*, 21 April 2000

10 Diane Sollee cited in article, 'Kids better off in two-parent families' by Sharon Jayson in USA TODAY, September 2005, posted on website; Azcentral.com/families/articles/0913marriagehealth. html

11 'Couples-education conference fights divorce, Coalition's annual couples-education conference fights high divorce rates', 12 July 2008, by Heidi Benson, *Chronicle* Staff Writer, http://www.sfgate. com/news/article/Couples-education-conference-fights-divorce-3277317.php

12 *The Psychotherapy Networker* - Nov/Dec, 2004: Cover story: 'The Citizen Therapist: Making a Difference - 5 therapists who dared to take on the wider world' by Rob Waters

13 'Shifting Gears : An Optimistic View of the Future of Marriage', Diane Sollee, MSW, Director, CMFCE at the Conference on Communitarian Pro-Family Policies, Washington, DC, 15 November 1996, sponsored by the Communitarian Network

14 Ibid.

15 Ibid.

16 *New York Magazine*, 'No Joy in Splitville', by Ariel Levy, 12 May 1997

17 Ibid.

18 Ibid.

19 Patty Howell, 'Marriage Education: An Important Investment in Cultural Change', California Association of Marriage and Family Therapists article

20 American Association for Marriage and Family Therapy website, Position Statement, AAMFT

Position on Couples and Families, http://www.aamft.org/iMIS15/AAMFT/MFT_Resources/MFT_Resources/Content/Resources/Position_On_Couples.aspx

21 'What Kind of Love? The Equal-Regard Marriage and Children', Don S. Browning, *American Experiment Quarterly*, Summer 2001, p48

22 Ibid. pp51-52

23 A press release promoting the June 2003 conference of the Coalition for Marriage, Family and Couples Education in Reno, Nevada

4

Couple relationship education in the UK

The ideas of the marriage education movement rapidly spread across the Atlantic to the fertile ground of the UK. As the last decades of the twentieth century were being characterised by record levels of divorce and a massive rise in the number of children born to single mothers, the UK was ready for a new initiative. Yet there was a distinct difference between the USA and the UK—whereas ideas about marriage still had some support in the US, in the UK marriage had been seriously devalued by the political classes and mass media, so much so that even the word 'marriage' was seen as being inconsistent with the government's diversity agenda. To defend marriage was held to be discrimination against single parents and same-sex civil partnerships. The political climate made it more acceptable to speak of 'relationships' or 'couple partnerships' rather than marriage.

The vehement anti-marriage view among the British establishment had come about as a result of a determined ideological assault on marriage during the last three decades of the twentieth century, led by feminists, socialists, prominent academics, celebrities and media personalities. Marriage had been so devalued in the eyes of the nation that there is no British political party that was prepared to give it unequivocal support. Prime Minister David Cameron paid tribute to Tony Blair's government for the way that it had legalised 'civil partnerships'. He said: 'I just want to say I am absolutely determined that this Coalition government will follow in that tradition by legislating for gay marriage in this Parliament.'[1] He has made it clear that he supports all types of family arrangements, not only the traditional family created by marriage.[2] Such is the sentiment against the biblical view of marriage that the terms 'husband' and 'wife' are no longer used in official government reports.

Marriage guidance changed to Relate

The ideological opposition to marriage is illustrated by the way the National Marriage Guidance Council, set up in the 1930s to help marriages that were in difficulty, changed its name to Relate in 1988 in order to keep in step with the social and political thinking of the time. This change of name, which dropped the word marriage, meant that Relate no longer focused on married couples, but on all types of sexual relationships, including those of single people, cohabiting couples and same-sex couples. According to the Relate website: 'We were renamed Relate to reflect that change, and now in 2008, we offer support, courses, counselling to couples, married or in a Civil Partnership or not, in the heterosexual and LGBT [lesbian, gay, bisexual and trans-sexual] population, as well as young people and whole families.'

Couple Relationship Education in the UK

The annual National Relationships Education Conference, which has been held since 2002, brings together a number of individuals and organisations that share an interest in what they have chosen to label 'relationship education'. Conference participants believe 'the most useful term is "Couple Relationship Education" (CRE) to cover our broader view of how relationship education should be applied and delivered. It is considered that relationship education should be widely available to all couples who wish to access it, as well as individuals who wish to learn about developing and nurturing a couple relationship.'[3]

The aim of relationship education is to ensure that all sexual relationships are seen to be of equal value. Marriage is not regarded as having any special value, for it is simply one of a number of equally valid sexual relationships, which include cohabiting, same-sex, and marriage. The implication is that no sexual relationship is to be regarded as being abnormal or immoral.

Regular participants at the Conference, as we saw in chapter 1, have included Relate, the largest provider of relationship support services in the UK. Also included are One Plus One, an organisation that does research and provides advice to the government and other public bodies on relationship issues; and family and parenting support organisations, including Parenting UK, Care for the Family, Marriage Care, and the

Marriage Course of Holy Trinity Brompton. As with the Coalition for Marriage, Family and Couples Education in the USA, the UK Conference includes both faith-based and secular organisations.

Building Strong Foundations

The report, 'Building Strong Foundations – The Case for Couple Relationship Education' (2009), is an important document produced in response to a recommendation from the 2007 Conference 'that a comprehensive case should be assembled, using the latest research evidence, for a much greater commitment to the provision of relationship education across the UK'.[4] The report reviews international evidence on the effectiveness of Couple Relationship Education in facilitating couple stability. According to the report, 'CRE is the communication and exploration of values, strategies and interpersonal behaviours designed to build harmony and intimacy in the relationship. It aims to increase stability and satisfaction for the couple and to assist individuals make good couple relationship choices. The report argues that relationship education is effective and under-utilised. A relatively small investment could lead to significant outcomes for the couples involved and society as a whole.'[5]

The report acknowledges that relationships are vital for the well-being of society – increasing health, happiness and life expectancy. 'A successful intimate long-term relationship is a strong aspiration for the vast majority of young people, and a key enabler to many other things they desire in life such as health and financial security. Such a relationship requires basic skills which it can no longer be assumed that people acquire from family and friends. Many will require specific training if they are to have the opportunity of a stable committed relationship.'[6]

What is interesting about this comment is the acknowledgement that men and women have an innate, natural desire to form a long-lasting sexual relationship. What this means is that those who are ideologically opposed to marriage have realised that it is natural for men and women to come together to form a sexual relationship. And so it becomes clear that the ideological opposition is not to sexual relationships per se, but to the biblical view of marriage. Indeed, the most effective way to destroy biblical marriage is to encourage and legitimise sexual relationships outside of marriage. The whole purpose of CRE is to provide an alternative to biblical marriage. What CRE is saying is that all sexual relationships, of whatever type, are now socially acceptable. They are doing their level best to destroy the traditional belief that for a couple to live together outside marriage is wrong, even sinful. In the eyes of CRE there is no such thing as sexual immorality, and therefore all types of sexual relationship are acceptable. Sexual sin and fornication have been placed on the dust heap of traditional values.

Another point to note is the claim that relationships founder not because of the sinful behaviour of the human heart, but because of a lack of 'basic skills'. This way of thinking entirely ignores the reality of sinful, selfish behaviour that is the real cause of broken relationships. The effect is to remove personal responsibility from the agenda and to ignore the consequences of sin, as people are encouraged to focus on acquiring basic skills.

According to 'Building Strong Foundations' the UK government should have a role to play in promoting relationship education. 'The cost of family breakdown is enormous both socially and economically. We suggest that the overall spending burden on the State can be reduced by supporting and encouraging relationships through couple relationship education (CRE).'[7] This is an important point, for the CRE movement wants the State to control relationship education. An underlying desire is to see all people equipped to achieve their aspirations for wellbeing in their relationships. 'What is clear is that for couples and individuals to achieve the good relationships to which they aspire, a comprehensive relationship movement is required; a movement that is recognized and supported by society generally, as well as by specific public policy, and positive media coverage… CRE delivered within such a "relational" atmosphere will be positively received, and much more likely to succeed in its aim.'[8]

A key recommendation is that funding the expansion of CRE should come from both central and local government.[9] To build momentum towards universal provision, the report proposes 'strategies similar to those adopted to change attitudes to smoking, seat-belt wearing and drink-driving where mass advertising sought to shift overall public perception, in parallel with measures targeting those most resistant to change.'[10] Here the argument is for the government to take over CRE. The State will teach its population how to live their lives. The population will be indoctrinated into accepting the State's version of how they should form sexual relationships. Here we have the ultimate version of the therapeutic State. The British people are now so demoralised by unbelief, and so given over to psychotherapy, that they need the government to teach them how to conduct their sexual relationships. Abandoning God's laws with regard to sexual relationships, as taught in the Bible, naturally leads to bondage and misery, as we see in today's society.

The aim of CRE is to create a relationship movement that changes the marriage culture within British society. The vision is for a society in which marriage gives way to a whole assortment of sexual relationships that are supposed to make people happy. Society is to be freed from the restriction inherent in traditional marriage. All types of sexual relationships, including cohabiting and same-sex partnerships, are to become the norm. CRE claims the ability to teach the basic skills necessary to produce happy relationships.

Care for the Family

Many in the Church have eagerly taken on board the agenda of the modern marriage psycho-education movement. Care for the Family has for the last 25 years been involved in marriage and family education. Rob Parsons, who founded Care for the Family as a charity to provide a Christian response to a world of need, is a key figure in the marriage education movement. As an acknowledged expert in marriage and family education, Parsons has spoken to hundreds of thousands of people about marriage in the UK and other countries across the world. Care for the Family claims that its key purpose is to promote strong family life and to help those hurting because of family breakdown. It has produced a marriage education programme, called '21st Century Marriage', which is discussed in chapter 16.

The Marriage Course

The Marriage Course has emerged from the Anglican church, Holy Trinity Brompton, London, home of the Alpha Course. The Marriage Course has been developed by Rev Nicky Lee and his wife Sila, and is by far the most popular marriage education course in the UK. Such is the attraction of its teaching that it has spread across the Christian world and is now in 76 countries, including the USA, and continues to grow at a rapid pace. In the UK, the Course is held in a whole range of churches, including mainstream evangelical Anglican churches (like All Souls, Langham Place), New Life charismatic churches and a range of independent evangelical churches. The Course is popular even among Roman Catholic churches. The Marriage Book (2000), which explains the philosophy of The Marriage Course, is discussed in chapter 17.

The National Couple Support Network

Christian marriage education is being actively promoted by The National Couple Support Network, a partnership between Care for the Family and the Family Life Department of Holy Trinity Brompton. This network aims to offer marriage preparation education to engaged couples throughout the country. The ambitious plan is to appoint a coordinator in each registration district across the UK, who will contact engaged couples through churches and registry offices.[11] Engaged couples will be offered a marriage preparation course, asked to complete a psychological questionnaire, and provided with a link to a support couple who have the task of discussing the issues that emerge from the results of their questionnaires. In this way these two organisations hope to take control of Christian marriage education across the UK.

Internet based couples education

A website with the strange name 2-in-2-1 was set up in 2000 by David Percival, who, with his wife Liz, has been involved with marriage and relationship education for over 20 years. While alluding to the Christian faith, the website appears to be multi-faith in ethos. David Percival is one of the authors of the 'Building Strong Foundations' report discussed above. The website is 'a business founded not only in the commercial potential of this particular market area, but also on the belief that marriage, as a lifestyle choice, is the foundation of a secure society. A core principle of 2-in-2-1 is its commitment to building a range of service offerings focused on sustainable relationships, not in a moralising or self righteous way, but in a holistic manner seeking to reach the deeper emotional as well as physical needs of the customers.'[12]

The purpose of the website is to draw together relationship support and education organisations to enable them to act more strategically. It provides a gateway for couples to access resources and services that assist them achieve their aspirations for their relationships. The website explains that its Marriage Clinic is 'here to help you face the tough times in marriage. All of us face tough times at different stages in life, and the clinic is the place to come for help. Whether your challenge is that a friend is turning to you in a crisis and you don't know where to start, or maybe you are struggling to come to terms with the fact (or even suspicion) that your partner is having an affair, you will find material in here to suggest some ways through. If you need to talk with someone, you will find contact details for the many different sources of counselling and support available nationwide.'[13] What is clear about this website is that it does not have a moral content and is not promoting a biblical view of marriage.

In Praise of Marriage

Even Reformed Anglicans have joined the marriage and relationships industry. A booklet from Reform, 'In Praise of Marriage' (2010), provides encouragement to mainstream evangelical Anglican churches to promote marriage education in their congregations, using the resources of Care for the Family and The Marriage Course. Many of the leaders of Reform are running The Marriage Course in their churches. So the face of Christian marriage education in the UK is made up of an alliance between Care for the Family, Holy Trinity Brompton and Reform. Together they all sing from the same hymnbook.

What works in Relationship Education?

A high-powered academic symposium to promote relationship education in the UK, organised by Care for the Family, working in collaboration with the Doha International Institute for Family Studies and Development based in Qatar, was held in London in September 2008. This prestigious event took place in the Jubilee Room in the Palace of Westminster, and brought together world experts to share their current research and experiences on what works in the field of relationship education.

David Percival of the website 2-in-2-1 was very excited by the event. He writes, 'Every now and then an event gets into my diary that makes the hairs on the back of my neck tingle with excitement – and the two days I have just spent as an invited guest at a private colloquium on "What Works in Relationship Education?" is one of those occasions.'[14]

The events of the two-day symposium have been recorded in the book, *What Works in Relationship Education?* written by Harry Benson and Samantha Callan. 'The primary purpose of this book is to gather together a wide range of scholarly papers and reviews that investigate whether and how both married and unmarried couples can improve their odds of success of staying together, of being happier, of fighting less.'[15]

An expert audience was invited to contribute to the symposium with the aim of integrating the research findings into service and policy design. 'Not only were the House of Commons and the House of Lords both represented but the event was sponsored by the All-Party Parliamentary Group on Sustainable Relationships. We were also joined by senior executives of many non-governmental organizations, researchers from top UK universities and practitioners who are working at the coalface of couples' relationships on a daily basis. Although some of these practitioners usually work therapeutically with couples, the emphasis of the whole event was on how to work preventatively in such a way that severe and pronounced relationship difficulties do not emerge or become full-blown.'[16]

The PREP programme, developed by Scott Stanley and his colleague Howard Markman, received a lot of attention. 'Their relationship education programme PREP has undoubtedly been studied more than any other, is probably the most widely used programme in the US, and has now been developed into several different variants for use in prison, in the military, amongst unmarried new parents and amongst singles.'[17]

The Marriage Course was presented as an example of relationship education in practice. According to Nicky and Sila Lee the content of The Marriage Course 'is based on Christian principles for practising love in a marriage. But the practical advice is accessible to those without any Christian faith or church background. Cohabiting couples are also encouraged to attend.'[18] Their goal is to make marriage education (both before and during marriage) available to every couple in the UK. 'At the moment most support is given through marriage counselling, but often by the time a couple goes for counselling it is too late. The Marriage Course seeks to empower couples to put in the foundations themselves to insure against a crisis and then to keep investing in their relationship. Making courses a "normal" activity is as important as making them available. And that requires a change of culture in the UK, a new way of thinking about marriage education. Hasten the day when taking the opportunity to learn the skills and attitudes to build a marriage is as normal as taking lessons to learn to drive a car or being coached to improve a golf swing.'[19] This kind of thinking, coming from the creators of the Marriage Course, trivialises marriage, placing it on a par with playing golf.

Self-improvement or work of the Holy Spirit?

Marriage education in the UK, under the banner of couple's relationship education, has made great strides in the last two decades. The relationship education movement is truly syncretistic in approach, as secular and Christian organisations work closely together. As in the USA, relationship education is held to be so important by the self-proclaimed experts that religious scruples need to be put to one side in the struggle to create happy long-term relationships. This syncretised approach means that the Christians involved have deserted the biblical view of marriage, for it is not acceptable to their secular friends. This compromise means that there is now a de facto consensus that all long-term sexual relationships are of equal value, and biblical teaching on sexual conduct and marriage has been conveniently forgotten.

The vision of the CRE movement is utopian in outlook. The idea that human beings can be taught skills and tools that will enable them to live successful lives and build happy relationships, is to deny the fundamental biblical truth of the sinful nature of the human heart. 'The heart is deceitful above all things, and desperately wicked; who can know it' (Jeremiah 17.9). For this reason the promises of CRE can only lead to disappointment and despair. So the self-improvement model promoted by CRE has no place in the life of a Christian. The promises of Scripture are completely different. The believer is a 'new creation' indwelt by the Holy Spirit and no longer a slave to sin. He has died with Christ to the ways of the flesh, and is exhorted to put off the works of the old sinful nature and to put on the works of the new nature, in true righteousness and holiness (Ephesians 4.22-24). A Christian husband and wife who 'no longer live for themselves, but for Him who died for them' (2 Corinthians 5.15), will manifest love for God and for each other. This love, described by the apostle Paul in 1 Corinthians 13, comes not by following secular methods and techniques, but from trusting and obeying the Word of God.

To fully understand the ideological battle over marriage, described in these first four chapters, we must understand what Scripture teaches about marriage. Only then shall we appreciate the large gulf between biblical marriage, based on Scripture, and the psycho-education version of marriage, which comes from flawed sociological research and the false theories of humanistic psychology.

(Endnotes)

1 *Daily Telegraph*, 'We will legalise gay marriage by 2015, says David Cameron', by Christopher Hope, Senior Political Correspondent, 24 July 2012

2 'The Coalition: our programme for government', Cabinet Office, London. Publication date: May 2010, p19

3 The Relationships Foundation, 'Building Strong Foundations - The Case for Couple Relationship Education', 2009, report by Michael Clark, Rose Lynas and David Percival, p21

4 Ibid. p3

5 Ibid. p7

6 Ibid. p7

7 Ibid p12

8 Ibid. p25

9 Ibid. p11

10 Ibid. p61

11 Engage website of Care for the Family, and National Couple Support Network

12 Website of 2-in-2-1, 'About Us', http://www.2-in-2-1.co.uk/admin/aboutus.html

13 Ibid. 'Marriage Clinic', http://www.2-in-2-1.co.uk/marriageclinic/

14 David Percival commenting on the 'What Works in Relationship Education' report, edited by Harry Benson and Samantha Callan, cited from website of 2-in-2-1, http://www.2-in-2-1.co.uk/articles/relcoll08/

15 Harry Benson, Introduction to 'What works in relationship education?' in H Benson and S Callan (Eds.), Doha, Qatar: Doha International Institute for Family Studies and Development, 2009, pp12-13

16 Ibid. Samantha Callan, Preface, 'Lessons from academics and service deliverers in the United States and Europe', pp 7-10.

17 Ibid. Markman H, Rienks S, Wadsworth M, Markman M, Einhorn L, Moran E, Mead Glojek N, Pregulman M, Gentry L, 'Adaptation: Fatherhood, individual, and Islamic versions of PREP', pp67-74

18 Ibid. Lee N & Lee S, 'Case study: The Marriage Course', pp 117-120

19 Ibid. p120

5

What the Bible teaches about marriage

The biblical view of marriage has always been at the foundation of Western civilisation. Since time immemorial it has been widely accepted that marriage is an honourable estate ordained by God for the union of one man and one woman. Marriage was part of a shared theological understanding of life and society. The vows of the traditional marriage ceremony – 'to have and to hold from this day forward, for better for worse, for richer for poorer, in sickness and in health, to love, cherish and obey, till death us do part, according to God's holy ordinance' – were so well known that they became part of Western culture. For centuries the idea that marriage is a lifelong union between a man and his wife has been widely accepted by virtually all in society.

In Great Britain the divine plan for marriage has been believed and accepted for countless generations and brought great blessing to the nation. In the USA there has not been the same deep belief in marriage, for right from the start of American history the people took a more pragmatic view of marriage and divorce, as documented in my book, *The Great Divorce Controversy* (2000). Towards the end of the eighteenth century a new way of thinking emerged in the USA, which believed that the main purpose of marriage is to make the couple happy. The traditional belief that the prime purpose of marriage is to have children and raise a family was replaced with the idea that the prime purpose is to meet the emotional needs of husband and wife.

As a consequence of America's ideas about marriage, its road to mass divorce was very different from that chosen by Britain. While Britain accepted divorce reluctantly and only after a fierce struggle, the American people right from the beginning yearned after divorce when they were no longer happy in their marriage. Whereas in the UK the debate revolved around the indissolubility of marriage, the American debate was more concerned with finding the right grounds for divorce.

So it is no surprise that the divorce rate in the USA is amongst the highest in the world. Divorce has become so ingrained in the social fabric that it is an accepted component of the American way of life.

In the first four chapters we have seen that traditional marriage is under serious and sustained assault on both sides of the Atlantic. Many in the psychotherapeutic world, together with their friends in sociological research, have led the assault with great passion. The eminent demographer Kingsley Davis has expressed the view that 'at no time in history, with the possible exception of Imperial Rome, has the institution of marriage been more problematic than it is today'.[1] There is indeed a profound ideological war on marriage, as the vow 'till death us do part', once part of Western culture, is being replaced with the sentiment 'as long as I am happy'. In this chapter, I argue that we can only understand the war on traditional marriage if we first understand the biblical view of marriage. It is only when we grasp the spiritual war around marriage that we are able to really understand the underlying battle lines and the real source of conflict.

Biblical view of marriage

God's plan for sexual conduct and marriage is one of the most profound teachings of Scripture, for it forms the basis of family life and of order in the Church. The divine plan for marriage and the family is indeed the foundation on which a stable society is built. In the New Testament the closeness and permanence of the marriage union between husband and wife is illustrated by the relationship between Christ and the Church (Ephesians 5.31-32). Because God's plan for sexual conduct is based in divine wisdom it has a great appeal to the human heart. Those who hear God's plan for marriage know in their conscience that what they are hearing is divine truth—sometimes they even yearn for this ideal, whatever their own reality may be. In his great wisdom, God ordained the institution of marriage as a lifelong union between husband and wife, and protected marriage with four virtues—chastity, modesty, chivalry and faithfulness.

Sexual nature of mankind

Scripture makes it clear that sex is God's idea. The God of the Bible, who created human beings in his own image, created mankind male and female. In his infinite wisdom God created human beings as creatures who would reproduce sexually. He could have chosen a non-sexual way of reproduction, but he did not do so. God had sex in mind for humanity right from the very beginning of creation. After God had created the first man (Adam) and the first woman (Eve), he saw that his creation, including our sexual nature, was 'very good' (Genesis 1.31). So our sexual nature is part of God's perfect creation, one of God's greatest gifts to mankind.

God's first command to mankind was to be fruitful and multiply (Genesis 1.28), which of course requires sexual relations. As we shall see, it is God's will that children should be born into the family created at the time of marriage. After God had created the man from the dust of the earth, he said, 'It is not good that man should be alone; I will make him a helper comparable to him' (Genesis 2.18). God caused the man to fall into a deep sleep, and created the woman from a rib taken from the side of the man. This is an important truth, for it shows the closeness of the relationship between the sexes.

But our sexuality has been distorted by the Fall. As a consequence society is given over to the lusts of the flesh and sexual temptation surrounds us daily, expressing itself in shameful practices. In his wisdom God provided marriage as a legitimate place for our sexuality, to keep us safe from fornication. The apostle Paul says, 'because of sexual immorality, let each man have his own wife, and let each woman have her own husband' and 'it is better to marry than to burn' (1 Corinthians 7.2, 9). The traditional marriage service says that marriage 'was ordained for a remedy against sin, and to avoid fornication'. Clearly, God's ordinance of marriage is the bedrock of a stable society and brings great blessing to men, women and children.

Marriage ordinance

The first marriage is described in the second chapter of Genesis. God brings the woman to Adam and he cries out with delight, 'This is now bone of my bones, and flesh of my flesh; she shall be called Woman, because she was taken out of Man' (Genesis 2.23). God ordained marriage with these words: 'Therefore a man shall leave his father and mother and be joined to his wife, and they shall become one flesh' (Genesis 2.24).

The symbolism of the rib provides a picture of marriage, for at marriage the rib symbolically returns into the man, as husband and wife become one flesh; they are no longer two separate individuals but one entity— a new family. This is why traditionally the woman takes the man's name, and so fully identifies herself and their offspring as one family. There is something so deep and wonderful in the marriage bond that we need spiritual insight to understand its divine significance. As we have already seen above, Scripture uses the unity between Christ and his Church as a symbol of the marriage union of husband and wife. Yet marriage is a creation ordinance, which means that it is for all people, not just Christians.

The Lord Jesus emphasised and confirmed the one flesh union created at marriage with the words: 'So then, they are no longer two but one flesh. Therefore what God has joined together, let not man separate' (Matthew 19.6). The one-flesh union is complete when the couple consummate their marriage union by sexual intercourse. Husband and wife lovingly share their sexual life, accepting that their union, in the providence of God, is likely to be blessed with children. They accept with joy the children that result, for they are the natural, legitimate products of their marriage—clear evidence that they are truly one flesh. The concept of one flesh is illustrated by the children who are born into the family. Both parents contribute equally to the genetic make up of their children, and their likeness to their parents witnesses to this fact. Biblical teaching makes it clear that a family is formed by the marriage of a man and a woman. Without marriage, there is no true family, only a de facto assortment of relationships.

According to the Lord Jesus, it is God who joins a husband and wife in marriage. And so we see a profound biblical truth— families are created by God, and not by man. Those who marry must understand that they have entered into a lifelong union; there is no turning back, no second chance, for the marriage vow is 'till death us do part'. This is why it is so important for husband and wife to remain faithful to each other.

Working together in partnership

The Lord God planted a garden in Eden and put the man in the garden to tend and keep it (Genesis 2.8,15). Here we see from Scripture that the prime task of man is to work the Garden of God, standing for this world in general. Even before the Fall it was God's intention that man, created in the image of God, should work to develop the world. This is a fundamental biblical truth—work is intrinsic to human life. And God created the woman to help the man work the Garden. God said: 'I will make him a helper comparable to him' (Genesis 2.18). And here we see an important truth about marriage that is largely forgotten in our day. The man and woman – united in marriage – are together, as husband and wife, to work the Garden. The primary task of a godly marriage is for husband and wife to work together to develop God's creation. The primary task of a Christian husband and wife is to work together to care for their family, to support others and to build the Church of God. This means that a godly marriage is a relationship that is directed toward God and is outward looking, in which husband and wife engage in their God-given task of working for others. The modern idea of the inward looking marriage, in which the prime task of husband and wife is to meet each other's emotional needs, is an aberration. Such a marriage, which focuses on the desires and wants and happiness of husband and wife, is a selfish enterprise that entirely fails to understand the purposes of God.

Maternal instinct

Because womankind is created in the image of God, women have an inborn understanding of the maternal role. The first woman was named Eve, 'because she was the mother of all living' (Genesis 3.20). God has created women in such a way that it is natural for most to desire marriage and motherhood. Most women understand that children should be born into a family created by marriage. God has placed within the conscience of womankind a natural inhibition to restrain them from abusing the gift of motherhood. Their conscience warns that sex outside marriage is wrong, and they fear the consequences of an unintended pregnancy. But the pressure of the permissive society, the growth of feminism and the collapse of traditional Christian morality, together with the loss of the shared societal consensus of what family should be, has smothered this innate instinct in many women, so that premarital cohabitation has become common. Yet even in our sexually permissive culture many women in cohabiting relationships are deeply unhappy, although many are reluctant to say so, for fear that they may lose their partner.

Biblical virtues

In his great wisdom God has instituted moral laws around human sexual conduct that are expressed in the four virtues mentioned above—chastity, modesty, chivalry and faithfulness. The divine plan has given us standards of moral conduct (virtues) to safeguard marriage, the family and children. While each virtue applies to an aspect of sexual behaviour, together they form a coherent inner belief system that expresses the biblical attitude to sex, marriage and the family. Sexual purity is the foundation on which these virtues are built. An attitude of mind that seeks after sexual purity is at the heart of biblical teaching. Implicit within the idea of purity is a spirit of obedience to God's moral law which renounces sensual and sexual pollution. A pure heart inculcates a duty of self-restraint and self-denial. The people of God desire purity in all areas of their lives, and especially in sexual relationships. Marriage flourishes when all four virtues are practised.

The concept of chastity flows from the holiness that is central to the character of God. Because God is holy, he demands sexual purity among his people. 'It is God's will that you should be holy; that you should avoid sexual immorality; that each of you should learn to control his own body in a way that is holy and honourable, not in passionate lust like the heathen, who do not know God... For God did not call us to be impure, but to live a holy life' (1 Thessalonians 4:3-7 NIV)[2].

Modesty is the virtue that reveals the inner beauty and moral strength of a woman. A woman's beauty does not come from her outward appearance, but from 'the hidden person of the heart, with the incorruptible beauty of a gentle and quiet spirit, which is very precious in the sight of God' (1 Peter 3:4). The true beauty of a woman comes from her moral character.

Like modesty in women, chivalry is a virtue that reveals the inner moral strength of a man. It is a mindset that compels a man to treat women with honour and respect, because they are the weaker partner in that they are sexually vulnerable through pregnancy, childbirth and motherhood. A chivalrous man is courteous and caring towards women, and does not take sexual advantage. He learns to practise self-control and is not ruled by sexual lust. He does not treat women as sex objects, and rejects casual sex as wrong. He strives to keep himself sexually pure.

The virtue of faithfulness comes from the character of God. 'Therefore know that the Lord your God, He is God, the faithful God who keeps covenant and mercy for a thousand generations with those who love Him and keep His commandments' (Deuteronomy 7.9). As God is faithful in all his promises to his people, so his people are to be faithful in their promises to each other. This is particularly the case between husband and wife, who have promised to live together for life.

Biblical Christianity lays down a clear moral framework for the behaviour of men and women, teaching that sexual activity should be confined to the marriage relationship. All forms of sexual immorality are condemned as sinful and a cause of harm to those involved. The Bible teaches that 'marriage should be honoured by all, and the marriage bed kept pure, for God will judge the adulterer and all the sexually immoral' (Hebrews 13.4 NIV). And most important of all, these are the God-given virtues that protect children from the ravages that result from sexual immorality.

Governance of marriage and the family

The roles and responsibilities of husband and wife and the way the family should be governed are set out in the Bible. The unity between Christ and his Church is used as a symbol of the marriage relationship—just as Christ and his Church are one, so husband and wife are one. The need for husband and wife to have a correct understanding of the significance of their marriage and the right attitude towards each other is emphasised. The Bible provides clear teaching about the roles of husband and wife. The apostle Paul in his letter to the Ephesians (5.22-33) and the apostle Peter in his first letter (1 Peter 3.1-7) give clear instructions to Christian believers on the way they ought to behave in marriage.

> Wives, submit to your own husbands, as to the Lord. For the
> husband is head of the wife, as also Christ is head of the church;
> and He is the Saviour of the body. Therefore, just as the church

is subject to Christ, so let the wives be to their own husbands in everything (Ephesians 5.22-24).

Husbands, love your wives, just as Christ also loved the church and gave Himself for her… So husbands ought to love their own wives as their own bodies; he who loves his wife loves himself. For no one ever hated his own flesh, but nourishes and cherishes it, just as the Lord does the church… This is a great mystery, but I speak concerning Christ and the church. Nevertheless let each one of you in particular so love his own wife as himself, and let the wife see that she respects her husband (Ephesians 5.25-26, 28-29, 32-33).

Wives, likewise, be submissive to your own husbands, that even if some do not obey the word, they, without a word, may be won by the conduct of their wives, when they observe your chaste conduct accompanied by fear… Husbands, likewise, dwell with them with understanding, giving honour to the wife, as to the weaker vessel, and as being heirs together of the grace of life, that your prayers may not be hindered (1 Peter 3.1-2, 7).

Headship of the husband

The Bible teaches that the husband is the head of the family. The headship of the husband is taught explicitly in Ephesians. 'For the husband is the head of the wife, as also Christ is the head of the church... just as the church is subject to Christ, so let the wives be to their own husbands in everything' (Ephesians 5.23-24). The apostle Paul explains, 'But I want you to know that the head of every man is Christ, the head of woman is man, and the head of Christ is God' (1 Corinthians 11.3). According to the Bible there is a hierarchy of authority within the family. The family is not to be leaderless, nor is it to be governed by whim or fancy, nor by the majority view. Instead the husband has been given by God the duty of leadership in the family. The husband, however, is to exercise his leadership role under the authority of Christ, who is his head and the example he should follow in exercising his role. As the leader, he has a responsibility to provide for and protect his wife and children, and is responsible, together with his wife, for the moral wellbeing of his family.

Male headship is carefully qualified so that it poses no threat to woman's worth or dignity. Male headship in no way implies female inferiority—it is about roles ordained by their Creator. Men and women are created in the image of God (Genesis 1.27), are both fully equal, but not equivalent. Headship is given to the man; and the woman is given the role of helper. She is given to the man as his glory (1 Corinthians 11.7). Also, the woman is created from the man (Genesis 2.21-22), and for the man (1 Corinthians 11.8-9). Paul explains that men and women are in fact mutually dependent, for the man comes through the woman (1 Corinthians 11.11-12). God's righteous judgement on the woman, as a consequence of her sin that led to the Fall, is that she would suffer at the hands of men (Genesis 3.16). Yet in true Christian marriage she is restored to something like her original glory.

The woman rejects the authority of her husband to her shame, to the detriment of her family and herself, and to the dishonour of God. For a husband not to accept his God-given leadership responsibility in marriage is to disobey God, fail his wife and family, and plant the seeds of dissension in the marriage. He has a unique leadership role in the family that he should not abdicate.

As we saw in chapter 2, the concept of male headship is anathema to the mindset of the psychotherapeutic world; it is condemned as the foundation of the patriarchal society and the cause of women's oppression. According to the thinking of the marriage and family therapist, marriage must be an equal-regard partnership where each submits to the other. But this is a dangerous teaching, for it denies biblical truth.

Submissive wife

The Bible teaches that the wife should accept the authority of her husband to lead the family, and submit herself willingly to his leadership. (Of course, the husband must never attempt to force his wife to submit.) This exhortation to the wife to submit to her husband is the universal teaching of the New Testament. Every passage that deals with the relationship of the wife to her husband tells her to submit to him. Colossians 3.18 tells wives to 'submit to your husbands, as is fitting in the Lord'; and Titus 2.5 instructs wives 'to be discreet, chaste, homemakers, good, obedient to their own husbands, that the word of God may not be blasphemed'.

She should not challenge his leadership, but should rather support and help him in this role, accepting that God has vested the leadership of the family in her husband. The wife should submit to her husband in the same way as the Church submits to its Lord. So the wife should not in any way undermine the authority of her husband, for that would damage the family unit of which she is an integral part; it would also damage her children. Moreover, not only should she submit with an attitude of willing acceptance, but also in everything (Ephesians 5.24). The Bible leaves no doubt about the importance of submission to the headship role of the husband. It mentions the holy women of the past who were submissive to their own husbands, like Sarah, who obeyed her husband Abraham, and called him her lord (1 Peter 3.5-6).

It is not difficult to see why the profession of marriage and family therapy, which is dominated by feminists and liberals, is so violently opposed to this Christian teaching. The idea that a wife should actually submit to her husband is unthinkable to the feminist mind, and goes against the most fundamental tenets of the marriage education movement. At the heart of modern feminism is the godless idea that the woman can live without reference to the man – her oppressor – if she so chooses. By extension, she can also live without the 'oppressive dictates' of the God of biblical Christianity.

Husbands, love your wives

The husband is to show a deep and sacrificial love for his wife. We have seen that God has joined the husband and wife together so that they become one flesh, one entity, and part of each other. The husband should love and cherish his wife as himself, because the Scripture says 'husbands ought to love their own wives as their own bodies' (Ephesians 5.28). As Christ loved the Church so the husband must love his wife. Christ's love was undeserved—he loved us although we did not love him. And he showed his love by giving of himself, for 'Christ also loved the church and gave Himself for her' (Ephesians 5.25).

Following this example, the husband must put the interests of his wife and family above his own. A loving husband will give of himself for the benefit of his wife. He will treat his wife with kindness, gentleness and courtesy. As Christ has forgiven him much, he will learn to forgive his wife from his heart. By loving his wife, he will bring great blessing on the family of which he is the head. And if he does not love his wife then he damages his family, his children and himself. As the Bible says, 'He who loves his wife loves himself' (Ephesians 5.28).

Wives, respect your husbands

We have seen that the wife must submit to her husband because he is the head of the family. Yet it is possible for her to do this without actually respecting him. But that would be wrong, for submission without respect means that the wife submits with a poor attitude, not really understanding why she should do so. She must respect her husband because he is the head of the family, the father of her children, and the provider and protector of the family home. She should respect her husband because God has commanded her to do so (Ephesians 5.33) and because it is the right thing to do. The husband has the major responsibility for maintaining order and discipline within the family; this is no easy task, and he needs the respect of his wife as he strives to fulfil his role. After all, how will the children respect their father if their mother does not do so?

Problems for the wife

We need to recognise that in today's feminist culture virtually all women are exposed to unbiblical, indeed anti-biblical, values from their earliest years. Education and the mass media inculcate in women a mindset of independence and self-determination. It follows that those converted to Christ out of this world come into the Church with deeply entrenched feminist views, and so gentle patience is needed to show a woman the biblical way, for she needs much grace to take on her biblical role at the best of times, how much more in a day heavily influenced by feminist ideas.

But to follow the biblical role brings great rewards. The headship of the man was never meant to be authoritarian. Man and wife are heirs together (1 Peter 3.7), equal in God's sight, living out together a godly partnership in service to him. This brings true blessing to both. The husband soon comes to rely implicitly on his wife, admiring her many gifts and capacities, trusting her intuitive instincts, confiding in her loving loyalty to himself. He sees in her many attributes that he knows he lacks. She complements and completes him.

And she needs him too, despite what the modern world may tell her, because – and this is heresy in our culture – her glory is to be a servant. The woman's role is predominantly one of service—to her husband, to her children, to her extended family, to her church. All Christians are servants, of course, but the servant-role is peculiarly the wife's. Our society despises the very concept of servanthood; it is abhorrent to our false sense of 'self-esteem'—a servile and demeaning state. But not in God's sight. For even our Lord Jesus Christ came not 'to be served, but to serve' (Mark 10.45). When the woman serves, she humbly walks in the footsteps of her Saviour and honours him. For both men and women are eternally destined to be servants of God (Revelation 22.3).

The ideal wife of Proverbs 31 was a servant, but certainly no drudge or doormat. She had the scope to make important decisions, to buy and sell, to run the household. Yet in all her tasks her eye was always on the good of her husband and family, and her husband only too willingly praised her. It would be good for the modern Christian woman, contemplating marriage, to learn from this biblical example. She should not put her preferences first, but ask the Lord to guide her to the man she could best serve. 'Many daughters have done well, but you excel them all' (Proverbs 31.29).

Parents – nurture and discipline your children

The action of the Lord Jesus following the dramatic encounter with the Pharisees over the reasons for divorce (Matthew 19.3-12) shows why marriage is so important and why divorce was never meant to be an option. After issuing his warning to married couples not to separate, the Gospel of Matthew records:

> Then little children were brought to Him that He might put His hands on them and pray, but the disciples rebuked them. But Jesus said, "Let the little children come to Me, and do not forbid them; for of such is the kingdom of heaven" (Matthew 19.13-14).

How the Saviour delighted in children! By his loving attitude towards children the Lord is showing that divorce is not even to be contemplated – for husband and wife, and especially father and mother, should never separate. The action of Christ, which is to love and care for children, graphically illustrates to the disciples the value God places on children. God's intention is that the marriage relationship should be fruitful and produce children. The Bible tells us that 'children are a heritage from the LORD, the fruit of the womb is a reward. Like arrows in the hand of a warrior, so are the children of one's youth. Happy is the man who has his quiver full of them' (Psalm 127.3-5). Children are a gift from God, and those parents who have many children – or as the psalmist would say, 'a quiver full of arrows' – are blessed by God.

The birth of children brings with it parental responsibilities as husband and wife become father and mother. Parents have a God-given responsibility to care for their children—it is unthinkable that they should not do so. The Proverbs of Solomon make it clear that the father and mother must teach and instruct their children, and children are advised to listen to their father's instruction and not forsake their mother's teaching (Proverbs 1.8). Within the family home, children are to be loved, taught and disciplined by both their mother and their father. This is God's plan. Parents, and especially fathers, have a duty to train and discipline their children. The Bible makes it very clear that all children need parental discipline, and that the father should take the lead in disciplining the children, 'For what son is not disciplined by his father?' (Hebrews 12.7 NIV).

Moreover, discipline is for the good of the children, for it teaches them that they cannot always have their own way; they need to develop self-control and self-discipline, and they need to recognise and respect the authority of their parents. Parental discipline warns children of the dangers of immoral behaviour. The discipline that parents exercise over their children is a sign of their love, for while any discipline seems unpleasant at the time, it produces a harvest of good in the long run (Hebrews 12.11). Parents are to teach their children the difference between right and wrong, and, by their behaviour, set an example for their children to follow. A major problem associated with family breakdown is that it separates parents from their children. This makes it difficult for parents to discipline their children and to teach them a moral foundation on which they can base their lives. By divorcing, parents show their children that marriage does not matter; by honouring their marriage vows, parents teach their children the importance of marriage and the family. Therefore divorce is one of the cruellest acts parents can inflict on their children.

The Bible teaches that a fundamental purpose of marriage is to provide a secure family home in which children are to be nurtured as they grow into adulthood. This biblical teaching is an eternal truth, and applies to all people, and for all time. And this point needs to be underlined—God's plan for marriage is not only for Christians, but is for all people. It is part of God's common grace; the Creator designed marriage for the good of all mankind. Those who are not Christian need to recognise the wisdom of the biblical view of marriage; to do so will bring great blessing to their family.

War of the two seeds

The war against marriage, described in the first four chapters, can only be fully understood when viewed in a biblical context. The third chapter of Genesis describes the Fall of man and its consequences. When Adam and Eve rebelled against God's command and ate the forbidden fruit, their eyes were opened and they knew that they were naked. So they sewed together fig leaves for coverings, and when they heard God walking in the Garden they hid themselves from his presence. When God asked Adam if he had eaten of the forbidden fruit, Adam blamed both God for giving him the woman and the woman for giving him the fruit of the tree, and the woman blamed the serpent, 'The serpent deceived me, and I ate' (Genesis 3.13). So God cursed the serpent, Satan, who had deceived the woman and said: 'And I will put enmity between you and the woman, and between your seed and her Seed; He shall bruise your head, and you shall bruise His heel' (Genesis 3.15).

Here we learn from Scripture of the battle between the seed of Satan, described by our Lord as, in effect, the seed of the devil (John 8.44), and the Seed of the woman, who is Christ and his Church. The apostle Paul refers to the prince of the power of the air (Satan), 'the spirit who now works in the sons of disobedience' (Ephesians 2.2).

According to the Bible commentator, Matthew Henry, 'A perpetual quarrel is here commenced between the kingdom of God and the kingdom of the devil among men; war is proclaimed between the Seed of the woman and the seed of the serpent.' This is a spiritual war against the rulers of the darkness of this age, against the spiritual hosts of wickedness in high places referred to in Ephesians 6. Today the war between the seed of the serpent and the Seed of the woman has reached a new intensity. The seed of the serpent is manifest in the godless ideology of secular humanism, an ideology that is at total war with the Christian Church.

Secular humanism is a worldview that rejects the God of Scripture and his moral law. Over recent decades it has become the dominant ideology in the UK, the USA and the West in general. It is represented by many leading academics in the fields of humanistic psychology, the human potential movement, sociology, and marriage and family therapy. It seeks to create a society that is ruled by (so-called) rational thought alone, without recourse to the God of Scripture. It rejects God's absolute moral law and opposes God's plan for marriage and the family, for it wants a godless society where every person is free to do what is right in their own eyes. Far from being 'rational', it is in fact hopelessly irrational, as it blindly follows its own flawed research and false dogma to the ultimate destruction of all that is right and good—all that is God-given.

At the heart of secular humanism is a deep hostility to God's plan for marriage and the family, and the biblical virtues that protect marriage. Secular humanism, and its offshoots of humanistic psychology and the human potential movement, has played a prominent role in the development of marriage education, which it uses as a vehicle for inculcating its godless ideas into society. Just as Satan deceived Eve in the Garden of Eden, casting doubt on the truth of God's Word, so today he deceives mankind by challenging God's plan for marriage as being no longer relevant in a modern world.

The marriage education movement is an important front in the spiritual war between the seed of the serpent and the Seed of the woman. To understand the motivation that drives the marriage educators we must recognise and understand the spiritual war that is being waged against the divine plan for marriage.

A new marriage culture

We have seen that the purpose of marriage education is to create a new marriage culture. Having rejected the biblical view of marriage, marriage psycho-education is proposing to propagate a psychological view of marriage that disregards the teaching of headship and submission, and replaces it with equal-regard marriage. This new culture, which does not see marriage as an exclusive relationship between one man and one woman, is seeking to change the meaning of the word 'marriage' to include a variety of sexual relationships. It promotes the idea that a same-sex relationship, a cohabiting relationship and a traditional marriage relationship are simply variations of the same thing. The version of marriage promoted by the marriage education movement is the very antithesis of biblical marriage.

In the chapters that follow the meaning of the new marriage culture that is being generated by the marriage educators will become increasingly clear. The place to start is probably with the most influential psychological thinker of the twentieth century, and one of the fiercest opponents of the biblical view of marriage, Carl Rogers.

(Endnotes)

1 Kingsley Davis, 'The Meaning and Significance of Marriage in Contemporary Society,' in Kingsley Davis (ed.), *Contemporary Marriage*, New York, Russell Sage Foundation, 1985, p21
2 The Holy Bible, New International Version, First South African edition, 1978, The Bible Society of South Africa

6

Carl Rogers' alternatives to marriage

In the previous chapter we saw that God ordained marriage at the time of creation, before sin entered into the world. It is God's will that a man and his wife should live together in a sexual relationship, and that they should have children as God blesses their marriage. It is through the family, created by God, that the divine plan for mankind to be fruitful and multiply, to fill the earth and subdue it, is to be fulfilled (Genesis 1.28).

We have learned from Scripture of the battle between two seeds, the seed of Satan and the Seed of the woman, who is Christ and his Church. This perpetual war has waged throughout the ages, and in our day is manifest in (amongst many other things) the humanistic psychology of Carl Rogers, who wrote *Becoming partners – marriage and its alternatives* (1972), to help people find alternatives to traditional marriage. As we shall see, humanistic psychology is really an extension of man's rebellion against the Word of God.

Marriage enrichment and the human potential movement

An early response to the divorce culture was the development of a number of marriage enrichment programmes, such as the Association of Couples for Marriage Enrichment (ACME), founded by David Mace in 1973, which helped couples to seek growth and enrichment in their marriages. These programmes, which paved the way for the marriage psycho-education movement founded by Diane Sollee, were developed as an offshoot of the humanistic psychology of Abraham Maslow and Carl Rogers. Maslow's psychology emphasised an individual's innate power to grow and to achieve self-fulfilment, or what he termed 'self-actualization'. Roger's client-centred therapy, which peaked in popularity in the 1950s, revolved around the assumed potential within every human being to experience personal growth. Humanistic psychology gave rise to techniques, such as sensitivity training and encounter groups, that placed great stress on self-expression and intense emotional experiences.

One of the early fruits of humanistic psychology was the human potential movement, of which marriage enrichment became an important aspect. The human potential movement, grounded in the ideas of Maslow and Rogers, embraced a set of values that rejects absolute moral truths. The basic notion is that through the development of human potential, human beings can experience an exceptional quality of life filled with happiness, creativity and fulfilment. Dr William Coulson, for many years a disciple of Rogers' humanistic non-directive therapy, identifies the fatal flaw in Rogers' approach. 'Humanistic psychology, the kind that has virtually taken over the Church in America, and dominates so many forms of aberrant education like sex education, and drug education, holds that the most important source of authority is within you, that you must listen to yourself.'[1]

Richard Hunt, Professor of Psychology at Fuller Theological Seminary, explains that humanistic psychology, 'which espoused the expression of feelings, the creation of effective relationships, and the fulfilment of personal potential, was one of the inspirations for marriage enrichment because it saw marriage as a major area in which each person can enact his or her inherent tendency toward growth and self-actualization, with respect to self and others.'[2] Hunt freely acknowledged the role of the human potential movement in forming an ideological foundation for the marriage enrichment process. He also recognised the link between Rogerian psychotherapy and marriage enrichment programmes, where 'participants can freely express their feelings and experience increased self-acceptance and knowledge, and increased acceptance of others and from others, especially their marital partner.'[3]

In *Couples in Treatment* (2001), psychologists Gerald Weeks and Stephen Trent confirm the link between marriage enrichment and the human potential movement. They write: 'The marriage enrichment movement predated and subsequently merged with the human potential movement of the 1960s. Although this movement never established a large foothold in the clinical field, many psychotherapeutic programs were developed to promote healthier, happier, more loving relationships.'[4]

Marriage enrichment, faithful to the human potential movement, holds an optimistic view of human nature that sees positive self-improvement as possible. According to Hunt, 'the keystone of marriage enrichment is growth and human potential, based on the premise that all persons and relationships have a great many untapped strengths and resources that can be developed.'[5] The goal of marriage enrichment is to help couples develop and use techniques that achieve self-growth and happiness. We are called to reject all negative thoughts that place a limit on human potential, persuading ourselves that we have the innate ability to achieve truly happy relationships. We are promised great marriages if we learn a set of psychological skills and put our minds to it.

Influence of Eastern mystical religion

Carl Rogers is probably the most influential psychologist of the twentieth century. A study published in 1982 in the journal *American Psychologist*, five years before Rogers' death, ranked the ten most influential psychotherapists, with Rogers rated as number one.

As a young man Carl Rogers attended the World Student Christian Federation's Conference in Peking, China, where he was deeply touched by the Eastern mystical religion of Taoism. His exposure to Far Eastern philosophies awed him, and upon his return to the USA Rogers did not consider himself a Christian. He came to believe that Christ was just a good man and certainly not the divine Son of God. Rogers was impressed by the Zen Buddhist tradition that taught that all the answers to life's problems are found within the person. Rogers returned to his college education so profoundly influenced by Taoism and Zen Buddhism that he removed himself from the practice of formal religion.[6]

The words of Lao-Tse, the first philosopher of the Taoist school of thought, had an enormous impact on Rogers: 'The Perfect man... does not interfere in the life of beings, he does not impose himself on them, but he helps all beings to their freedom.'[7] Taoism insists that the individual find answers within himself, and this idea became central to Rogers' non-directive therapeutic model. Indeed, a psychology graduate, after reading a book on Taoism, argues that Rogers' one great original idea was in fact an idea that was over two-thousand years old.[8]

And so Rogers as a young man rejected the Christian faith and what he regarded as its repressive moral code. In later life he developed a deep commitment to the cause of secular humanism, and in 1964 was elected humanist of the year by the American Humanist Association. But there is no doubt that Carl Rogers was greatly influenced by the teachings of Tao, and his humanistic psychology has clear Eastern perspectives.[9]

The modern marriage education movement is deeply committed to Rogers' therapeutic ideas. In many ways Rogers can be seen as the prophet of modern marriage education, for it is his psychotherapeutic ideas that form the foundation of marriage and family therapy, and most marriage therapists have been trained in the skills of his client-centred, non-directive counselling model. So to really understand the marriage education movement, we need to understand the psychotherapeutic model of Carl Rogers.

The starting point of Rogers' philosophy is the presupposition that human nature is basically good. He asserted that 'the basic nature of the human being, when functioning freely, is constructive and trustworthy.'[10] He wrote of the 'growing recognition that the innermost core of man's nature, the deepest layers of his personality, the base of his "animal nature", is positive in nature – is basically socialised, forward-moving, rational and realistic.'[11] He was resolutely opposed to the Protestant Christian tradition, for it had 'permeated our culture with the concept that man is basically sinful, and only by something approaching a miracle can his sinful nature be negated'.[12]

Because of his strong aversion to the Christian faith, Rogers accepted no moral authority outside of himself and his own experience. He writes, 'Experience is, for me, the highest authority. The touchstone of validity is my own experience. No other person's ideas, and none of my own ideas, are as authoritative as my experience. It is to experience that I must return again and again, to discover a closer approximation to truth as it is in the process of becoming in me.'[13] And lest there be any doubt he goes on, 'Neither the Bible nor the prophets – neither Freud nor research – neither the revelations of God nor man – can take precedence over my own direct experience.'[14]

In *On Becoming a Person* (1961), Rogers says that when life is at its best the flow of his experience carries him in a direction which appears to be forward, toward goals of which he is but dimly aware; there are no fixed points, no closed system of beliefs, no unchanging set of principles which he holds. 'Life is guided by a changing understanding of and interpretation of my experience. It is always in process of becoming. I trust it is clear now why there is no philosophy or belief or set of principles which I could encourage or persuade others to have or hold.'[15] His ambition is to 'give others the permission and freedom to develop their own inward freedom and thus their own meaningful interpretation of their own experience. If there is such a thing as truth, this free individual process of search should, I believe, converge toward it.'[16]

As a committed humanist, Rogers makes it clear that he does not believe in God and that he has no idea whether there is such a thing as truth. He rejects the moral teachings of Scripture and believes in no moral framework other than his own experience. He taught that authority to make choices lies within the self, rather than in Scripture, society or another person. He said that the individual must recognise that it rests within himself to choose; that the only question which matters is, 'Am I living in a way which is deeply satisfying to me, and which truly expresses me?'[17] According to Rogers, it's me first—satisfying my desires is all that counts. He has no moral compass, no moral reference point and appears to glory in his unbelief and self-centredness. Moreover, he wants others to share his freedom from moral restraint, so that they can feel good about following his self-centred, amoral lifestyle.

Feelings and emotions

Rogers placed a great emphasis on feelings; and his ideas have been eagerly taken up by marriage education, as we shall see. To be a real person we must learn to own, experience and communicate our deepest feelings. He asserted that most people blocked their true feelings, and therefore lived a pretence that prevents them from becoming a real person. To be a real person, with real emotions and true feelings, we must change from a position of fixity to what he called 'flowingness'. In a position of fixity, feelings and personal meanings are neither recognised nor owned, and there is no desire to change. 'The individual has little or no recognition of the ebb and flow of the feeling life within him... He does not communicate himself, but only communicates about externals.'[18] Rogers wants people 'to feel their own feelings, live by values which they discover within, and express themselves in their own unique ways.'[19]

He believed that the good life involved developing our potential to the full. To experience a good life a person must be 'free to live his feelings subjectively, as they exist in him, and also free to be aware of these feelings'.[20] He says that for those individuals who are able to trust their reaction to a new situation because they are open to their experience, doing what 'feels right' proves to be a trustworthy guide to behaviour which is truly satisfying.[21] His belief in the innate ability of humans beings to experience the good life has emerged from his flawed view of human nature.

Rogers emphasised the importance of feelings in order to communicate in family relationships. 'Experience in therapy seems to bring about change in the way our clients live in their family relationships. They learn something about how to initiate and maintain real two-way communication. To understand another person's thoughts and feelings thoroughly, with the meanings they have for him, and to be thoroughly understood by this other person in return – this is one of the most rewarding of human experiences, and all too rare... When we are living behind a façade, when we are trying to act in ways that are not in accord with our feelings, then we dare not listen freely to another.'[22] But when a client expresses his real feelings in the situation in which they occur, 'when his family relationships are lived on the basis of the feelings which actually exist, then he is no longer defensive and he can really listen to and understand another member of his family'.[23]

Rogers says that sharing feelings, and a willingness to be vulnerable and take a risk, is an important part of communicating with our partner. He explains: 'I will risk myself by endeavouring to communicate any persisting feeling, positive or negative, to my partner – to the full depth that I understand it in myself – as a living, present part of me. Then I will risk further by trying to understand, with all the empathy I can bring to bear, his or her response, whether it is accusatory and critical or sharing and self-revealing.'[24]

Based on Rogers' advice, virtually all marriage education programmes, both secular and Christian, teach that real communication involves revealing and sharing our deepest feelings. However, a problem with this emphasis on feelings is that it makes us concentrate on ourselves. The feelings of an unregenerate heart are nearly always self-centred, for they reflect the desires, wants, lusts, anger, envy and jealousy of a sinful heart. Scripture says that 'a fool vents all his feelings, but a wise man holds them back' (Proverbs 29.11). The emotions of believers are moulded and controlled by God's Word. We are encouraged to have the mind of Christ and to set our mind on things that are above, not on things on the earth, and certainly not on ourselves. So we do not focus on our feelings, but on Christ and his Word.

Rogers on marriage and its alternatives

Rogers was upfront that his mission in writing *Becoming Partners – Marriage and its Alternatives* (1972) is to find alternatives to traditional marriage. He developed his vision for a new type of marriage as he gathered first-hand experience of the struggles that men and women have in trying to create meaningful relationships. He writes, 'So there began to form in my mind the thought that I might have something to offer to them in some of their pioneering struggle to build new kinds of marriage and alternatives to marriage. Not a stupid book of advice, certainly, but perhaps something that was *new*.'[25]

Rogers tells us something of his marriage to Helen. He says that they did not agree about 'whether there is an element of possessiveness in a good marriage. I say no. She says yes. I formed a real attachment to another woman, an attachment which to my mind did not exclude Helen, but was in addition to my love for her. She did not see it the same way at all, and was very upset. It was not so much jealousy as it was a deep anger at me which she turned inward, feeling that she was "on the shelf", and inadequate.'[26] This statement speaks volumes about the morality of Carl Rogers—in his self-centred arrogance he sought to justify his adulterous relationship, caring little for the deep hurt that this caused his faithful wife.

Rogers interviewed a range of couples in his determination to find alternatives to marriage. He also freely expressed a view of how he hoped sexual relationships would develop over time. He said that the trend towards greater freedom in sexual relationships, in both adolescents and adults, is likely to continue, whether this direction frightens us or not. He predicted that the attitude of possessiveness, 'which historically has dominated sexual unions—is likely to be greatly diminished. It is certain that there will be enormous variation in the quality of these sexual relationships—from where sex is a purely physical contact... to those in which the sexual aspect is an expression of an increasing sharing of feelings, of experiences of each other... Some temporary unions thus formed may be legalized as a type of marriage—with no permanent commitment... It is becoming increasingly clear that a man-woman relationship will have permanence only to the degree to which it satisfies the emotional, psychological, intellectual, and physical needs of the partners... There may be a mutual agreement as to whether or not the marriage includes sexual faithfulness to one's mate.'[27]

With this powerful statement the humanistic psychologist declared total war on the biblical view of marriage. He was a fierce warrior in the perpetual war between the seed of Satan and the Seed of Christ, who took pleasure in sounding the death knell of traditional marriage as he sought to legitimise a new way of looking at marriage and sexual relationships. He cultivated the idea that the *purpose of marriage was to satisfy the emotional needs of the partners*. The future was a new kind of 'marriage' ordained by the wisdom of Carl Rogers.

Marriage education

Carl Rogers was one of the first to grasp the potential for marriage education to change the way society viewed marriage. He claims that his theories offer something of value to people in 'their pioneering struggle to build new kinds of marriage and alternatives to marriage'.[28] Rogers' underlying premise is that conventional marriage is a failing institution that has had its day. He says the present-day young person 'tends to have a distrust of marriage as an institution. He has seen too many flaws in it. He has often seen it fail in his own home. Instead, a relationship between a man and a woman is significant, and worth trying to preserve, only when it is an enhancing, growing experience for each person... The young person today is not impressed by the fact that, religiously, a marriage should last "until death do us part". Rather he tends to regard the vows of complete permanence in marriage as clearly hypocritical.'[29]

Rogers taught that adultery was an enriching experience, as long as both husband and wife agreed to it.[30] He believed that married couples may feel the need to date others or to have sexual intercourse with others, and wrote that such relationships should not be called by such negative expressions as 'extramarital affairs', and adultery should not be regarded as immoral.[31]

Rogers says that learning to be partners is a basic need. 'An individual can get a college degree today without ever having learned anything about how to communicate, how to resolve conflict, what to do with anger and other negative feelings... though modern marriage is a tremendous laboratory, its members are often utterly without preparation for the partnership function.'[32] He advocates learning groups (led by people who do not cause psychological damage) to teach about partnership skills. 'The communication of real feelings, positive and negative; the resolution of conflicts and antagonisms; the pathway to self-accepting personhood – all of these might be at least partially achieved.'[33] So Rogers outlines the classic psychological syllabus for marriage education—communication skills, learning to express real feelings, conflict resolution, and affirmation.

Marriage roles of husband and wife

Rogers has a strong aversion to the traditional roles prescribed by Scripture to husband and wife. He chooses life in a Mexican village to present a caricature of biblical marriage. Speaking of a young woman, he says that if both sets of parents approved, 'you would be married in a church... as a young wife you conformed to your husband's wishes, were passive and obedient, and submitted to his sexual demands... you were not lively and warm, but compliant and acceptant of your husband's domination of you.'[34] A young wife needed to ask her husband's permission before taking any action of significance, for her whole training up to this point had been to obey and submit. 'She was supposed to obey her husband, and keep her children submissive to his wishes.'[35] The aim of Rogers is to 'permit real people, *modern* people, to reveal themselves in their fumbling attempts to establish a better kind of partnership'.[36] He says that the 'role behaviour expected by society of a man and a woman, a husband and wife, constitute a heavy burden on the individual'.[37]

In Rogers' eyes, the dissolution of roles in marriage is an important issue. 'To live by role expectations seems consistently in opposition to a marriage which is going somewhere, which is in process.'[38] The woman, who is submissive to her husband because she is supposed to be that way, is in 'a relationship which is static or going downhill. So in the only marriages which seem enriching and satisfying, roles play a lesser and lesser part… to follow—more or less blindly—the expectations of one's parents, of one's religion, of one's culture, is to bring to disaster the ongoing, differentiating process of a developing partnership.'[39] According to Rogers, we must live by our own choices and must not 'be shaped by the wishes, the rules, the roles which others are all too eager to thrust upon us'.[40]

He makes his hostility to the biblical view of marriage abundantly clear. He rejects the idea that the husband is the head of the household, and that the wife should submit to her husband. He ridicules the biblical view of marriage, and he encourages people to reject marriage roles and follow their own way. Rogers is a rebel against God, and he wants everyone to follow his rebellion.

New approaches to marriage

Rogers says that marriage and the nuclear family constitute a failing institution, a failing way of life.[41] So what should we do? 'We need laboratories, experiments, attempts to avoid past failures, exploration into new approaches… new ways of relating, new kinds of partnerships are being tried out, people are learning from mistakes and profiting from success.'[42] He applauds young people who are 'inventing alternatives, new futures, for our most sharply failing institutions, marriage and the nuclear family to conventional marriage'.[43]

Rogers complains that young people are not being supported as they experiment with changes in the institution of marriage. He says we are back in the Middle Ages, as 'we still hold that tradition and religious sanctions, and codes of morality taken from the past, must never be broken, and woe to the person whose values, discoveries, and ways of living violate these sanctions'.[44]

Influence of Carl Rogers

The philosophy of Carl Rogers has had a massive impact on the marriage education movement. He reached three conclusions in his search for alternatives to marriage. First, he concludes that traditional, conventional marriage, in which husband and wife have clear and distinct roles, is a failed institution that needs to be replaced with alternatives. Second, he concludes that we need to experiment to find what types of partnerships work. 'We need laboratories, experiments, attempts to avoid past failures, exploration into new approaches.'[45] We need freedom from moral censure in order to experiment with new types of partnerships. We must rid ourselves of the old-fashioned concepts of living in sin, committing adultery, fornication, homosexuality, lewd and lascivious conduct, for these 'are actions engaged in by individuals struggling to find a better pattern of partnerships'.[46] In effect, he is saying that we must learn to live by the lusts of the flesh. Third, he concludes that partnership education must teach the four 'pillars' of good relationships—communication skills, learning to express real feelings, conflict resolution, and affirmation. These pillars have ever since formed the basis of all modern marriage psycho-education programmes.

So we see that the ideas of Carl Rogers – a godless man without a moral compass, a man who openly promoted selfishness, a man who shamelessly promoted adultery and who actually committed adultery whilst his faithful wife was dying of cancer – has laid the foundation of marriage education. He wanted young people to be freed from the moral demands of biblical marriage. He was especially opposed to a view of marriage that imposed roles on husband and wife, and so he proposed that the roles be dissolved. He wanted a husband and wife to be freed from moral restraints so that they could 'become' themselves and get closer to their inner feelings. He said that the value of an experience is not determined by what your partner says, or by your parents, or by your church, 'but by the way it "feels" to you in your very deepest level of experiencing'.[47]

Rogers was one of the intellectual leaders of the 'if it feels good, do it' movement that contributed greatly to the destruction of the moral standards of millions of Americans and many others in the West, from the 1960s onwards. His book, *Becoming Partners*, published in 1972, undoubtedly had a major impact on the world of marriage and family therapy. Most psychotherapists and family counsellors were trained in the principles of his non-directive counselling techniques, and absorbed his amoral view of life. Surely the rotten foundations underlying so much of modern marriage education must be clear to all. The human potential movement and marriage education were the natural products of Rogers' permissive humanistic philosophy. For more on Rogers see my book, *The Dark Side of Christian Counselling*, the Wakeman Trust, 2009. We now turn to the mother of family therapy, Virginia Satir, the woman who eagerly followed in Rogers' footsteps.

(Endnotes)

1 Cited from Issues, Etc website, 'Meet Dr. Bill Coulson, Thoughts from the man who, together with Carl Rogers, pioneered the practice of encounter groups', edited by Don Matzat. http://www.mtio.com/articles/aissar74.htm

2 Richard Hunt, Larry Hof, Rita DeMaria, *Marriage Enrichment*, 1998, Brunnel/Mazel, pp35-36

3 Ibid. p36

4 Gerald Weeks and Stephen Treat, *Couples in treatment*, Brunner-Routledge, second edition, 2001, p110

5 Richard Hunt, Larry Hof, Rita DeMaria, *Marriage Enrichment*, p 15

6 'A Historical Look at the Anti-Religious Bias in the Social Sciences and its Effect on the American Family', an article by Julia Witham, Paul Robinson and Emily Naegle, Brigham Young University, Provo, Utah: http://aabss.org/Perspectives2006/AABSS2006Article2AHISTORICALLOOKATTHEANTI.pdf

7 Cited from *A Practitioner's Guide to Understanding Indigenous and Foreign Cultures*: 'An Analysis of Relationships Between Ethnicity, Social Class and Therapeutic Intervention Strategies', by George Henderson, Spigner-Littles Dorscine, Virginia Millhouse, Charles C Thomas Pub Ltd; 3 edition, 2006, p148

8 Comment by Brett Strohl, who has a Masters Degree in counselling and psychology theory, on A Ku Indeed! website, page entitled, 'Taoism, Confucianism and Humanistic Psychology' oolongiv.wordpress.com/2008/02/21/taoism-confucianism-and-humanistic-psychology/

9 Cited from *A Practitioner's Guide to Understanding Indigenous and Foreign Cultures*, p148

10 Carl Rogers, *On Becoming a Person*, Houghton Mifflin, Boston, 1961, p194

11 Ibid. p91

12 Ibid. p91

13 Ibid. pp23-24

14 Ibid. p24

15 Ibid. p27

16 Ibid. p27

17 Ibid. p119

18 Ibid. p133

19 Ibid. p175

20 Ibid. p188
21 Ibid. p189
22 Ibid. pp323-324
23 Ibid. p324
24 Carl Rogers, *Becoming Partners – Marriage and its Alternatives*, Constable and Company, (first published in 1972), reprint 1988, p210
25 Ibid. p11
26 Ibid. p34
27 Ibid. pp17-18
28 Ibid. p11
29 Ibid. pp20-21
30 Richard M. Ryckman, *Theories of Personality*, 4th edition, Brooks/Cole, Pacific Grove, California, 1989, p389
31 Ibid.
32 Carl Rogers, *Becoming Partners*, p221
33 Ibid. pp221-22
34 Ibid. p82
35 Ibid. p83
36 Ibid. p86
37 Ibid. p52
38 Ibid. p211
39 Ibid. p211
40 Ibid. p212
41 Ibid. p217
42 Ibid. p217
43 Ibid. p217
44 Ibid. p218
45 Ibid. p217
46 Ibid. p218
47 Ibid. p213

7

Virginia Satir – mother of family therapy

Virginia Satir is the woman referred to by many as the pioneer of family therapy. Her ideas have had an enormous influence on shaping the profession that we now know as marriage and family therapy. She was significantly influenced by Carl Rogers' humanistic psychology, and was voted the fifth most influential therapist of all time by the *Psychotherapy Networker*. Such was her status that in 1988, shortly before her death, she was appointed to the Steering Committee of the International Family Therapy Association and became a member of the Advisory Board for the National Council for Self-Esteem in the United States.

Her claim to psychotherapeutic fame is that she was one of the first therapists to see the whole family together. In the early 1950s, as a young therapist, she realised the importance of counselling family members together as the best way to get the complete picture. Although her ideas went against the therapeutic thinking of the day, she nevertheless developed and taught family therapy courses at the Mental Research Institute in California. In 1962 the Research Institute obtained a grant from the National Institute of Mental Health to begin what would be the first formal family therapy training programme. Her first book, *Conjoint Family Therapy* (1964), established her as a pioneer in new ways of helping people in need. She travelled extensively throughout the 1960s and 1970s, conducting workshops and seminars to spread her philosophy of family therapy.

Satir gained a reputation as a creative, forceful and charismatic therapist. While she was gifted in developing new ideas, she had little interest in doing research. Over her long career she achieved international fame as a family therapist and was best known for her work in self-esteem. She wrote, 'It is not surprising that occasionally a low pot person [her terminology for low self-esteem] under overwhelming pressure will resort to drugs or suicide or murder. I truly believe that most of the pain, problems, ugliness in life – even wars – are the result of someone's low pot, which he really can't talk straight about.'[1] The dogma of low self-esteem, which Satir championed, was destined to gain great influence in society, and even within the pastoral ministry of the Church.

Satir's ideas have undoubtedly had a very large impact on the profession of marital and family therapy and on the marriage education movement. Such is her legendary status that she is acknowledged as the honorary founding chairperson of PAIRS, a hugely popular marriage education programme that is described in chapter 11.

The Universal Life Force

Satir's beliefs about religion and spirituality were central to her worldview and therapeutic ideas. As a young person Satir took a cursory look at Christian Science, the religion of her mother. In an interview with Sheldon Kramer, cited in *Transforming the inner and outer family: humanistic and spiritual approaches to mind-body systems therapy* (1995), Satir said: 'I knew that life was something that I didn't make and nobody else made. Therefore there had to be a higher power. Life was the result of the Higher Power and had nothing to do with the human mode. So very early I remember taking God as life and nature as life… how can we grow up and be connected if a God up there is going to kill me if I don't do right?'[2] Satir said that one of the hardest things is to recognise life as energy. 'And what we do to ourselves is we put up a wall and contain the energy so that it isn't free to move. And so all of these experiences have to do with flow. This is life flowing. In the flow of everything… Life is energy. I don't see it's anything else, and it's an energy that permeates everything.'[3]

Like Carl Rogers, Satir rejected the Christian faith and chose to follow a form of spirituality that had much in common with Eastern religions. She believed that growth was the 'Universal Life Force' revealing itself. 'I believe that we have a pipeline to universal intelligence and wisdom through our intuition, which can be tapped through meditation, prayer, relaxation, awareness, the development of high self-esteem, and a reverence for life. This is how I reach my spirituality.'[4] She used techniques that blended Eastern meditation and spirituality, and incorporated meditation and affirmation into her work. She said that 'dreams and wishes go together', and she encouraged her students to use such affirmations as, 'I own me. I can engineer me.'[5]

Human potential movement

As her vision broadened, Satir became a leading advocate for the human potential movement. She served as director of training at the Esalen Institute, California, which was founded in 1962 as an alternative educational centre devoted to the exploration of human potential – the world of unrealised human capacities that lies beyond the imagination. She was especially keen to learn more about meditation. Her approach to therapy, which was based on the idea of personal growth, and her understanding of family systems were integrated into many of the Institute's healing and personal growth programmes.[6] She was concerned with the health and healing of each individual human spirit, which she believed could be achieved by connecting with a universal life force.

Her best-selling work, *The New Peoplemaking* (1988), revised shortly before her death, provides a clear statement of her ideology. She wrote the book 'to support, emphasize, educate and empower the family'. She believed that a new evolution in humankind was afoot. 'All people who are working toward becoming more fully human will be bridges to that new time... Our challenge now is to develop human beings with values—moral, ethical and humanistic—that can effectively utilize this development. When we achieve that, we will be able to enjoy this most wonderful planet and the life that inhabits it. We are on the way.'[7]

From her experience as a family therapist she noticed that there were two groups of families—troubled families and nurturing families. She realised that troubled families had low self-worth, poor communication, and worst of all, rules that were inhuman, rigid and everlasting. In contrast, untroubled families are characterised by high self-worth among its members, communication that is clear and specific, and rules that are flexible, humane and subject to change. Members of a nurturing family feel free to tell each other about their feelings.[8]

She profoundly believed that all human beings have an innate drive to grow and evolve a positive energy that moves them towards becoming, as she put it, more fully human. Her approach towards people was always positive.[9] She believed that 'all people are manifestations of the Life Force, and, as people, we all have the internal resources we need in order to cope successfully and grow'.[10] She held high hopes in the ability of the human spirit to make this world a better place to live in. Her vision was to help empower people to reach their full potential.

Marriage and family

The marital history of the pioneer of family therapy is surely relevant to our understanding of her teaching. She married at the age of 25 after a war-time romance, and divorced her first husband after eight years of marriage in 1949. She married her second husband, Norman Satir, in 1951, but this marriage also ended in divorce six years later. She chose not to marry a third time. She wrote that 'divorce is coming to mean more of a desirable social necessity and not a personal calamity'.[11] Her teaching was profoundly opposed to the traditional view of marriage, and she often used role-plays 'to demonstrate the destructive results of typical and traditional family patterns of dominance and submission'.[12] She also used role-plays to teach family members what she saw as the alternative—to communicate as equals.[12a]

She was highly sceptical about traditional sexual morality. She said we should not be critical of 'some people whose level of interest is short and so they choose one mate after another. Instead of considering this a shortcoming, what would happen if we treated this as a simple variation? Such people could enter a limited contract; say from one to five years... Perhaps the married people who have heterosexual relationships outside the marriage are not simply "adulterers", but are people with a human need. After all, polyandry and polygamy were once respected forms of marriage. And why not have group or communal marriage?'[13] She rejected the biblical view of marriage out of hand. She asked: 'Why does it have to be limited to just one man and one woman?'[14]

Satir was a firm advocate of what she called 'positive pairing', which she promoted as a counter to the submission/headship model of Scripture. She said that 'various forms of submission and domination characterized the pair model that most of us grew up with. I will henceforth refer to this model as the threat-and-reward model.'[15] We are told that although learning how to pair positively is new to many of us, we need to enter a 'new world of equality of value with all other human beings... The stakes are high: replacing the threat-and-reward model with one of positive pairing could improve global as well as personal relations.'[16]

Here we should pause to take on board the fact that Virginia Satir, with her profound hostility to the biblical view of marriage and the traditional family, is accepted and venerated as one of the pioneers of marriage and family therapy.

Human nature is basically good

Like Abraham Maslow and Carl Rogers before her, Satir believed that human nature is basically good at its core. She claimed that 'everyone's intentions were positive, no matter how horrible their behaviour was, and she used these positive intentions as a firm foundation of agreement from which to search for more positive feelings, communications and behaviour... She believed that, at the core, people mean well—even when they do mean things.'[17] As a consequence she never blamed anyone for their behaviour, for 'she presupposed that hurtful or destructive behaviour was simply a result of limited opportunities to learn how to respond more favorably'.[18]

Flowing from her positive view of human nature, Satir's work with a client was guided by four questions: 'What do you want?'; 'How will you know when you've got it?'; 'What stops you now?'; 'What do you need to do in order to get it?'[19] She believed that helping people to get what they want would move them in a positive direction and develop their potential.

Satir's therapeutic beliefs

Satir was unshakable in her confidence that human growth is natural and moves in a positive direction. She reasoned that because human beings are all unique manifestations of the same 'Universal Life Force', they can connect in a positive, accepting, loving way.

The Satir Growth Model is a set of beliefs, tools and experiential exercises that support positive change in individuals, family systems and communities.[20] It is based on the assumption that change is possible—'the Satir Process Model provides a road map for assisting individuals, couples, and families through a transformational shift in their basic belief or understanding of themselves. The process of change is a way to assist people in making choices that increase self-esteem, provide self-accountability, and move a person toward a more congruent sense of self. The transformation that is experienced is an internal process where the universal yearnings to be loved, acknowledged, and accepted can be met by the individual self.'[21]

In the early development of her model Satir focused on communication. She felt that, when placed under stress in relationships, people needed to find a way to protect the positive nature of their inner self. 'She found that there are common patterns of how people cope. She labelled them placating (pleasing), blaming (projecting), super-reasonable (analyzing) and irrelevant (distracting). These coping stances indicate the behaviours, feelings, thoughts and expectations of the people using them and became the basis for her early work.'[22]

Later in her career, she 'developed a number of creative vehicles and interventions to help people access their own internal wisdom for growth'.[23] By the end of her life, she was more open about including her spiritual beliefs about people in her teaching and therapy sessions, often presented as her meditations and visualisations. The deep therapeutic work she did with people and families was viewed with awe, as the clients she worked with discovered their own internal resources and made choices to heal.

Satir made the following declaration of her self-esteem: 'I am Me. In all the world, there is no one else exactly like me. Everything that comes out of me is authentically mine, because I alone chose it—I own everything about me: my body, my feelings, my mouth, my voice, all my actions, whether they be to others or myself. I own my fantasies, my dreams, my hopes, my fears. I own my triumphs and successes, all my failures and mistakes. Because I own all of me, I can become intimately acquainted with me. By so doing, I can love me and be friendly with all my parts.'[24]

Satir believed that the therapist's self-esteem is crucial to the therapeutic process, and so she focused on helping therapists to do their own inner healing during her training programmes. She taught that a therapist must heal their own internal world before they can heal their clients' internal and external family systems. Therapists who are able to increase their own self-esteem will be more effective.[25]

Significance of Satir

Satir was more than a therapist—she was a revolutionary who was fighting for a new way of living, a new moral order in which people achieve self-worth, in which relationships are more positive, loving and happy, and in which families are more nurturing. And she knew that she was engaged in a battle against the Christian faith and its teachings on marriage and the family. 'Let us remember that old, traditional, entrenched, familiar attitudes die hard... I am working on the side of nurturing the new ways, and I invite you to join me.'[26] Family therapy was to be a key weapon in the battle to propagate the new ways. Here we see just another example of man's search for a new way to happiness and meaning. Like Adam and Eve in the Garden, Satir was not satisfied with God's way.

Her thinking was heavy influenced by Carl Rogers. She followed most of Rogers' therapeutic ideas and incorporated them into her family system. Her ideas on self-worth and communication are straight from Rogers. Like the humanist psychologists, she rejected entirely the Christian view of life. We see this in her rejection of what she called rigid, non-negotiable and everlasting rules—clearly a reference to biblical laws.[27] In particular she did not like the absolute biblical view of sexual conduct that condemned fornication and adultery as sin. She wanted flexible, changing rules that were able to accommodate and tolerate human sin. She was also profoundly opposed to the biblical view of marriage, and especially the teaching of submission and headship taught by the apostle Paul in Ephesians 5.

Her influence has been widespread and pervasive, and clearly has had a large influence on the profession of marriage and family therapy and on the marriage psycho-education movement. Yet in many ways her ideas and writings are simplistic and hopelessly utopian. Her own special contribution was to make spirituality and meditation acceptable ideas to the therapeutic industry. Spiritual enlightenment and openness to the 'Universal Life Force' was central to her system. She promoted the notion of living in the flow of life, an idea that would come to fruition in the positive psychology movement of the late 1990s, as we shall see in chapter 9.

(Endnotes)

1 Virginia Satir, *Peoplemaking*, Souvenir Press, first published 1972, reissued in paperback 1989, p23

2 Sheldon Z. Kramer, *Transforming the inner and outer family: humanistic and spiritual approaches to mind-body systems therapy*, The Haworth Press, 1995, p3

3 Ibid. p3

4 Virginia Satir, *The New Peoplemaking*, Science and Behavior Books, 1988, p338

5 Cited from website of Women's Intellectual Contributions to the Study of Mind and Society, article on 'Virginia Satir (1916-1988)', http://www.webster.edu/~woolflm/satir.html

6 Website of Northwest Satir Institute, Virginia Satir (1916-1988), http://nwsatirinstitute.org/virginia.html

7 Satir, *The New Peoplemaking*, preface, px-xi

8 Ibid. p4

9 Cited from paper 'Peace for the New Millennium' by Kathlyne Maki-Banmen, Website of the Satir Institute of the Pacific, http://www.satirpacific.org/uploads//documents/Publications/Peace

10 Website of Northwest Satir Institute, Virginia Satir

11 Satir, *Peoplemaking*, p303

12 Steve Andreas, *Virginia Satir: the patterns of her magic*, Science and Behavior Books, 1991, p6 Cited from http://www.steveandreas.narod.ru/en_satirpatterns_10.html

12a Ibid

13 Satir, *Peoplemaking*, p298

14 Ibid. p299

15 Satir, *The New Peoplemaking*, p326

16 Ibid. p329

17 Andreas, *Virginia Satir: the patterns of her magic*, p4

18 Ibid. p5

19 Ibid. p3

20 Website of Satir Institute of the Southeast, 'Overview of the Satir Growth Model' http://www.satirinstitute.org/CLDW.php

21 Cited from abstract of the article 'Transformational Change—Based on the Model of Virginia Satir' by Carl Sayles in *Contemporary Family Therapy*, vol 24, issue 1, March 2004, pp93-109

22 Cited from paper, 'Applications of the Satir Growth Model, Introduction', by Dr. John Banmen and Kathlyne Maki-Banmen, 2006

23 Ibid.

24 'My Declaration of Self-Esteem', Virginia Satir, cited from website, International Human Learning Resources Network, http://www.ihlrn.org/about_virginia_satir.html

25 Cited from 'Therapist's Self' by Wendy Lum, in *The Wisdom Box*, The Official Newsletter of the Satir Institute of the Pacific, May 2003, Spring Issue

26 Satir, *The New Peoplemaking*, p385

27 Ibid. p4

8

John Gottman's marriage research

John Gottman is the man who has taken on the mantle of Carl Rogers. In chapter 6 we saw Carl Rogers emphasise the need for experimentation to find what types of partnerships really work. He said that 'we need laboratories, experiments, attempts to avoid past failures, exploration into new approaches'.[1] He also said that to do proper research we need freedom from moral censure. We must, therefore, rid ourselves of old-fashioned concepts, such as living in sin, committing adultery, fornication, homosexuality, lewd and lascivious conduct, for these 'are the actions engaged in by individuals struggling to find a better pattern of partnerships'.[2]

John Gottman claims to have done the research that helps us understand the reality of relationships—what makes them work, and what causes them to fail. He has taken up the challenge of Rogers' plea for exploration to find new approaches to relationships. After three decades of research Gottman is widely accepted as the foremost world authority on marriage and relationships. In the field of positive psychology he is well-known for his 5-to-1 ratio of positive to negative language, and how this ratio predicts the success of relationships.

In 1986 Gottman joined the Department of Psychology at the University of Washington, and started the Family Research Laboratory, which has been the site for numerous studies on marriage, gay and lesbian couples, domestic violence, parenting and child development. The work of the Laboratory is held to be so important that it has consistently received long-term funding from the National Institute of Mental Health. Gottman's research has earned numerous major awards, which include the American Association for Marriage and Family Therapy

Distinguished Research Scientist Award, and a Presidential citation for outstanding Lifetime Research from the American Psychological Association Division of Family Psychology.

Gottman's Family Research Laboratory, popularly known as the Love Lab, is actually a well-appointed apartment with a one-way mirror, cameras for recording every word and facial expression, and sensors for tracking physiological signs like heart beat and blood pressure. A couple admitted to the Love Lab are carefully observed and their physiological signs recorded. After separately completing a questionnaire about their relationship, the couple have an interview with one of the researchers. They are then prepared for a 'conflict discussion', when they are wired up so that their physiological response to the conflict session can be monitored. A video monitor focuses on each partner as they are asked to discuss distressing issues, or to tell the story of how they met. A box of tissues is placed near each chair to help deal with the tears that result. Some couples are so upset by this exercise that they need 20 minutes to recover from the stress and anger that has been generated.

Gottman has stated the purpose of his research programme in bold terms. 'My goal has been nothing more ambitious than to uncover the truth about marriage—to finally answer the questions that have puzzled people for so long: Why is marriage so tough at times? Why do some lifelong relationships click, while others just tick away like a time bomb? And how can you prevent a marriage from going bad?'[3] We are being asked to accept that his sociological research, based on observing couples with video cameras, has the ability to reveal 'truth' about marriage. In effect, Gottman is asserting that the 'truth' generated by his research is to be placed above the truth of Scripture, which we set out in chapter 5.

After three decades Gottman has studied over three thousand couples, and claims to be able to predict the likelihood of divorce with 91 percent accuracy. He says that his guidance for strengthening good marriages and repairing troubled ones is based on scientific principles. His philosophy of marriage education, built on the foundation of this research, is expressed in two books, *Why Marriages Succeed or Fail and How to Make Yours Last* (1995) and *The Seven Principles for Making Marriage Work* (1999).

The successful relationship ratio

Gottman's major contribution to sociological research is the supposed finding that successful relationships are those which exist in a rich climate of positivity. He apparently discovered that happily married couples keep 'their negative thoughts and feelings about each other (which all couples have) from overwhelming their positive ones... The more emotionally intelligent a couple—the better able they are to understand, honor, and respect each other and their marriage—the more likely that they will indeed live happily ever after. Just as parents can teach their children emotional intelligence, this is a skill that a couple can be taught.'[4] Gottman says that it all comes down to a mathematical formula. 'Our research suggests that what really separates contented couples from those in deep marital misery is a healthy balance between their positive and negative feelings and actions towards each other... that magic ratio is 5-to-1. In other words, as long as there is five times as much positive feeling and interaction between husband and wife as there is negative, we found marriage was likely to be stable. It was based on this ratio that we were able to predict whether couples were likely to divorce: in very unhappy couples, there tended to be more negative than positive interaction.'[5] The conclusion is 'that your marriage needs much more positivity than negativity to nourish your love. Without it, your relationship is in danger of withering and dying.'[6]

Gottman describes what he calls 'The Four Horsemen of the Apocalypse', which are very bad for the marriage relationship. 'In order of least to most dangerous, they are criticism, contempt, defensiveness and stonewalling. As these behaviours become more and more entrenched, husband and wife focus increasingly on the escalating sense of negativity and tension in their marriage.'[7] The 'Four Horsemen' are dangerous because they sabotage attempts to keep negativity from overwhelming a relationship. 'By unsettling a marriage's healthy ecology – that 5-to-1 ratio in favour of positive interaction – the horsemen can throw a happy couple into a dangerous tailspin... However, if you learn to recognize what is happening to your once-happy marriage, you can still develop the tools you need to regain control of it.'[8]

Scripture identifies these 'horsemen' as the works of the flesh, described in Galatians 5. The believer is exhorted to: 'Walk in the Spirit, and you shall not fulfil the lust of the flesh' (Galatians 5.16). The command of Scripture is that we put off the old sinful nature, with its lustful desires, and be renewed in the spirit of our mind, putting on the new nature in true righteousness and holiness (Ephesians 4.22-24). Gottman's 'Four Horsemen' do not rule in the life of a believer who obeys Scripture.

Tips for developing a positive mindset

Gottman gives examples of how 'stable couples showed their positivity. It translates into a useful list of ways to put more weight on the positive side of the equation in your marriage.'[9] Examples include being 'actively interested in what your partner is saying. Your wife, for example, complains about an employee who is irresponsible and makes her miss her bus. You say, with feeling and energy, "He really did that? I can't believe he came late again and you had to stay and miss your bus!".'[10] Another example is to show your affection by 'touching or holding hands while you watch TV, intertwining your feet while you read the Sunday paper together'.[11] You could show you care by small acts of thoughtfulness, which is a powerful way to boost the positivity in your marriage. Here are some examples: 'You are shopping and you pass a florist; you buy your wife some flowers she'd like. Or you're in the grocery store and you think of getting your husband's favourite ice cream.'[12] You must learn to be appreciative of your marriage. 'You put positive energy into the marriage simply through appreciating it—thinking about and remembering positive moments from your past, thinking fondly about your partner, and so on.'[13]

You can be empathetic by showing your partner an emotional resonance. 'You can show that you really understand and feel what your partner is feeling just through an expression on your face that matches your partner's.'[14] You can be accepting, 'even if your partner is saying something you don't agree with, let your partner know what he or she is saying makes sense and is important—that you respect it'.[15] This shows that you accept the feelings that are being expressed.[16] These, according to Gottman's theory, 'are the marks that keep your marriage on the positive side of that 5-to-1 ratio'.[17]

Gottman gives four key strategies for improving your marriage. The first is to calm down and to learn to relax when in a disagreement with your partner.[18] The second is to learn to speak non-defensively to your partner. It is important 'to have a positive mindset about your spouse and to reintroduce praise and admiration into your relationship'.[19] You must understand 'the importance of praise and admiration and some blue-print for reintroducing them into your marriage'.[20] He makes the rather obvious point that 'everyone, including your spouse, responds to genuine praise, thanks and simple heartfelt compliments on a regular basis. At first, you may need to remind yourself to speak your positive thoughts.'[21] He gives a few examples of the sorts of simple things that we should learn to say: 'I really appreciated your cooking dinner tonight'; 'You really handled that contractor well'; 'You were a very considerate father tonight'; or even, 'You were really funny tonight. I just love your sense of humor.'[22]

The third strategy is validation. 'Letting your spouse know in so many little ways that you understand him or her is one of the most powerful tools for healing your relationship.'[23] Validation is simply putting yourself in your partner's shoes and imagining his or her emotional state, and letting them 'know that you understand those feelings and consider them valid, even if you don't share them'.[24] The fourth strategy is to keep on practising the above skills. 'You and your spouse have to practice these skills even when you don't necessarily feel like it... if you practice, practice, practice these skills you will have gone a very long way toward improving your marriage.'[25]

It seems amazing that it took a large research programme to establish the obvious common-sense truth that lasting relationships are built on kindness, encouragement and mutual support, whilst hatred, hostility and selfishness cause relationships to break down. This we know from Scripture, which tells us that to be spiritually minded is life and peace, while the works of the flesh are hatred, contentions, outbursts of wrath, selfish ambitions and dissensions (Galatians 5.20).

Concept of the new husband

Gottman discusses what he calls the concept of the 'new husband'. He asserts that 'the emotionally intelligent husband' is the next step in social evolution. 'He has simply figured out something very important about being married that the others haven't—yet. And that is how to honor his wife and convey his respect to her.'[26] This new husband is able to accept influence from his wife. He is also familiar with his children's world, and 'because he is not afraid of emotions, he teaches his children to respect their own feelings—and themselves.'[27]

Gottman paints a dismal caricature of the husband who believes in the biblical concept of male headship. The traditional husband is a very sad story, for 'he responds to the loss of male entitlement with righteous indignation, or he feels like an innocent victim. He may become more authoritarian or withdraw into a lonely shell, protecting what little he has left... He will not accept his wife's influence because he fears any further loss of power.'[28] Of course, no husband who holds to the biblical view of male headship refuses to accept his wife's influence; he simply maintains God has ordained that he is the ultimate decision-maker in the marriage.

According to Gottman, sharing marital power is a relatively new concept that has come about in the wake of vast social changes over the past few decades. While 'wearing the pants' was once the norm for a husband the times have changed. 'Maybe all of this sounds like a feminist line, but it's also the reality... it's understandable that some men have problems with the shift in the husband's role. For centuries men were expected to be in charge of their families.'[29] While some men may resist being influenced by their wives, that is a forlorn hope according to Gottman, for 'there is scientific evidence that we are living through a cultural transformation that will not come undone'.[30] Note how Gottman makes the assertion that there is 'scientific evidence' to support his ideological position that the biblical view of male headship is a thing of the past, and that its demise cannot be undone. This simply shows the weakness of his teaching. The ordering of authority in a marriage does not come from so-called 'scientific evidence', but from the teaching of Scripture.

Gottman concedes that 'not all marriages have become more egalitarian. Many men are still disengaged from family life. Yet a growing number are seeking guidance in coping with the cultural change... The challenge for each man is to decide how to deal with this great transformation. Our research clearly indicates that the only effective approach is to embrace the change rather that to react with anger and hostility.'[31] Husbands are persuaded that to 'willingly cede power to your spouse

[is] a hallmark of an emotionally intelligent marriage'.[32] Notice again the appeal to 'our research'.

This is Gottman's attack on male headship as taught in Scripture. He asserts that the biblical role of the husband is crumbling and in irreversible decline. Therefore, the new husband must be taught to share marital power with his wife, for marriage must be an equal-regard relationship. The emotionally intelligent husband is the one who willingly relinquishes headship of the family and cedes power to his wife. So we see that three great pillars of the marriage education movement – Carl Rogers, Virginia Satir and John Gottman – have all disparaged the biblical model of marriage and the ordering of authority in the family.

Housework

Gottman is adamant that housework should be shared between husband and wife. He is very critical of the husband who thinks that a woman's role is to be the homemaker. He labels husbands who don't share the housework as slackers. 'But many were raised in traditional homes where their father did no housework at all. A husband may pay lip-service to the notion that times have changed and that it isn't fair for his wife to work a second shift when she gets home while he pops open a beer. But old ways die hard. On some level many men still consider housework to be a woman's job… Men have to do more housework!'[33] Scripture teaches young wives to be 'homemakers, good, obedient to their own husbands, that the word of God may not be blasphemed' (Titus 2.5). Actually, although the wife always welcomes a helping hand from her husband, she is far from wanting him let loose in the house. The home is the wife's domain and very precious to her, which she prefers to run along her own lines, without interference from an over-helpful husband!

Forgive Yourself

This is Gottman's master stroke. He tells us about the man who is full of self-criticism. There is a voice inside that says he is not good enough. 'He continually searches for approval but cannot enjoy it or even accept it when it is offered… If you consider yourself inadequate you are always on the lookout for what is not there in yourself and your partner... If you recognize yourself in the description of the self-critic, the best thing you can do for yourself and your marriage is to work on accepting yourself with all of your flaws. As I look back on my own life so far, I realize the immense difference it has made in my role as a husband and a father for me to forgive myself for all of my imperfections.'[34]

So Gottman's advice for the man with a troubled conscience is that he should work on accepting himself with all of his flaws. Scripture, in contrast, offers such a man – who is dead in his sins – not forgiveness of self, but salvation in Christ. Our Lord said, 'Come to Me all you who labour and are heavy laden and I will give you rest' (Matthew 11.28). And Gottman claims for himself the power to forgive all of his 'imperfections'. What he is really saying is that he has the power within himself to forgive all his own sins. Scripture teaches that God alone has the authority to forgive sin.

An exercise in thanksgiving and praise

Gottman gives us an exercise in thanksgiving to help overcome our negative feelings. The first step is to try to focus on what is right. 'Search for things to praise. Begin with simple things. Praise the world... Utter some silent words of thanksgiving (to no one in particular) for these small wonders in your day. This will begin to change your focus on the negative.'[35] Step two is to 'give at least one genuine, heartfelt praise to your spouse each day for an entire week. Notice the effects of this exercise on your partner and yourself... Remember this all has to be genuine and heartfelt. Don't be phony. Notice these positive qualities. Enjoy them... As you stretch the period of thanksgiving one day beyond a week, and then another day, and then another, you'll receive a great gift: You will begin to forgive yourself. Grace and forgiveness will enter your world.'[36]

Here we see the fruit of Gottman's vast research enterprise. When all is said and done all he has to offer is an exercise in positive psychology—pseudo-scientific research, dressed up in pseudo-spiritual vocabulary and banal platitudes. He tells us that we are to learn how to focus on the positive, forgive ourselves, praise our spouse and accept ourselves as we are—and men are to do more housework.

The Art and Science of Love

The Art and Science of Love is the marriage education programme of John Gottman and his wife, Dr Julie Schwartz Gottman. It is presented as a couple's workshop that, according to the website, is designed to strengthen your marriage or relationship: 'If you have a strong relationship, this workshop will provide you with insights and tools to make it a great one... This two-day workshop will give you new insights and research-based relationship skills that can dramatically improve the intimacy and friendship in your relationship and help you resolve conflict in a healthy, productive way.' The Gottmans say that 'for relationships to be strong, the ideal climate is one teeming with positive interactions.'[37]

Workshop topics include learning how 'love maps' provide a solid foundation for intimacy. You are taught to use the 'fondness and admiration system' to renew respect and care for one another. You are shown how to create an 'emotional bank account' that you can draw upon in times of stress. You are helped to develop your problem-solving skills, including the four techniques of effective conflict resolution. And best of all, you will find out how you can make your dreams and aspirations come true for you, your partner, and your relationship.

A satisfied client gives this endorsement: 'The Gottman Method is a tool that we use to stay happy and keep ourselves together. It takes a lot of work, but I think there are places that a relationship can go that can only be attained with further knowledge and new techniques.'[38]

The promotion of self-reliance

This quotation, taken from among numerous testimonials on the Gottman Relationship Institute webpage tells us all we need to know about what they sell to people with 'troubled' relationships. The goal is to provide 'tools' which people can employ using their own effort to improve their relationships. But the message of Scripture is that the pursuit of self-improvement is a futile exercise that has no place in the Christian life. Believers should no longer be children, tossed to and fro by every new teaching, taken in by every claim of the marriage educators, deceived by the cunning craftiness that passes for marriage research.

Gottman's theory of marriage education is based on the central idea 'that your marriage needs much more positivity than negativity to nourish your love'. His 5-to-1 ratio of positive to negative interactions is widely known and frequently quoted.[39] His ideas lie at the heart of positive psychology discussed in the next chapter.

(Endnotes)

1 Carl Rogers, *Becoming Partners – Marriage and its Alternatives*, Constable and Company, (first published in 1972), reprint 1988, p217

2 Ibid. p218

3 John Gottman and Nan Silver, *The Seven Principles for Making Marriage Work*, (first published 1999), paperback edition published by Orion Books, 2000, p2

4 Ibid. pp3-4

5 John Gottman, *Why Marriages Succeed or Fail and How to Make Yours Last*, (first published 1995), paperback edition published by Bloomsbury Publishing, 2007, p57

6 Ibid. p57

7 Ibid. p72

8 Ibid. pp101-102

9 Ibid. p59

10 Ibid. p59

11 Ibid. p59

12 Ibid. p59

13 Ibid. p60

14 Ibid. p60

15 Ibid. p60

16 Ibid. p60

17 Ibid. p61

18 Ibid. p176

19 Ibid. p181

20 Ibid. p182

21 Ibid. pp183-184

22 Ibid. p184

23 Ibid. p195

24 Ibid. p195

25 Ibid. pp200-201

26 Gottman, *The Seven Principles for Making Marriage Work*, p109

27 Ibid. p110

28 Ibid. p110

29 Ibid. pp110-111

30 Ibid. p111

31 Ibid. p113

32 Ibid. p117

33 Ibid. p205

34 Ibid. p265

35 Ibid. pp265-266

36 Ibid. p266

37 Cited from website of *Positive Psychology Daily News*, 'Gottman's Art and Science of Love', by Amanda Horne, 3 November, 2009: http://positivepsychologynews.com/news/amanda-horne/200911034418

38 Testimonial from The Gottman Relationship Institute, http://www.gottman.com/SubPage.aspx?spdt_id=2&sp_id=100747&spt_id=1

39 Gottman,. *Why Marriages Succeed or Fail*, p61

9

Positive psychology – the recipe for happiness

Positive psychology has come to the fore over the last two or three decades. It is a new branch of psychology that seeks to find the best in people and to inspire them to focus on their strengths and live out their potential. The marriage education movement, which for years has been promoting psychological skills and tools of self-improvement, such as positive emotions, effective communication and conflict resolution, found its ideological home in the school of positive psychology. As we shall see, the aims of both marriage education and positive psychology are to a large degree the same—namely, to build skills and provide tools that enable people to achieve the best things in life and marriage. So the advent of positive psychology in the late 1990s simply enhanced and strengthened the marriage education movement.

The Active Marriage and Best Practices programme provides a good example of the common ground between marriage education and positive psychology. Developed by Kelly Simpson, a licensed Marriage and Family Therapist with a Masters Degree in Psychology from Southern Methodist University, Dallas, the programme is advertised as combining 'the best ideas, tools, and exercises from the fields of marriage education, relationship skills, positive psychology and conflict resolution'.[1] Topics and skills covered include: effective communication styles, skills for happiness, anger management, the importance of compassion and forgiveness, conflict resolution, healing the emotional wounds of infidelity, the biology of love and romance, and wise choices for partners.

As we shall see in the chapters that lie ahead, marriage education, both the secular and Christian versions, is now immersed in positive psychology. As a cleverly disguised imposter – a wolf in sheep's clothing – it secretly slips into the Church as an angel of light to help couples to think positively and acquire the skills needed for a successful marriage. Christians need to be aware of this deceptive teaching that is misleading many people. The purpose of this chapter is to show how the tools, skills and techniques of positive psychology are being used to propagate the ideology of the marriage education movement.

The humanistic foundation of positive psychology

The positive psychology movement has been built on the foundations of humanistic psychology laid by both Carl Rogers and Abraham Maslow. The last chapter in Maslow's book, *Motivation and Personality* (1954), is entitled 'Toward a Positive Psychology'. He was disappointed that the 'science' of psychology had concentrated on the negative side of life rather than on the positive side. 'It has revealed to us much about man's shortcomings, his illness, his sins, but little about his potentialities, his virtues, his achievable aspirations, or his full psychological height.'[2] Maslow realised that if human nature is basically good, as he believed, then human potential for growth would be better served by focusing on the positive. Rogers, who also saw the human being as basically good, trustworthy, reliable and constructive, claimed that in the counselling situation, after negative feelings have been fully expressed, they are followed by faint and tentative expressions of positive impulses that make for growth.[3] His philosophy of the good life, and the way to personal growth, are ideas that have become part of positive psychology.

Norman Vincent Peale

Norman Vincent Peale (1898-1993), author of the runaway bestseller, *The Power of Positive Thinking* (1952), is the father of 'positive thinking'. He is credited as one of the top five most influential religious figures of the twentieth century. As a gifted inspirational speaker he had a remarkable talent for combining the ideas of humanistic psychology and the Bible into an appealing method of self-improvement. He believed that human beings 'are inherently good—the bad reactions aren't basic'.[4] He frequently used New Age terminology, such as 'the life force', 'energy', 'the Source', 'inward power' and 'our deepest desire', when referring to God.

Reared in a Methodist home, Peale was educated at Ohio Wesleyan University and Boston University School of Theology. In 1932 he was appointed pastor of Marble Collegiate Church, a Reformed church in New York. When he arrived the church had 600 members, and by the time he retired in 1984 it had over 5,000. Early in his career Peale established a clinic with Freudian psychiatrist Dr Smiley Blanton in the basement of Marble Church. The clinic, based on the theories of Jung and Freud,[5] expanded to employ around 20 psychiatric doctors and psychologically trained ministers, and eventually became known as the American Foundation for Religion and Psychiatry.

In his ministry Peale cleverly merged theology and psychology. Harold Ellens, the editor of the *Journal of Psychology and Christianity*, commented: 'Norman Peale saw psychology and Christian experience as very compatible... he had the courage to stand pat on this position in spite of the opposition of the entire Christian church for nearly half a century. His genius was that he... translated psycho-theology into the language of the people.'[6] His optimistic messages of positive thinking, expressed in Christian jargon, proved to be massively popular and his sermons were mailed to 750,000 people every month. Back in 1955, in an article for *Life* magazine, the editor of *Christian Century*, Paul Hutchinson, said that Peale 'preaches to probably the largest audience ever gathered by an American cleric'.[7] For 54 years his weekly radio programme, 'The Art of Living', was broadcast on NBC.

The Power of Positive Thinking was on the *New York Times* bestseller list for 186 consecutive weeks, and by the late 1980s had sold over 15 million copies in many different languages. It became the best-selling non-fiction book by a single author in the history of publishing. Peale himself credited his doctrine of positive thinking to Ernest Holmes, founder of the United Church of Religious Science—a Unitarian body.[8] Peale's so-called 'practical Christianity' was in fact a euphemism for his unique version of New Thought, a therapeutic, mystical message driven by the needs of his audience. In *God's Salesman* (1993) Carol George says that although Peale mentioned 'Jesus' throughout his ministry, 'it was as friend and as Way-Shower in the New Thought sense and not as the incarnate Christ'.[9] According to his critics, 'it was a kind of shadow religion, a distorted and dangerous adaption of the real thing.

Peale's cosmic and transcendental concept of divinity was viewed as blasphemous because it seemed to reduce God to human proportions and to make God the servant of humanity'.[10]

Peale says *The Power of Positive Thinking* 'is written with the sole objective of helping the reader achieve a happy, satisfying, and worthwhile life'.[11] If you 'sincerely and persistently practice the principles and formulas set forth herein, you can experience an amazing improvement within yourself... You will become a more popular, esteemed, and well-liked individual.'[12] You are told to believe in yourself, for 'self-confidence leads to self-realization and successful achievement. Because of the importance of this mental attitude, this book will help you believe in yourself and release your inner powers.'[13]

According to Peale, two important techniques for re-educating your mind are to reject all negative thoughts and to frequently affirm positive thoughts. By constant repetition of affirmations you bypass your conscious mind and implant suggestions into your unconscious mind where they operate automatically. He said, 'Let them sink into your unconscious and they can help you overcome any difficulty. Say them over and over again. Say them until your mind accepts them, until you believe them – faith power works wonders.'[14] Peale promised that if we follow his techniques we will always think positively and remove all negative thoughts and attitudes from our lives. 'It is important to eliminate from conversations all negative ideas, for they tend to produce annoyance and tension inwardly.'[15]

In his article, 'Confidence Man', historian Donald Meyer is highly critical of Peale's teaching around positive thinking. He wrote, 'In more classic literature, this sort of pretension to mastery has often been thought to indicate an alliance with a Lower rather than a Higher power.'[16] He asserted that Peale's repetitive techniques are actually a well-known form of hypnosis and called Peale's book 'The Bible of American auto-hypnotism'.[17]

Virginia Satir and John Gottman

Virginia Satir (chapter 7), the mother of family therapy, was another pioneer of positive psychology. She eagerly taught that everyone's intentions are positive, no matter how horrible their behaviour. She used positive intentions to search for more positive feelings and communications.[18] We have seen how 'marriage expert' John Gottman used sociological research to establish his 5-to-1 ratio of positive to negative interactions, which, he claims, can predict successful relationships.[19] Indeed, many of Gottman's ideas, such as the power of praise and acceptance, the power of a positive mindset, the power to forgive yourself, and the power of affirmation are skills and tools that are central to the school of positive psychology.

The beginnings of positive psychology

In the first week of January 1999, American psychologist Martin Seligman – widely regarded as the father of the modern positive psychology movement, hosted a six-day seminar in Akumal, Mexico, for eighteen of the brightest and best young people in the field of positive psychology. Within a few months of this meeting Seligman was approached by the Templeton Foundation, which proceeded to award large grants for research in the field of positive psychology. Here we should note that the Foundation, set up by billionaire Sir John Templeton to explore the interface between religion, psychology and science, has strong New Age sympathies, as we shall see in chapter 10. According to *Time* magazine, 'The result was an explosion of research on happiness, optimism, positive emotions and healthy character traits. Seldom has an academic field been brought so quickly and deliberately to life.'[20]

And so the new positive psychology movement was launched in the late 1990s, during Martin Seligman's term as president of the American Psychological Association. Its focus was on such topics as happiness, leadership, creativity, strength and virtue. According to the *Authentic Happiness* newsletter, 'Positive Psychology is founded on the belief that people want more than an end to suffering. People want to lead meaningful and fulfilling lives, to cultivate what is best within themselves, to enhance their experiences of love, work, and play. We have the opportunity to create a science and a profession that not only heals psychological damage but also builds strengths to enable people to achieve the best things in life.'[21]

With Templeton's money the experts in positive psychology have embraced a rigorous programme of scientific research. Two papers presented at the Second International Positive Psychology Summit, held in 2003, explicitly focused on happiness. One paper claimed that 'psychologists have already learned some of the ways by which people not only maintain but even can increase their level of happiness. From the standpoint of the average person on the street, this may constitute the single most noteworthy question addressed in the field. If positive psychology can reliably teach people how to become and remain happier, it will have made an immense contribution to human life, and these articles begin to show the way to how this can be done.'[22] The Summit ended with an invitation to psychologists of all backgrounds to join the exploration of the positive side of life. The movement is searching for the 'holy grail' of the secret of happiness, which it believes can be uncovered through vigorous scientific research.

In his book, *Authentic Happiness* (2002), Seligman claims that the new research into happiness 'demonstrates that it can be lastingly increased. And a new movement, Positive Psychology, shows how you can come to live in the upper reaches of your set range of happiness.'[23] But he identifies a profound obstacle to our life of happiness, what he calls the 'rotten-to-the core' dogma. 'If there is any doctrine this book seeks to overthrow, it is this one. The doctrine of original sin is the oldest manifestation of the rotten-to-the-core dogma.'[24] He says that this dogma pervades the understanding of human nature even in the arts and social sciences. 'In spite of the widespread acceptance of the rotten-to-the-core dogma in the religious and secular world, there is not a shred of evidence that strength and virtue are derived from negative motivation.'[25] He says that positive psychology offers a road out of a meaningless life with few pleasures. 'This road takes you through the countryside of pleasure and gratification, up into the high country of strength and virtue, and finally to the peaks of lasting fulfilment: meaning and purpose.'[26]

So the basic premise of positive psychology is that human nature is good, and therefore capable of achieving self-improvement with the appropriate psychological techniques. The great obstacle to this, Seligman maintains, is the biblical doctrine of original sin. As the book of Romans says: 'For there is no difference; for all have sinned and fall short of the glory of God', and 'For as by one man's disobedience many were made sinners' (Romans 3.22-23 and 5.19a). This fundamental biblical truth about the human condition is vehemently opposed by the positive psychology movement.

In his book, *Learned Optimism: How to Change Your Mind and Your Life* (2006), Seligman says that optimism can set us on the path to happiness. 'The skills you will read about here can increase the duration and intensity of your positive emotions. These skills can enable you to use your highest strengths and talents more effectively. Finally optimism is invaluable for the meaningful life.'[27] Optimism is about trusting in our own power to make our life and future better. It's about developing positive beliefs, expectations, choices and strategies. Seligman says that we must learn to accept that we are responsible for improving our life.

Seligman describes the purpose of the new psychology with these words: 'We believe that a psychology of positive human functioning will arise that achieves a scientific understanding and effective interventions to build thriving in individuals, families, and communities.'[28] Here we see a movement that promises abundant life through its psychological interventions. This promise stands in direct opposition to the Christian faith, for Christ has come that through faith in him we may have life and life more abundantly (John 10.10). So the hope of an abundant life through the 'effective interventions' of positive psychology is a false hope that misleads many.

Positive psychology believes that cultivating spirituality can produce positive outcomes. Professor Jonathan Haidt's views on spirituality are so popular that in 2001 he was awarded the Templeton Prize in Positive Psychology. In his book, *The Happiness Hypothesis* (2006), he makes the following recommendations to build spirituality: 'For five minutes a day, relax and think about the purpose of life, and where you fit in; for five minutes a day, think about the things you can do to improve the world or your community; read a religious or spiritual book, or go to a religious service every day; explore different religions. You can do this by going to a library, looking on the Internet, or asking your friends about their religions; spend a few minutes a day in meditation or prayer; invest in a book of affirmations or optimistic quotes. Read a few every day.'[29]

Positive emotions

Promoting positive emotions is a key aspect of the new psychology. A leading scholar, Dr Barbara Fredrickson, of the University of North Carolina at Chapel Hill (she moved there from the University of Michigan in 2006), has focused her research on positive emotions and human flourishing. She set up the Positive Emotions Laboratory at the University in order to study how positive emotions affect people's thinking patterns, social behaviour and physiological reactions. The ultimate goal of this research is to understand how positive emotions might transform people's lives for the better.

She is supported by grants from the National Institute of Mental Health in the USA, and her work is so influential that in 2000 she received the prestigious Templeton Prize in Positive Psychology, awarded by the American Psychological Association. According to Martin Seligman she is the genius of the positive psychology movement, who developed the 'broaden-and-build' theory for positive emotions, as well as the 3-to-1 ratio for a flourishing life. Fredrickson confesses that her practice of 'mindfulness meditation' deepened after an awe-filled week of instruction with experts in the field.[30]

In a paper presented to The Royal Society of Biological Sciences in London, Dr Fredrickson outlined her broaden-and-build theory of positive emotions. She concluded: 'People should cultivate positive emotions in their own lives and in the lives of those around them, not just because doing so makes them feel good in the moment, but also because doing so transforms people for the better and sets them on paths toward flourishing and healthy longevity. When positive emotions are in short supply, people get stuck. They lose their degrees of behavioural freedom and become painfully predictable. But when positive emotions are in ample supply, people take off. They become generative, creative, resilient, ripe with possibility and beautifully complex. The broaden-and-build theory conveys how positive emotions move people forward and lift them to the higher ground of optimal well-being.'[31] The research for this paper was funded by the Templeton Foundation.

In her book, *Positivity* (2009), Fredrickson makes this promise to her readers: 'With positivity, you see new possibilities, bounce back from setbacks, connect with others, and become the best version of yourself... You will never look at feeling good the same way again. You'll understand and appreciate the potency of positive emotions in ways that will prove to be astonishingly useful. There's a side of positive emotions that you don't know yet. Once your eyes are opened to this side – the scientifically tested side – you'll have a fuller understanding of your self and your potential. With this more complete self-knowledge, you'll function more fully and be empowered daily. *Positivity* presents an opportunity to step up to the next level of existence: to broaden your mind and build your best future.'[32]

She extols the benefits of positivity. 'The first core truth about positive emotions is that they open our hearts and our minds, making us more receptive and more creative.'[33] She says that negativity holds us back. 'Negativity and neutrality constrain your experience of the world. In consequence, they also constrain your knowledge of the world.'[34] The second core truth is that 'positivity transforms us for the better. By opening our hearts and minds, positive emotions allow us to discover and build new skills, new ties, new knowledge, and new ways of being.'[35]

She is dismissive of the Protestant work ethic, which she caricatures as 'a philosophy that holds that enjoyment and leisure are sinful'.[36] She says that those who practise Buddhist meditation experience greater positivity in daily life. She promises to tell us 'how meditation works and how you can make it work for you'.[37]

Fredrickson has developed a 'tool kit' to decrease negativity and increase positivity. The technique of cognitive behavioural therapy is used to dispute negative thinking. 'Capture your inner critic, that voice in your head that's sceptical of you, of others, and of everything around you—the voice of ill will.'[38] She instructs her reader to make a list of negative thoughts and then to loudly dispute them. But the Bible teaches that this inner voice is our God-given conscience which warns us against wrong-doing. When we break God's moral law our conscience makes us feel guilty, and the positive psychologists don't like that, so they want us to dispute with our conscience.

Another useful tool, according to Fredrickson, is 'loving-kindness meditation'. The goal is to arouse warm and tender feelings to loved ones, yourself, and all people and creatures of the earth. She explains:

'Traditional loving-kindness meditation comes with a set of statements that you repeat silently to yourself… May I be safe. May I be happy. May I be healthy. May I live with ease.'[39]

She concludes with an exhortation—and while acknowledging that as a scientist she is not in a position to advance religious doctrine, she does so anyway: 'Even so, the complex evolved systems of negativity and positivity may well be the core of karma. Viewed in this way, there needn't be any score-keeping deity up in the sky drawing up a list of who's naughty and nice. Positive consequences emerge from positive emotions simply as the unfolding of a natural process. If you plant seeds of positivity you flourish… Become like a plant and turn toward the light, in all its spiritual, earthly, and human forms.'[40] She finishes with this remarkable statement: 'By making more moments glisten with positivity, you make the choice of a lifetime: you choose the upward spiral that leads to your best future—and to our best world.'[41]

Dr Fredrickson's commitment to New Age and Buddhist practices is clear from her writing and research. Her approach to positive psychology, expressed in the following words from her website, read as a statement of New Age belief: 'You have – within you – the fuel to thrive and to flourish, and to leave this world in better shape than you found it… Where is this fuel within you? You tap into it whenever you feel energized and excited by new ideas. You tap into it whenever you feel at one with your surroundings, at peace. You tap into it whenever you feel playful, creative, or silly. You tap into it whenever you feel your soul stirred by the sheer beauty of existence. You tap into it whenever you feel connected to others and loved. In short, you tap into it whenever positive emotions resonate within you.'[42]

The claim of Fredrickson that she is a scientist has a hollow ring. With generous funding from the Templeton Foundation, she appears to be on a mission to lead people away from the God of Scripture into a life of 'mindfulness meditation'. In truth, when Fredrickson offers 'to broaden your mind and build your best future', she is hoping to do so through the practice of Buddhist meditation. This leaves us with a big question. Where does positive psychology end and New Age begin, or are they in fact just a different manifestation of the same thing?

How to be happy

In her book, *The How of Happiness: a Scientific Approach to Getting the Life you Want* (2007), Sonja Lyubomirsky, Professor of Psychology at the University of California, Riverside, tells us how to discover the real keys to happiness. She shows us how to find happiness activities that fit our interests, values and needs. Happiness activities include expressing gratitude, cultivating optimism, avoiding over-thinking, practising acts of kindness, learning to forgive, increasing 'flow experiences' and savouring life's joys. We are reminded that behind sustainable happiness is positive emotion. The book explains what can be done to bring us all closer to the happy life we all want for ourselves. We are offered a potentially life-changing programme of positive psychology that helps us to understand our innate potential for joy and happiness.

Lyubomirsky cites an avalanche of studies to show that 'meditation has multiple positive effects on a person's happiness and positive emotions, on physiology, stress, cognitive abilities, and physical health, as well as on other harder-to-assess attributes like "self-actualization" and moral maturity.'[43] Once again we see New Age sentiments wrapped up in positive psychology.

Positive psychology and Buddhism

Marvin Levine, a well-known researcher and theorist in cognitive-experimental psychology, in his book, *The Positive Psychology of Buddhism and Yoga – Paths to A Mature Happiness* (2009), which is strongly recommended by Martin Seligman, draws out the similarities between Buddhism and Western Psychology. He shows that both are concerned with alleviating inner pain and emotional suffering; both are humanistic and naturalistic in that they focus on the human condition and interpret it in natural terms; both teach the appropriateness of compassion, concern and unconditional positive regard towards others; both share the ideal of maturing or growth. 'Buddhism, Yoga, and Western Psychology, especially the recent emphasis on positive psychology, are concerned with the attainment of deep and lasting happiness. The thesis of all three is that self-transformation is the surest path to this happiness.'[44]

Indeed there is much common ground between Buddhism and positive psychology, for both are opposed to the most fundamental doctrines of the Christian faith. Both deal with our inner pain and offer us techniques for enhancing our levels of positivity; both promote meditation to increase our inner peace and positive emotions; both offer to unveil the secret of happiness; both see happiness as the goal of life; both deny the problem of sin and believe in self-improvement and personal growth without the God of the Bible. But neither is able to deal with the problem of a sinful heart; neither is able to offer salvation from sin. Scripture warns, 'There is a way that seems right to a man, but its end is the way of death' (Proverbs 14.12).

Positive psychology and the Smart Marriages Conference

The annual Smart Marriages Conference, discussed in chapter 3, has included a number of sessions with a positive psychology message. A workshop in 2010 entitled, 'Positivity Transforms Relationships', presented by a psychologist trained at the Gottman Relationship Institute, claimed to show how the concepts of positive psychology can help couples build gratitude, compassion, curiosity, admiration, and other skills to transform relationships and boost satisfaction and success.[45]

In July 2008, The Marriage Garden programme, developed at Arkansas University by Dr Wallace Goddard, and Dr James Marshall, was presented at the Smart Marriages Conference. The programme claimed to be based on new discoveries in positive psychology that cultivate flourishing relationships. In their book, *The Marriage Garden* (2010), the authors assert that decades of intensive research on marriage have provided the key to building strong relationships.[46] We are told that 'some thoughts and experiences help us feel more peaceful and happy. Others make us feel more tense and angry... if we privilege our positive feelings—if we dwell on them and trust them—we are likely to get happier. Positivity snowballs. We feel grateful for our partners, we act more kindly, and the relationship grows. We find ever more positives.'[47] The authors refer to the work of Martin Seligman, John Gottman and others in the positive psychology movement.

Another Smart Marriages workshop, entitled 'Heart Rhythm Practice', was led by trainers from the Institute of Applied Meditation. Couples are taught 'a new way to reduce stress, heal old wounds, increase trust, optimism and connection by synchronizing heart, body and brain in a positive, energetic state.'[48] The Institute has 'always insisted that meditation, the most powerful of all techniques, be applied in very practical ways, advancing our health, relationships and accomplishments in life.'[49] Clearly many of the marriage education programmes promoted at Smart Marriages conferences are built around the principles of positive psychology.

Conclusion

We have seen that positive psychology is a product of the minds of Abraham Maslow, Carl Rogers, Virginia Satir, John Gottman, Norman Vincent Peale and Martin Seligman. It is a human philosophy that claims to have found the secret of happiness and the abundant life. We are promised that the 'effective interventions' of positive psychology open the way to the pleasant life and personal fulfilment. The claim is that even 'normal' people, not just the mentally ill and depressed, need to be nurtured toward greater happiness. The clients of positive psychology are taught certain nebulous skills, such as mindfulness, flow, learned optimism, pathways thinking, and so on, by which to build for themselves 'character strengths and virtues', which, when put into daily practice, will assure them of the 'pleasant life'. Thus positive psychology has gathered together the myriad psychotherapies that promise self-improvement via self-effort.

Marriage psycho-education is in actuality a branch of positive psychology. Both have emerged from the same roots and teach the same philosophy of the good life. Both claim to have found the secret to a happy life and successful marriage without God. Both promote positive emotions, positive thinking and positive affirmations. Both ignore Scripture and the reality of sin. The only significant difference is that positive psychology is more deeply entrenched in meditation and New Age mysticism than marriage education.

As we have seen in this chapter, the central concepts of positive psychology are personal growth and human potential. The promise is that by learning certain skills we can change our lives and marriages for the better. We have encountered a utopian philosophy that strives to create a world of happiness by way of self-improvement. We see human wisdom, which is foolishness in God's eyes (1 Corinthians 1.19-20), designing tools and skills that are supposed to make people happy and successful. But Scripture teaches that the 'foolishness' of God, revealed in the Cross of Christ, is wiser than the wisdom of positive psychology (1 Corinthians 1.25). The idea that sinful men and women can in reality improve themselves and solve their own problems without God is a wicked delusion, for no flesh will glory in his presence (1 Corinthians 1.29). Those who rely on positive psychology soon discover that they are on the road to disappointment and despair, for they have based their hope on the wisdom of men and not the wisdom of God.

(Endnotes)

1 Active Relationships Center, website, Programs for couples: http://www.activerelationships.com/programs_for_couples.htm

2 Abraham Maslow, *Motivation and Personality*, Harper, 1954, p354

3 Carl Rogers, *On Becoming A Person*, Houghton Mifflin, Boston, 1961, pp26-27

4 Cited from Way of Life Literature website, the article 'Dangers in Christian Bookstores' quotes an interview published in *Modern Maturity* magazine, December-January 1975-76, when Peale was asked if people are inherently good or bad: http://www.wayoflife.org/database/dangersbookstores.html

5 Carol V.R. George, *God's Salesman: Norman Vincent Peale and the Power of Positive Thinking*, Oxford University Press, 1993, p90

6 Cited from an article entitled, 'Norman Vincent Peale – highlights of a life' on the Ohioana authors website: http://www.ohioana-authors.org/peale/highlights.php

7 Paul Hutchinson, 'Have we a New Religion?', *Life*, April 11, 1955, p148

8 'Norman Vincent Peale – The Father of Positive Thinking', by Ian Ellis-Jones, an expanded version of an address delivered at the Sydney Unitarian Church, 10 December 2006: http://www.sydneyunitarianchurch.org/NVP_Positive_Thinker_revsd.pdf

9 Carol VR George, *God's Salesman*, Oxford University Press, 1993, p145

10 Ibid. p145

11 Norman Vincent Peale, *The Power of Positive Thinking*. Prentice-Hall, New York, 1952, Introduction, px

12 Ibid. px

13 Ibid. p1

14 Ibid. p103

15 Ibid. p24

16 Donald Meyer, 'Confidence Man', *The New Republic*, July 11, 1955, pp. 8-10, cited from Wikipedia article 'Norman Vincent Peale', http://en.wikipedia.org/wiki/Norman_Vincent_Peale

17 Donald Meyer, *The Positive Thinkers*, Pantheon Books, 1965, p264

18 Steve Andreas, *Virginia Satir: the patterns of her magic*, Science & Behavior Books, June 1991, p4

19 Cited from website of *Positive Psychology Daily News*, 'Gottman's Art and Science of Love', by

Amanda Horne, 3 November, 2009: http://positivepsychologynews.com/news/

20 *Time* Magazine, 'The New Science of Happiness' by Claudia Wallis, 17 January 2005

21 Cited from Authentic Happiness Newsletter Center, University of Pennsylvania: http://www.authentichappiness.sas.upenn.edu/newsletters.aspx

22 *Positive Psychology at the Summit*, 'Review of General Psychology', by the Educational Publishing Foundation, 2005, Vol. 9, No. 2, 99–102

23 Martin Seligman, *Authentic Happiness*, Nicolas Brealey Publishing, first published 2002, reprinted 2007, pxii

24 Ibid. pxii

25 Ibid. pxiii

26 Ibid. pxiv

27 Martin Seligman, *Learned Optimism; How to Change your Mind and Your Life*, Vintage Books, 2006, piv

28 Seligman, Martin E.P.; Csikszentmihalyi, Mihaly (2000). 'Positive Psychology: An Introduction', *American Psychologist* 55 (1): 5-14.

29 Cited from Authentic Happiness website, University of Pennsylvania, 'Spirituality' by Ben Dean: http://www.authentichappiness.sas.upenn.edu/newsletter.aspx?id=74

30 Barbara L. Fredrickson, *Positivity*, Crown Publishers, 2009, p169

31 'The broaden-and-build theory of positive emotions', by Barbara L. Fredrickson; Published online 17 August 2004. Published in Phil. Trans. R. Soc. Lond. B (2004), p1375: http://rstb.royalsocietypublishing.org/content/359/1449/1367.full.pdf

32 Fredrickson, *Positivity*, pp12-13

33 Ibid. p21

34 Ibid. p23

35 Ibid. p24

36 Ibid. p28

37 Ibid. p30

38 Ibid. p204

39 Ibid. p210

40 Ibid. p230-231

41 Ibid. p231

42 Website of University of North Carolina, The Positive Emotions and Psychophysiology Laboratory: http://www.unc.edu/peplab/purpose.html

43 Cited from Amanda Horne, April 2008, 'Wellbeing, Meditation and Mindfulness', At the 1st Australian Positive Psychology and Well-being conference: http://www.amandahorne.com.au/newsletter/Apr08-WellbeingMeditationMindfulness.htm

44 Marvin Levine, *The Positive Psychology of Buddhism and Yoga: Paths to A Mature Happiness*, 2009, Routledge, Product Description on Amazon

45 Workshop in Smart Marriages 2010 brochure, 411, 'Positivity Transforms Relationships' by Vagdevi Meunier

46 Wallace Goddard, James Marshall, *The Marriage Garden*, published by Jossy-Bass, 2010, p2

47 Ibid. p6

48 Cited from Smart Marriages website, Workshop in Smart Marriages 2010 brochure, 215, 'Heart Rhythm practice', Dan McMannis, Jana Staton,

49 Cited from The Institute for Applied Meditation website: http://www.appliedmeditation.org/IAM-U/index.php

10

Positive psychology and New Age thinking

We saw in the last chapter that marriage psycho-education has found its ideological home in the school of positive psychology. Our analysis revealed positive psychology to be little more than a pseudo-scientific enterprise founded on human pride and expressed in pseudo-spiritual terms and utopian promises. But for us to grasp the real agenda of the positive psychology movement, we need to be aware of the massive financial support provided by the John Templeton Foundation. Without question the rapid growth of this movement has taken place largely through the generous funding provided by this Foundation. Indeed, it is probably true to say that without this support there would be no positive psychology movement.

The Templeton Foundation

Sir John Templeton (1912-2008) was a financial wizard who made a large fortune on the stock market. As a multi-billionaire he set up a foundation to investigate what he referred to as the deep things of life and to promote his spiritual interests. He wanted his philanthropy to reach scientists, theologians and opinion leaders, but his ultimate audience was all of humanity.[1] The overarching goal of Sir John was to discover new spiritual information, and to see progress in our understanding of religious truths and the deepest realities of human nature. He encouraged opinion leaders to become more open-minded about the possible character of ultimate reality and the divine.[2]

The Templeton Foundation serves as a philanthropic catalyst for research into what it calls the 'Big Questions'. 'We support work at the world's top universities in such fields as theoretical physics, cosmology, evolutionary biology, cognitive science, and social science relating to love, forgiveness, creativity, purpose, and the nature and origin of religious belief. We encourage informed, open-minded dialogue between scientists and theologians as they apply themselves to the most profound issues in their particular disciplines.'[3]

However, not everybody is impressed with the way Templeton's money is being used to promote the positive psychology bandwagon. Barbara Ehrenreich, a well-known American author, is distinctly underwhelmed with the claims of positive psychology, as she makes plain in her book, *Bright-sided: How the Relentless Promotion of Positive Thinking Has Undermined America* (2008). She is highly sceptical of the way Templeton's money is being used to support religious and psychological research. 'But the Templetons' most famous baby is the young field of Positive Psychology, launched by University of Pennsylvania's Martin Seligman after his five-year-old daughter accused him of being a "grouch" and he resolved to improve his outlook. Pos Psych carves out everything ordinary psych, with its bent toward pathology, ignores, which is in itself an admirable ambition. In practice, though, it tilts dangerously, for something that considers itself a science, toward the prescriptive. If you're not happy – or optimistic or upbeat – you better get to work on that now, and we have the "coaches" to help you.'[4]

Barbara Ehrenreich attended the Sixth Annual International Positive Psychology Summit conference in Washington, DC, in 2007, 'to see what was up, and am happy – make that also optimistic, hopeful and almost positive – to report that this Templeton-spawned group could probably not plot its way out of a paper bag. The presentations I sampled occupied the full range from mediocrity to silliness.'[5]

Religious views of Sir John Templeton

An article in *The Nation*, the oldest continuously published weekly magazine in the United States, describes Sir John Templeton's religious beliefs. 'Though a lifelong Presbyterian, he imbibed the wisdom of religions both Eastern and Western, ranging from his friend Norman Vincent Peale, the prophet of the organization man, to Ramakrishna. Early on, his mother exposed him to the Unity School of Christianity, a turn-of-the-century movement that emphasized positive thinking and healing through prayer.'[6]

Sir John, disappointed at the resistance of numerous Christian leaders to innovation and change, came to the conclusion that many highly educated people felt that 'religion sometimes seems like a kind of history museum which lacks the excitement and vibrancy of other aspects of life that constantly experience innovation'.[7] He therefore proposed that religion pursue the same strategy that has led to progress in other fields of human endeavour: 'Progress comes from constructive competition, and churches and religions can benefit greatly from it... Only an inferior religion needs to discourage competition, lest its inferiority be exposed for all the world to see.'[8]

Templeton was well aware that such a view might be objectionable to those who consider the Bible to be the exclusive source of true spiritual wisdom, but he suggested an alternative view of divine revelation: 'Christians think god appeared in Jesus of Nazareth two thousand years ago for our salvation and education. But should we take it to mean that education and progress stopped there, that Jesus was the end of change, the end of time? Is such a notion compatible with the divine, free, open, creative nature of the universe? To say that god cannot reveal himself in a decisive way again, because he did it once centuries ago, can seem sacrilegious.'[9] Clearly, for all his spiritual experience and exploration, he appeared to have little understanding of the Christian faith.

Templeton was an ardent supporter of the Association of Unity Churches International. He writes: 'Although I have been a lifelong member of the Presbyterian Church, my mother imbued in me something of the spiritual philosophy of the Unity School of Christianity. I have benefited by reading the Unity books and magazines for more than sixty years.'[10] He did not accept that heaven and hell were literal places and believed in the divinity in humanity.[11] In his book, *The Humble Approach* (1998), he wrote: 'God is billions of stars in the Milky Way and He is much more... Time and space and energy are all part of God... God is five billion people on Earth... God is untold billions of beings on planets of millions of other stars... God is the only reality... God is all of you and you are a little part of Him.'[12]

Templeton saw the Bible as an old-fashioned, largely irrelevant book. He wrote: 'Suppose you went to your priest and asked for help — he would refer you to the Bible, but if you went the next day to your medical doctor, and he referred you to the book of Hippocrates, which was written at about the same time as the Bible, you would think that was old-fashioned.'[13] His book, *Wisdom from World Religions: Pathways toward Heaven on Earth* (2002), is designed to offer people of all ages and all nations an opportunity to learn more about the laws, principles and teachings of a variety of religions worldwide. It offers a selection of readings from the teachings of Buddhism, Christianity, Confucianism, Hinduism, Islam, Sikhism, Taoism, Zen, and other religions. The hope of the author is that the spiritual gleanings of his book may be used as effective, practical and workable tools for creating a better life.

Positive thinking

Templeton's belief in the power of positive thinking undoubtedly came from his friend Norman Vincent Peale. In the booklet, *Views, Values, & Vision*, he tells us that when his first wife died in 1951 he was left with the care of three small children and had to learn to be both mother and father to them while trying to build a business and earn a living. 'It wasn't an easy period, but, along with my abiding faith in God, there were three qualities I began to develop more fully in myself: mind power, positive thinking, and willpower. I learned to quietly release negative thoughts. I would even say to these thoughts: "I lovingly release you to the vast nothingness from whence you came... Mind power, positive thinking, and willpower—they will take you far on your quest for wholeness".'[14]

Templeton's money

John Templeton showed an interest in the positive psychology movement right from its beginnings in the late 1990s, and funded numerous initiatives and research projects over the years. The Templeton Positive Psychology Prize was established to encourage scientific investigation of the benefits produced by optimism, thanksgiving and the power of positive thinking. In 2000 Barbara Fredrickson, then of the University of Michigan, won the $100,000 prize for her work on the beneficial effects of positive emotions.

In 2001 a grant of $2.2 million helped Martin Seligman to establish the Positive Psychology Center at the University of Pennsylvania. According to the grant documentation, 'The field of Positive Psychology is founded on the belief that people want to lead meaningful and fulfilling lives, to cultivate what is best within themselves, and to enhance their experiences of love, work, and play.' A grant of $8.2 million helped to establish the Institute for Research on Unlimited Love in 2001. The philosophy of the Institute comes from Sir John's book, *Pure Unlimited Love: An Eternal Creative Force and Blessing Taught by All Religions* (2000). Through scientific research and education the Institute aims to significantly increase humanity's understanding and knowledge of what is commonly called 'unconditional love'.

Meaning of positivity

We need to take a brief look at the concept of 'positivity' which forms the common ground between positive psychology, marriage education and the Templeton Foundation. What does it mean to have positive thoughts, positive emotions, and positive morality? Where does the concept of positivity come from?

As a starting point we should note that neither the word 'positive' nor the word 'negative' is used in Scripture. The terms 'positive' and 'negative' when used in regard to ideas, conduct and morality are relativistic and have no relationship to the absolute truth of the Bible. In biblical thinking, attitudes, ideas and conduct are true or false, right or wrong, good or evil. Christians should think and speak in biblical concepts and avoid the relative morality expressed by the terms 'positive' and 'negative'.

Scripture does not instruct Christians to think positive thoughts or to reject negative thoughts, but rather to think on 'whatever things are true, whatever things are noble, whatever things are just, whatever things are pure, whatever things are lovely, whatever things are of good report' (Philippians 4.8). In other words, things which reflect the holy character of God, not the self-flattering fantasies of positive psychology. A believer, who has the mind of Christ (Philippians 2.5), is to 'seek those things which are above, where Christ is sitting at the right hand of God. Set your mind on things above' (Colossians 3.1-2). The mind of a Christian is renewed by the Holy Spirit, 'that you may prove what is that good and acceptable and perfect will of God' (Romans 12.2).

The so-called 'negative thoughts' referred to by positive psychology are in fact the thoughts of guilt, fear and shame that come from a life of unrepentant sin. Clearly, sinful mankind is subject to what positive psychology refers to as 'negative thoughts'. And so Martin Seligman, in his folly, seeks to overthrow the doctrine of original sin in the forlorn hope that to do so will abolish the 'negative thoughts' that result from sin. It is important to understand that the emphasis on positive thinking and the rejection of negative thinking has nothing to do with the Christian faith.

Positive thinking in Buddhism

The concept of positive thinking is central to Buddhism. According to its teachings, we are 'to abandon negative thoughts and develop positive thoughts in the Noble Eightfold Path and it is up to us to tread this path towards Nibbâna. Avoiding negative thinking and thinking positively can require a lot of effort and training on our part, but the result would be happier minds and happier lives. A positive mind is a pure mind.'[15]

Buddhism also teaches that 'happiness comes from positive minds such as love, patience and wisdom. By purifying the mind of its negatives and increasing its positive states we can attain increasingly happy states of mind. When the mind is completely pure we attain the ultimate happiness of enlightenment and become a Buddha.'[16] Loving-kindness meditation 'is a meditation practice taught by the Buddha to develop the mental habit of selfless or altruistic love... Loving-kindness is a meditation practice, which brings about positive attitudinal changes as it systematically develops the quality of loving-acceptance. It acts, as it were, as a form of self-psychotherapy, a way of healing the troubled mind to free it from its pain and confusion. Of all Buddhist meditations, loving-kindness has the immediate benefit of sweetening and changing old habituated negative patterns of mind.'[17]

Positive thinking in paganism

Pagans believe that thoughts have strong magic. The Pagan Grove website explains: 'Positive thoughts help us grow and achieve our desires, while negative thoughts are limiting and often destructive.'[18] A basic precept of paganism 'is that each of us are responsible for what we think and that we have the power to change our reality. Positive thought can liberate you from false ideas about yourself and the world around you.'[19] According to Pagan Space website, 'positive thinking brings about positive action. Positive thinking reinforced with positive emotions brings about change. I'm talking about life changes. With positive thinking you progress the soul which opens up all the doors you thought were closed to you... The challenge in this world is to think positive in any situation. If you start thinking positive the universe will put you in situations that promote your thinking and attract people to you. You are the company you keep and your company affects everything around you... There are two types of people in this world—negative people and positive people. Everyone else is the in-between. But we're all still connected. Negativity just disconnects us. It's never permanent because it's never too late to change.'[20] So encouraging positive thinking is a central tenet of paganism.

Positive thinking in New Age

New Age thinking, popularised during the 1970s, is an alternative spiritual subculture that focuses on so-called 'positive energy', and has an interest in such things as meditation, channelling, reincarnation, crystals, psychic experiences and holistic health. New Age adherents believe that all that exists is derived from a single source of divine energy. 'All that exists is God; God is all that exists. God is at once the entire universe, and transcends the universe as well. This leads naturally to the concept of the divinity of the individual, that we are all Gods. They do not seek God as revealed in a sacred text or as exists in a remote heaven; they seek God within the self and throughout the entire universe.'[21] So the New Age 'God' is an impersonal Higher Energy. All things, including man, are a part of the Higher Energy, also called the Universal Mind, The Source, Universal Self, Cosmic Consciousness, Universal Presence, or Inner Voice.

'Life Positive', a New Age website, says there is no greater joy than a positive life. 'You feel exhilarated, energetic, happy and on top of the world. A sense of total wellbeing permeates your mind. The future looks bright. You feel good to be alive. Great, but how do we get out of our innumerable worries, tensions and fears that the increasingly competitive life burdens us with? Simple! Tell yourself that you are good, healthy and capable. That is the power of positive affirmations. Such affirmations are also called self-suggestions. It is a powerful tool for transforming your inner self into an amazing health generating, self-healing entity. You can record these affirmations on a tape synchronized with pleasant instrumental music and replay them often to make them more effective and permanent.'[22]

This quote reads like a page from a manual on positive psychology. The great emphasis on self, the life-goal of happiness, the promotion of positive feelings and positive affirmations are all ideas common to positive psychology.

Interpreting positive psychology

We must understand that behind positive psychology is the Templeton Foundation and its New Age agenda. While positive psychology claims to focus on the positive side of life, to help us live lives that are flourishing and happy, the truth is that it is little more than New Age thought masquerading as psychology. It seeks to persuade us that the secret to a happy life is through positive affirmation and 'deep mindful meditation', which is, in effect, the ancient practice of Buddhism.

Positive psychology tells us to reject negative thoughts, yet it has no real explanation for these negative thoughts. Where do they come from? Why are so-called negative thoughts universal to all people? We find the answer in Scripture—thoughts of shame, fear and guilt arise in the conscience because God has written his law in the heart of man. This means that all people know in their conscience that they are guilty sinners before a righteous God. The sense that we face eternal judgement, when we will be called to account for all our actions, lies deep in the human condition. As Scripture warns, there is no peace for the wicked (Isaiah 48.22). When Adam and Eve, as the representatives of the human race, disobeyed God's Word, they felt shame, fear and guilt, and tried to hide from God. Their rebellion against God's command troubled their God-given consciences, and they experienced what positive psychology has chosen to call 'negative thoughts'.

So the negative thoughts that positive psychology seeks to abolish through its various techniques, are the thoughts of a guilty conscience before a holy God that point to our need for salvation through the Cross of Christ. Positive psychology, because it rejects God's Word, is seeking to present an alternative way of salvation from a guilty conscience. It proclaims salvation through self-improvement and psychological techniques that deny the Cross of Christ, and leave us without God and without hope.

For us to reach a true assessment of the marriage psycho-education programmes discussed in the next chapters, we must be clear in our minds about the ideas, motives and techniques of positive psychology and how they contradict what is taught in God's Word.

(Endnotes)

1 John Templeton Foundation website, 'The Philanthropic Vision of Sir John Templeton', http://www.templeton.org/sites/default/files/the-philanthropic-vision-of-sir-john-templeton.pdf
2 John Templeton Foundation website, 'Science & the Big Questions', http://www.templeton.org/what-we-fund/core-funding-areas/science-and-the-big-questions
3 Cited from the booklet, 'Does the universe have a purpose?' The John Templeton Foundation, http://www.templeton.org/purpose/pdfs/bq_universe.pdf
4 'John Templeton's Universe', by Barbara Ehrenreich, in *The Nation*, October 10, 2007: http://www.thenation.com/article/john-templetons-universe
5 Ibid.
6 'God, Science and Philanthropy', by Nathan Schneider, June 3, 2010, this article appeared in the June 21, 2010 edition of *The Nation*.
7 John Templeton, *Possibilities for Over One Hundredfold More Spiritual Information: The Humble Approach in Theology and Science*, Templeton Foundation Press, 2000, p9
8 Ibid. p122
9 Ibid. p38
10 John Templeton, booklet *Views, Values, & Vision*, p2, Sir_john_booklet_web.pdf.pdf
11 Association of Unity Churches International, *Contact* Magazine, Vol. 42, Issue 5, October/November 2008, 'A Financier of Prosperity', by Susan EngPoole, pp36-37
12 John Templeton, *The Humble Approach*, Templeton Foundation Press, revised edition, June 1998, pp37-38
13 John Templeton Foundation, website, quotes: http://www.templeton.org/newsroom/press_releases/sir_john_templeton/quotes
14 Templeton, *Views, Values, & Vision*, p8
15 'Buddhist Positive Thinking' by Rasika Wijayaratne, 8 February 2006, Namo tassa Bhagavato Arahato Sammâ Sambuddhassa!: http://www.docstoc.com/docs/70977902/Buddhist-Positive-Thinking
16 Cited from the website, Zentraveler on the art of Happiness: http://vanscott.wordpress.com/2010/03/22/zentraveler-on-the-art-of-happiness
17 Cited from 'An Overview of Loving-kindness Meditation', by Ven Pannyavaro: http://www.buddhanet.net/metta_in.htm

18 Pagan Grove website, The Power of Positive Thought, http://www.pagangrove.com/2011/06/13/the-power-of-positive-thought/

19 Ibid.

20 Cited from Pagan Space website, 'The Domino Effect & Some Spiritual Boundaries', posted by Faxon on 5October, 2009: http://www.paganspace.net/profiles/blogs/the-domino-effect

21 Cited from the Shangra-la website, 'Glossary of Key Terms', http://www.shangrala.org/father/RELIGIONS/11NewAge/Glossary.html

22 Cited from Life Positive website, 'Positive Thinking - Think positive' by Ernest Vinaya Kumar: http://www.lifepositive.com/mind/psychology/positive-thinking/live-healthy.asp

11

PAIRS relationship skills

We have looked at the ideology and thinking behind the marriage education movement. Now we turn to the practice—that is, what does marriage education look like at the grass roots? To do so, we first examine a purely secular programme before turning to the Christian versions of marriage education.

In his testimony before the US House of Representatives Committee on Ways and Means in 2002, John Crouch, a divorce lawyer from Arlington, Virginia, asserted that marriage education is a proven success. He said that 'the leading programs have been around for decades, like the Maryland-based Relationship Enhancement curriculum, or the Florida-based PAIRS program, which has been adapted by the American Bar Association for use in the public schools. The PREP program, from the University of Denver, has been used in the public sector for years. It is taught in the Army.'[1] These three programmes are prominently represented at the Smart Marriages Conference, and Diane Sollee (see chapter 3) has referred to PAIRS as the Cadillac of marriage education programmes. According to Virginia Satir (see chapter 7), whose philosophy is woven into the fabric of the programme, 'PAIRS works because it offers practical, usable ways to accomplish joy in relationships.'[2] In this chapter we examine the PAIRS programme, in order to understand the agenda of secular marriage education.

In 1975 marriage and family therapist Lori Gordon, a faculty member of the School of Counseling at the American University in Washington, D.C., developed the concept of a psycho-educational approach to save marriages. Her idea was to use the best tools and skills from psychology to create an educational programme. By the late 1980s Gordon's concept had been developed into the PAIRS (Practical Application of Intimate Relationship Skills) programme that is now widely used across the USA. It integrates a wide range of theories and methods from psychology and psychotherapy, and presents them in an educational format. It acts to bridge therapy, marital enrichment, and marriage and family development. The PAIRS Foundation was established in Northern Virginia in 1983 and relocated to South Florida in 2000.

Today PAIRS is one of the leading marriage psycho-education programmes in the USA and is available in many other countries. It claims to have 'helped tens of thousands of men and women across the world create and sustain enhanced levels of love, pleasure and happiness in their most cherished relationships'.[3] According to its website, 'the Mission of PAIRS is to teach those attitudes, emotional understandings and behaviors that nurture and sustain healthy relationships and to make this knowledge broadly available on behalf of a safer, saner, more loving world.'[4] The overarching goal 'is to establish positive attitudes, behaviors, and patterns of emotional expression that lead to healthy habits for loving family relationships'.[5] So we see that the PAIRS programme aims to deliver skills and strategies for enhancing pleasure, happiness, and love in marriages, families and other intimate relationships.

Central to the PAIRS approach is a commitment to invite and never to inflict. Classes are offered in a variety of formats, ranging from 9 to 120 hours in length. Courses are designed to accommodate the needs of different types of participants, from weekend intensives, through multi-week seminars, to a complete semester-long Mastery Course.[6] The courses claim to provide an environment that is safe and accepting for trying out new skills. They also allow people to see courage and growth in others. They provide a comprehensive system to enhance self-knowledge and to develop the ability to sustain pleasurable intimate relationships. There are programmes for children and youth, which are taught in schools; for churches and community organisations; and for the Military. Classes are taught by chaplains, counsellors, family service workers and PAIRS National Trainers. PAIRS also has faith-based programmes for the Jewish, Catholic, and other Christian church communities.[7]

The goal of PAIRS is to create 'a relationship that both partners can live with joyfully. For this to happen, each partner must become able to identify his or her own feelings and needs, and learn to communicate them in such a way that they can get met... Easily and fully meeting each others' needs is the foundation of intimacy, fulfilment, and happiness.'[8] PAIRS teaches tools for communication, such as 'confiding, complaining, and clarifying and for effective problem solving such as managing anger, expressing anger safely, fighting fairly for change and eliminating dirty fighting'.[9] It also addresses pleasure and satisfaction by teaching skills to enhance bonding, sensuality and sexuality in marriage. It teaches 'the Relationship Roadmap, to understand relationship success and to understand relationship mishaps and know what to do about them'.[10]

PAIRS claims that 'sustaining a pleasurable intimate relationship does not work by magic. It depends upon a set of skills and understanding that can be learned.'[11] The programme teaches specific skills, which include emotional literacy; skills for building and maintaining intimacy; and practical knowledge, strategies and attitudes for sustaining positive marriage and family life.[12] Altogether, PAIRS teaches over 60 skills that become the PAIRS Tool Box for ongoing relationship maintenance.[13]

Daily Temperature Reading

The Daily Temperature Reading (DTR), created by Virginia Satir, a pioneer in the field of humanistic psychology, is a step-by-step guide to help communication with our partner. Satir introduced the original DTR in the 1970s. Since then it has been refined, adapted and shared by PAIRS leaders for many tens of thousands of diverse participants across the world, claiming to be one of the most powerful exercises for deepening and sustaining relationships.[14] On a daily basis we must allow ourselves to navigate the following five steps.

The first step is appreciation. We must take turns acknowledging each other, sincerely and specifically. Appreciation builds up credit in the 'love bank'. Heartfelt words will help maintain goodwill, boost self-worth and self-esteem, and create an environment in which we can work together to constructively address the challenges, obstacles and differences that are a natural part of every active relationship.[15]

The second step is new information. We must be intentional about keeping each other up-to-date on what's happening in our lives. We must share the events of our lives, allowing our partner to know what we're thinking about and feeling. This helps to create the strong emotional bond that we all need as human beings.

The next step is 'puzzles'. This is our chance to ask questions about anything we are wondering about. It's an important step to make sure we are not acting upon inaccurate assumptions. The idea is to clear up big or little mysteries before they become suspicions, jealousy, false assumptions, or resentments.

The fourth step is expressing concerns with recommendations. This is really about dealing with conflict in a positive way. According to PAIRS, 'it's vitally important to develop the habit of listening with empathy and a desire to understand when someone we love shares a concern. This is easier to do when we're comfortable with our own sense of self-worth and can be quite difficult when our self-esteem is low. When sharing a concern with a recommendation, be specific about the behavior you're concerned about (don't attack, judge, blame or criticize), share how you feel (not think) when the behavior happens, and ask for exactly what you want instead.'[16]

The fifth and final step in the DTR is expressing our wishes, hopes and dreams. This is about describing things we hope for in our life. PAIRS website says, 'Creating a life in which our dreams have an opportunity to come true involves actively (and passionately) sharing them with others; enrolling those closest to us to support and encourage the fulfilment of our goals and ambitions; and waking up each day learning the lessons and taking the actions necessary to breathe life and potential into those dreams we most desire.'[17]

Conclusion

PAIRS is indeed the Cadillac of marriage psycho-education programmes. It is an eclectic programme that has taken the 'wisdom' of the human potential movement, the thinking of Virginia Satir and the new ideas of positive psychology, to design the finest programme that human wisdom is capable of creating. Undoubtedly, PAIRS has been developed from the very best psychological research to become the pinnacle of psycho-education programmes. It teaches over 60 skills that are supposedly necessary for maintaining successful relationships. Among the most important skills are: the ability to listen empathetically, the ability to communicate our feelings, and the ability to resolve conflict.

The problem with PAIRS is that it is the product of human wisdom—it is a way that seems right to man that has entirely excluded the God of Scripture and the true spiritual dimension of life. At its heart is the hopelessly naïve belief in the goodness of human nature. This utopian view comes from Virginia Satir's claim that human intentions are positive and good, and that with the right education people are capable of almost unlimited self-improvement and therefore the ability to live flourishing and successful lives. The unrealistic hope is that once people have grasped the power of the psychological tools available to them, they will be able to overcome all their relationship difficulties.

Secular marriage education has endowed human beings with almost the qualities of deity. The claim that we are able to improve ourselves and overcome our problems with the right psychological training is simply wishful thinking. It entirely ignores the undeniable biblical truth that the human heart is sinful; that man is incapable of improving his own sinful heart. It entirely misses the point that difficult human relationships come from the innate sinful nature of man. We fight and quarrel because we want our way, because of our selfish desires and fleshly lusts (James 4.1). Secular marriage education is doomed to fail, because it ignores the reality of sin and the true nature and purpose of marriage. All the psychological skills and tools in the world are no substitute for biblical truth.

With our understanding of positive psychology and secular marriage psycho-education, we now turn to the Christian marriage educators.

(Endnotes)

1 Testimony of John Crouch on Marriage Education in TANF Reauthorization U.S. House of Representatives Committee on Ways and Means Human Resources Subcommittee April 11, 2002

2 Cited from website of PAIRS Communication Skills For Couples, taught by Edie Stone: http://www.ediestone.com/PairsWorkshop.html

3 Cited from PAIRS website, 'PAIRS questions and answers', http://participant.pairs.com/faq

4 Ibid. 'PAIRS Mission', http://instructor.pairs.com/history.html

5 PAIRS website, 'Teach', http://www.instructor.pairs.com/

6 PAIRS website, 'PAIRS questions and answers', http://participant.pairs.com/faq

7 PAIRS website, 'About PAIRS', http://participant.pairs.com/about

8 Ibid. 'About PAIRS'

9 Ibid.
10 Ibid.
11 Ibid.
12 Ibid.
13 Ibid.
14 PAIRS website, 'PAIRS daily temperature reading: Five steps to thriving relationships': http://dtr.pairs.com/
15 Ibid.
16 Ibid.
17 Ibid.

12

Gary Smalley – America's relationship doctor

Dr Gary Smalley is the trailblazer of 'Christian' marriage education and regarded by many as America's relationship doctor.[1] A trained psychologist, he also holds a master of divinity degree from Bethel Seminary in St Paul, Minnesota. During the four decades of his ministry, he has built a reputation as the foremost Christian expert on marriage and family relationships. He is the author of 50 best-selling books and videos that have connected with more than 12 million people. He has been featured on hundreds of TV and radio programmes across the U.S. With confident presentation skills, he has appeared on national televisions programmes such as The Oprah Winfrey Show and Larry King Live. Such is Smalley's celebrity status that he is listed as an inspirational speaker by the All American Speakers Bureau, a celebrity booking agency and talent buyer which supplies celebrity talent worldwide. The fee range for an 'inspirational talk' by Gary Smalley is $10,000 to $20,000.[2]

The Smalley website

The Official Smalley website provides a good insight into the ministry of Gary Smalley and his two sons, Greg and Michael. The site provides access to a wide range of Smalley marriage education products, such as books, DVDs, seminars and conferences.[3] An online marriage assessment is offered free of charge: 'How healthy is my marriage?' shows how safe your spouse feels in their relationship with you. And do you know about your personality type? No! Then Gary Smalley can help you. He offers a personality test, developed jointly with marriage and family counsellor Dr John Trent, based on the Lion, Otter, Golden Retriever, and Beaver system, to evaluate your personality style and that of your spouse (based on the supposed characteristics of these animals), and then prints out a report, based on who you are and what you need to do, to honour your spouse's personality and resolve conflict together![4]

The Smalley Intensive is a powerful marriage education event that claims to give you the skills necessary to thrive in your marriage. 'Our Marriage Intensive is unique because it focuses on building practical relational skills that provide a framework for you to improve your ability to communicate and resolve conflict. We help you create the environment for understanding and win-win solutions, leading to greater intimacy and connection... No matter what state your marriage is in, our intensives will make a profound impact on your marriage. Couples who are stressed will learn why they are stressed and actually be able to significantly increase their marital satisfaction through learning practical and applicable relationship skills like conflict resolution, communication, forgiveness, and more.'[5]

The Smalley website offers a range of seminars. The Love & Laughter Marriage Getaway is promoted as an event that 'is guaranteed to make you laugh until your sides bust! The Love & Laughter Marriage Getaway is custom made for you and your spouse to bring some fun and adventure back to your marriage... Dr Gary Smalley (known for his hilarious stories about his own marriage) and special guests will take you into all the details you need to rekindle that adventure you've always wanted.'[6] Other seminars are Embrace with Michael and Amy Smalley, and The Comedy of Love with Michael Smalley.

Understanding Smalley

Two early books, *If Only He Knew: Understanding Your Wife* (1979), and *For Better or for Best: Understand your Man* (1979), provide an insight into Gary Smalley's philosophy of marriage education. He believes 'the ideal marriage evolves when the wife concentrates on meeting her husband's needs and the husband concentrates on meeting his wife's needs'.[7] He argues that it is ridiculous to expect 'men to build strong, loving relationships without any education at all'.[8] A man must be educated in the skills of love. So Smalley, calling on his psychological and theological training, plans to educate men and women to help them achieve better and more fulfilling marriages.

The book for men, *If Only He Knew*, sets out to explain a woman's deepest needs, and to show a man how to meet those needs by ten simple steps. Smalley aims to help a man 'to understand not only how to respond to a woman's feelings, but also how to make her feel important. Using humorous and touching illustrations from his own life, as well as case histories and biblical examples, Gary Smalley maps a blueprint to a better marriage.'[9] Co-author, Steve Scott, says the book made him realise that for years he had not been meeting his wife's emotional needs. 'For years, she had put up with a husband whose callousness and indifference had forced her to suffer through day after day of not having her deeper needs satisfied.'[10] Smalley says that husbands generally do not know what their wives need. 'Since understanding and meeting your wife's needs is a golden key to a fulfilling marriage, the rest of the book deals with that subject.'[11]

The book for women, *For Better or for Best*, aims to help a wife improve her husband's performance so that he can meet her deepest needs. Because a man enters marriage 'with such a low level of knowledge and skill to meet a woman's needs, it is essential that his wife teach him what her needs and feelings are and, ultimately, show him how he can meet those needs'.[12] A woman's great strength is her sensitivity; she is like a sensitive butterfly, whereas her husband is like an insensitive buffalo.[13] The thrust of this book is that most problems in marriage are caused by insensitive men who simply do not understand their wives' feelings and deepest needs. A wife's task is to educate her insensitive husband. 'You can be your husband's most effective teacher. He needs to learn from you *why* it's important to listen to you and *how* to listen.'[14] A wife must just accept the fact that her husband needs to be taught how to meet her needs. 'Remember, you are in the process of teaching him, and he is in the process of learning.'[15]

One of the most important chapters tells a wife how to increase her husband's sensitivity to her emotional needs and desires. A wife must make a list of the needs and desires she would like to see her husband fulfil. 'But delve into your feelings until you believe your list is complete. Condense the list into the smallest number of vital needs so it doesn't appear overwhelming. As you explain the list to your husband, remember to discuss one need at a time until you've covered each subject.'[16]

A wife must express a positive attitude at all times. 'If you want your husband to yearn for quality time with you, then it is essential that you develop and express a positive attitude.'[17] Smalley says that 'negative thinking, especially about ourselves, is a major cause for an overall negative outlook on life'. So we must avoid negative thoughts at all costs. 'If our thinking and actions are positive, then our feelings will be positive in a matter of hours.'[18]

It is interesting to note that much of Smalley's advice given in 1979 is consistent with the approach of positive psychology. Moreover, his insistence that a wife should educate her insensitive, rather ignorant husband is contrary to Scripture. The apostle Paul teaches that the head of the woman is the man (1 Corinthians 11.3). Therefore, 'I do not permit a woman to teach or to have authority over a man' (1 Timothy 2.12).

American theologian Al Dager is critical of Smalley's approach to marriage. He says that 'both books approach the marriage relationship from a selfish wife's viewpoint. They comprise a course on how to get the husband to meet the needs of his wife, with only a cursory explanation in *For Better or for Best* of how the wife can meet the needs of her husband—and this with the ulterior motive of inducing him to meet her needs… Essentially he [Smalley] wants them to give in to their wives' every whim, regardless of whether wisdom or God's leading direct otherwise.'[19]

Al Dager continues his analysis: 'An example of the lopsided approach to Smalley's marital counseling is the constant reference that the wife's book makes to the husband's book. This is to encourage the wife to get her husband to read his book so she can "motivate" him to shape up. Yet there is virtually no reference to her book in his. Thus the husband is unknowingly being "set up" for correction as a kind of conspiracy between Smalley and the wife.'[20] Al Dager concludes: 'And therein lies an essential problem with Smalley's philosophy. It is predicated upon the blanket proposition that all men are by nature lowbrow creeps whose only redeeming value lies in their brute strength which, if "harnessed" by women, as Smalley implies, might be put to some good use—like helping with the housework.'[21] Thus Smalley's psychological advice reverses biblical truth with regard to male-female roles, making the woman dominant.

A perceptive review on Amazon rather agrees with Al Dager: 'The overall tone of both books is guidance on how the woman wants the

133

man to behave and how she can teach him to behave the way she wants. In Smalley's seminars, he credits his program with an approval from a leading feminist. In other words, the feminist movement concurs with Smalley on how men should behave.'[22]

A man who followed Smalley's advice offers this comment: 'This book's advice will make you into a dancing monkey for your woman. To my embarrassment, sorrow and regret I followed Smalley's advice way too many times… The advice in this book will lead you to nothing but heartache.'[23] What is clear is that Smalley's advice is not soundly based in Scripture, but appears to be following a feminist agenda—the man is demeaned, while the woman is elevated. The effect is to overturn the divinely ordained ordering of marriage.

The Language of Love

In *The Language of Love* (1988), published by Focus on the Family, Gary Smalley offers the key to what he calls a life-transforming communication method—emotional word pictures. He explains the importance of left-brain/right-brain theory as follows: 'The sex-related hormones and chemicals that flood a baby boy's brain, cause the right side to recede slightly, destroying some of the connecting fibres. The result is that, in most cases, a boy starts life more *left*-brain orientated.'[24] According to the theory, females are much more two-sided in their thinking. The consequence is that men are more logical and factual in their thinking, whereas women are more in touch with their feelings and emotions. These differences result in communication difficulties between the sexes.

Fortunately there is a way for a man to boost his communication skills. Smalley says that 'if a woman truly expects to have meaningful communication with her husband, she must activate the right side of his brain. And if a man truly wants to communicate with his wife, he must enter her world of emotions. In both these regards, word pictures can serve as a tremendous aid. Indeed, a world of colorful communication waits for those who learn the skill of bridging both sides of the brain.'[25]

To illustrate the concept of emotional word pictures, Smalley suggests that Nathan the prophet (in 2 Samuel 12) succeeded in activating the *right side* of the King David's brain by using 'an emotional word picture that would change the course of a kingdom and echo throughout the ages... [David was] shattered by the blow of one emotional word picture... for the first time he was forced to face the evil he had done, to feel some of the emotional trauma he had caused to others.'[26]

Dave Hunt of the *Berean Call* comments: 'Talk about a trivialization of Scripture! It was the Holy Spirit who convicted David! Not only does a technique (activating the right brain and thereby arousing the emotions through the use of "word pictures") become the key, but its appeal is not to conscience or truth but to feelings.'[27]

Such was Smalley's popularity as an author that he was invited to give the key note address at the Christian Booksellers Association annual convention held in Dallas in 1988. But Dave Hunt was highly critical: 'His speech was humanistic nonsense. His entire talk was based upon today's popular left-brain/right-brain myth spawned by pop psychology—a myth which brain researchers call "whole-brain half-wittedness." I was embarrassed because of the many non-Christians present who knew that what Smalley was saying was ludicrous. Yet they observed hundreds of Christian leaders, representing the cream of evangelical publishing, applauding in enthusiastic approval... Moreover, instead of biblical truth that sets free, a deluding lie that would enslave was being passed off upon trusting Christians who thought that the "expert" addressing them knew whereof he spoke.'[28]

Following this criticism, Dave Hunt (at their request) met with Smalley and his pastor in Phoenix, Arizona. The outcome was that in subsequent editions of *The Language of Love* references to left-brain/right-brain mythology were removed.[29]

Smalley believes in research

Smalley's understanding of marriage comes largely from listening to the views of other people and from paying attention to the latest research findings. He says that the first five years of his marriage were very frustrating for his wife, Norma. 'Many of our arguments went unresolved. We were losing the love we had for one another. That's when I began interviewing women and counselors and reading books on the subject. Over time I found that women had a built-in marriage manual: They seem able to explain what makes up a good relationship and how to arrive at that kind of relationship… I kept doing research, asking couples what they needed, what worked and what didn't work. About three years ago I discovered Dr Howard Markman and Dr Scott Stanley of Denver University. I found them to be professional and scientific in their approach to marriage and the family… The basis of their findings became the heart of *Making Love Last Forever* (1996). Their scientific evidence reinforced some of the things I had already learned. Today I can speak with tremendous confidence about what hurts a marriage and what keeps it alive. The greatest killer of marriage and love is anger stored away in the heart.'[30] This was Smalley in 1997— yet by 2001 he had discovered and written *The Secrets to Lasting Love*, and by 2004 he had discovered nothing less than a new paradigm for relationships (*The DNA of Relationships*) that he promised would change our lives and our culture—which is a claim of the utmost significance or complete nonsense.

Smalley firmly believes that marriage and family research has helped us to know what it takes to make marriages survive. He is thankful for the input of four psychologists who helped him develop his video series for national TV. 'They met with me for days at a time and imparted their wisdom and research. Then after I had taken their instruction and developed each session, they would again listen to my sessions, and evaluate the accuracy and validity of each session. In short, they have not only greatly enriched my life over the past few years, but they have been truly great friends in stretching me to learn so many terrific things about marriage and life.'[31] Here Smalley openly acknowledges that his approach to marriage education is based in the theories of psychology and not Scripture.

Journey toward intimacy

In *Secrets to Lasting Love* (2001), we are shown how to feel safe enough to share our deepest needs with one another—how to dive into the deepest levels of our emotions.[32] Smalley refers to a relationship revolution taking place in America, and is enormously impressed with the marriage psycho-education programmes led by 'experts' like Drs John and Julie Gottman, Harvel Hendriks, Sherod Miller, and Steven Covey. Smalley writes, 'I am overwhelmingly convinced that if couples received instruction by using any of these programs, both before and after marriage, America could see the divorce rate significantly lowered within 10 years.'[33]

Although he had written numerous books on relationships, Smalley says that this new material has had a dramatic effect on his own marriage. 'When I find techniques that can help lost couples find their way back to happiness and contentment, I can't let those skills remain a secret.'[34] So Smalley takes us on a journey to find the ultimate relationship. 'Every fully realized relationship is a trip from surface emotions down into the depths, descending through five distinct levels of intimate communication that move from the shallow levels to the fifth and deepest level. At this fifth level, a couple feels absolutely safe and accepted for what they feel and need as unique individuals. Throughout this book I am going to show you how to accelerate your journey through these levels, arriving at the deepest level in the short-est, most effective amount of time.'[35]

The journey toward intimacy is like 'diving into' your relationship. 'You want to dive in deeply, to leave the shallow waters of superficial-ity and delve into, and revel in, the depths of intimacy.'[36] The journey involves learning to communicate at the deepest level. The first three superficial levels of communication are: clichés; sharing facts; sharing opinions. At level four you are 'sharing your deepest and truest feelings with each other. At this level, you help each other feel safe to share your deepest emotions. You each know that you will both do your very best to listen and value what the other is sharing. Each of you can accept the other as unique and special, a creation made up of all your history, personality, and family background.'[37]

At level five you are sharing your most important relational needs. This is the deepest level of love and marital satisfaction. 'But the most intimate part of loving communication is when both of you feel safe to reveal your unique needs to one another. This shows that you know you will be accepted and valued by your mate for who you are.'[38]

Smalley's new secret is that true and lasting love is based on sharing our deepest feelings. But this is not new and it is not a secret—years ago Carl Rogers taught that we must learn to delve into our deepest feelings in order to become real people. Rogers said we must move from a position of emotional fixity to what he called 'flowingness'. A real relationship should be lived on the basis of real feelings, rather than on the basis of a defensive pretence. Real communication, according to Rogers, is about understanding 'another person's thoughts and feelings thoroughly, with the meanings they have for him, and to be thoroughly understood by this other person in return – this is one of the most rewarding of human experiences, and all too rare'.[39] Smalley is simply regurgitating Carl Rogers' teaching on feelings that we read about in chapter 6. Here we should make the point that most Christian marriage education programmes are built on the false premise of Rogers' humanistic psychology, namely, that real communication involves sharing our deepest feelings.

Purpose of Smalley's ministry

In *The DNA of Relationships* (2004), Smalley explains the purpose of his ministry. 'For the past thirty-five years I have felt passionate about helping couples, families and individuals to strengthen, deepen and enrich their most important relationships. That is what God has called me to do. In this quest to improve relationships, I am always searching for what works and identifying what doesn't work. I love to take relationship theories, apply them to my own relationships, and see if they work for me personally. It makes no difference if I make the discovery on my own or if the new relationship idea comes from someone else. I'm always hunting. So for three and a half decades I've travelled all over the world delivering my message about how to improve relationships... That's why I'm constantly on the lookout for anything that really *works* for the vast majority of people I meet'[40] [Smalley's italics].

The above statement makes it clear that Smalley does not believe that Scripture definitively teaches how we should relate to each other. Indeed, he suggests that God has left his people in the dark when it comes to relationships. Therefore we need the research and guidance that comes from the marriage education industry to understand what makes relationships work. This attitude fundamentally denies the sufficiency of Scripture, and implies that those who lived before the advent of modern psychological theories were seriously handicapped in their relationships, Scripture not having provided instruction on how humans beings should relate to each other. Smalley places more faith in the psychological theories of Carl Rogers than Christ's Sermon on the Mount.

Smalley's new discovery

In his constant search for information to improve relationships, Smalley made what he says is the greatest discovery of his lifetime. And this great discovery came from observing his son Greg (who has a doctorate in psychology) doing intensive marriage counselling with couples on the brink of divorce. Having been 'enlightened' by his great discovery, he promises that the *new paradigm* for relationships that he has unveiled in *The DNA of Relationships* will change our lives. Indeed, Smalley believes that 'the message of this book can have a profound impact on our culture'.[41] So profound is this new 'truth', that he is working 'to recruit an army of a million relationship champions who will gather weekly with a small group of other champions to help one another learn and apply the DNA of relationship principles... We're also actively praying for 100,000 churches to join us as we work to ignite the relationship revolution that will transform our country and our world... In short, we'll be here for you until you understand this new message and can apply it easily in your life and relationships. We believe that we've found a relational gold mine, and we want you to profit from all its awesome riches.'[42] And Smalley reiterates his message: 'God has called me to hunt for and discover what actually works in strengthening the relationships of couples, families, and singles... Believe me, this new stuff works.'[43] These are grand claims indeed from the trailblazer of the Christian marriage psycho-education movement.

What is remarkable is that Smalley, who claims his ministry of thirty-five years is from God, has only now discovered what makes relationships work. So what has he been teaching all these years? Why has he only now discovered what makes relationships work? Does God's Word not teach his people how they should relate to each other? Are Christian people not to be conformed to the image of Christ and to live by the fruit of the Spirit? But Smalley evidently feels that God's Word is not enough, so he runs to psychological research to find what really makes relationships work. And Smalley has the audacity to claim that his new message will not only transform our lives, but our culture and the world. Having rejected the wisdom of Scripture, Smalley has chosen to follow the wisdom of psychology and is calling on others to follow him. By doing so he is leading others to deny the God of Scripture and place their trust in the foolish, man-made theories of psychology. Our Lord's comments on blind leaders in Matthew 15.14 spring to mind.

Smalley's doctrine of man

So what exactly is this new discovery, this new revolutionary truth that is going to transform society? Research from the marriage intensive seminars, led by Greg and Michael Smalley, found that every couple was involved in a 'destructive dance' that was based on *fear*. 'Every husband and wife was acting out of a core fear. Let me be so bold as to say that every person on the planet wrestles with some core fear... I mean things like fear of failure or fear of not being loved or fear of being alone.'[44] Smalley says that all mankind has a fear button, and when this button is pushed it produces a reaction. It is therefore important for you to identify your core fear. 'Without identifying your own core fear and understanding how you tend to react when your fear button gets pushed, your relationships will suffer.'[45] *So we all wrestle with our core fear*. And when someone pushes our fear button, 'we get stuck in a destructive Fear Dance that involves our hurts, wants, fears and reactions', and that destroys our relationships.[46]

In Smalley's eyes the basic problem of mankind is a *core fear*, like the fear of failure or the fear of not being loved. This is the great new discovery. But his view of man is based on psychological theory, and there is no recognition of the sinful nature of man; no acceptance that the lusts of the flesh war against the soul; no understanding of the destructive power of sin in human relationships. In addition, Smalley claims to have found the secret that will help us to break the rhythm of the Fear Dance and thereby overcome our core fear and restore our relationships.

Smalley's way of salvation

Smalley longs for you (his reader) to experience and enjoy the same new found life and vitality in relationships that he claims to have experienced in the past few years. His plan is to teach five new dance steps that will revolutionise your relationships. The first step is learning how 'to become completely empowered to choose how you feel within all of your relationships.' Second is to learn about safety. 'Just imagine friends, couples, and kids feeling completely safe to open up and share their deepest thoughts with others who love them.'[47]

Third is to learn about 'how God wants you to take care of yourself so that you can become a channel of his love to others'.[48] The problem is that 'we do not appreciate how God designed us to function as fully emotional beings. Why are emotions so important? Think of your emotions as God's information system. They inform you about your needs and your deepest beliefs.'[49] So you must identify your feelings. Smalley says, 'listen to your emotions, let them inform you about danger signs. Then tend to yourself spiritually, emotionally, intellectually and physically. Keep your battery charged. And when you do, you will be prepared for deeply satisfying relationships.'[50]

Smalley's assertion that we should think of our emotions as God's information system is suggesting that God's speaks to us through our emotions. But this is entirely false, for God does not speak to believers through their subjective, changing emotions, but through his eternal, unchanging Word. God does not reveal his truth through our feelings, but through his Word, which is truth (John 17.17).

The fourth step is to learn the message of emotional communication. 'We'll show you how to find the emotional nugget that leads to effective and fulfilling communication, enabling you to feel confident that you will be understood.'[51] He says that the real message is often the emotion beneath the words. 'You have to ask yourself, *What is this person feeling?*'[52] [his italics]

The final step is to adopt 'a no-loser policy that will help you walk in harmony and complete unity with your spouse, family members and friends so that you never again have to worry about losing an argument. We'll show you how to identify the obstacles that make your relationships difficult, as well as how to remove those hurdles.'[53]

There is, of course, nothing new in Smalley's new discovery. Just more of the same psycho-education—again we see that his model is built around Carl Rogers' theories on feelings and emotions, that we must be in touch with our emotions and communicate our feelings to others. This is false teaching that contradicts Scripture and leads away from the Gospel of truth.

141

Smalley's 'infomercials'

With great acumen Smalley foresaw the business opportunity presented by Christian marriage education. He realised that 'Christian marriage education' was a product which, with skilful marketing, would have a wide appeal among church-going people. To advertise his array of products, such as books, videos and DVDs, and his marriage seminars, Smalley developed so-called 'infomercials' that have been broadcast widely across the USA. (Infomercials are an advertising vehicle to both inform and to persuade people to buy products that help them become beautiful, rich and successful.)

Smalley produced his first infomercial, the award-winning 'Hidden Keys to Loving Relationships', in 1988. It has been screened all over the world, and helped him sell video cassette programmes worth millions of dollars. These infomercials featured four or five couples sitting around a living room saying how much Gary's videos helped them. Nestled on a couch next to American football celebrity Frank Gifford, his wife Kathie Lee (American television host) proclaimed, 'Anybody who knows us knows that nothing is more important than our children and our relationship with each other. It is a source of tremendous joy and security.'[54] Smalley's marketing strategy was remarkably successful, and the 18-videotape series sold over 4 million copies. He wrote: 'With the sale of all those tapes and steady stream of book royalties coming in you can imagine how much money we had to handle.'[55]

In 1999 Gary Smalley asked Diane Sollee, doyen of the world of marriage psycho-education and founder of the Coalition for Marriage, Family and Couples Education (discussed in chapter 3), to use her network to generate an audience for the taping of his infomercial, 'Love is a Decision'. Gary explained the purpose of his latest theory to Diane: 'The new material shows that all married couples move in and out of five levels of intimate communication every day and that there are four main "divorce producing relationship germs" that can develop at the third level of intimacy. Without understanding or training, many couples "hit a wall" at the third level of intimacy and can be blocked from entering the fourth and fifth levels of intimacy where real marital satisfaction takes place. We have developed three main relationship skills that move a couple through the wall, destroying the four "germs" and allowing the couple to enter the two deepest levels of intimacy. It's a fascinating concept and I'm looking forward to having it finished. This is what I'll be teaching at the Smart Marriages Conference this summer.'[56] Smalley's appeal for help shows that he regards the Coalition as a natural ally of his ministry.

Smalley's money and celebrity status

The fruit of Smalley's ministry was great financial success and even greater celebrity status. In his book, *Your Relationship with God* (2006), he speaks of the first three decades of his ministry. He writes: 'Here I was, with more money than I'd ever seen and a ministry that was going off the charts in terms of growth. Even though my passion was with the ministry, not with making a lot of money, all of a sudden both the ministry and the money were begging for my attention, and God was only somewhere in the mix. I was becoming distracted from my primary relationship by the sheer volume and pace of life.'[57]

His ministry was so successful that as time went on he began acquiring things—investment properties, new cars, snowmobiles, a boat. 'I told myself these things were all for my family's enjoyment, but being able to provide these nice things was just as much about satisfying my own ego.' He continues: 'People continued to treat me like a celebrity, and I began to act like one. I expected special treatment in restaurants and on airplanes, and I always traveled with an assistant to keep people from getting too close to me. How's that for a so-called relationship expert?'[58]

And here is the testimony of the man who for years and years had been teaching Christians about marriage and relationships. 'Throughout my life, and particularly during the years leading up to my kidney transplant... I succumbed to the desire to have more of everything all the time—more money, more possessions, a bigger house, a nicer car, a secure future. I wanted my reputation to be such that people would recognize me and say, "Now there is one successful man." Driven by greed and impurity, I was given to anger and malice when I didn't get my way.'[59] He confesses that a cantankerous outlook and deep anger ruled his life. So it seems that when he was far from God, when his life was given over to materialism and selfish ambition, he was busy writing books, producing DVDs and holding seminars to teach Christians about marriage and the keys to successful relationships. Who was he serving, God or mammon? Who was he seeking to please, God or men? What was the source of the wisdom behind his teaching?

When he was 65 years old, after three decades of teaching about marriage, Smalley says that God renewed his life. 'God's word can change our hearts each and every day of our lives. No other book can correct, teach, rebuke, bless, inspire, encourage, and sustain us. God's word is really alive... Colossians 3.1-17 has deeply affected me since the renewal of my relationship with God.'[60] As he claims to have come to his senses, to have renewed his relationship with God, to have realised the power of God's Word, he must surely realise that his teaching about marriage has not been based on God's Word, but on human wisdom that stands opposed to the Word of God. Is he going to repent for teaching millions of people to place their faith in psychology, and not the truth of God's Word? He says that God has separated him 'from addiction to the things of this world. He has lifted me from my negative emotions.'[61] Wonderful! Is Smalley now going to repudiate the Christian marriage psycho-education industry he has helped to construct? Apparently not. His seeming repentance over his own bad conduct merely becomes another money-spinning book; but the real issue is not addressed. Here we see the hypocrisy of the Christian marriage industry in all its horror, for Smalley in spite of what he says is still engaged in promoting the messages of positive psychology through the marriage psycho-education programme of Focus on the Family, as we shall see in chapter 15.

What do we make of Smalley?

Smalley's approach to marriage education is based on the seductive theories that come from psychological research. He accepts psychological research at face value, and eagerly follows the psychological way. Throughout his career Smalley has claimed the ability to uncover hidden keys for the Church. He boasts to have uncovered the 'secret' of successful relationships on a number of occasions. He is, in effect, a modern-day Gnostic who claims to have access to a special hidden knowledge that we all need to live a successful life.

Smalley is also an expert businessman. He admits that he made a lot of money and acquired many possessions from his ministry. His infomercials were blatant advertising ploys to increase the sale of his never-ending supply of books, videos and DVDs. Smalley has made a lot of money through his business, which he describes as a 'ministry'. But this is a false understanding of true ministry. Rather than a minister of the Gospel, he has all the appearances of a skilful salesman. And at this point we must understand that with a heart given over to greed and a mind given over to psychology, he wrote his books and developed his seminars with scant regard to biblical truth. He has used superficial psycho-education to mislead millions of naïve Christians with his un-biblical promises.

Smalley has freely associated with the ways and thinking of the world, and established a close working relationship with the decidedly secular approach of the Smart Marriages Conference. The effect of Smalley's ministry has been to trivialise the meaning and purpose of marriage in the eyes of society, and to lead Christians to believe that they need a range of man-made psychological tools and techniques to achieve a successful marriage. He has singularly failed to teach a biblical view of marriage, in fact, one could question whether he even understands what Scripture actually teaches about marriage and the family.

He has opened the way for many other so-called Christian marriage educators to market their products. There are now a host of Christian psychologists that have entered the Church and are accepted as the experts on marriage. Most of these 'experts' are Smalley clones, celebrities skilled at presenting their latest psycho-programme with a smile, expert marketeers who are full of stories and utopian promises, yet devoid of biblical truth. It is no surprise that the Church is now inundated with books, DVDs, websites and the like that promote marriage psycho-education, to the detriment of the truth of biblical marriage.

(Endnotes)

1 Gary Smalley, *Your relationship with God*, Tyndale House, 2008, Paperback, back cover: http://www.christianbook.com/your-relationship-with-drawing-closer-everyday/gary-smalley/9781414304465/pd/304465

2 All American Speakers website, allamericanspeakers.com/celebrity: http://www.allamericanspeakers.com/speakers/Gary-Smalley/4692

3 The Official Gary Smalley website: http://smalley.cc/

4 Ibid. Free Personality Test: http://smalley.cc/free-personality-test

5 Ibid. What is a Smalley Intensive?: http://smalley.cc/the-smalley-center/what-is-a-smalley-intensive

6 Ibid. Conferences: http://smalley.cc/smalley-seminars/love-laughter-with-gary-smalley-and-guests

7 Gary Smalley, *For Better or For Best*, Zondervan, first published 1979, revised edition 1988, p8

8 Gary Smalley, *If Only He Knew*, Zondervan, first published 1979, revised edition 1988, p26

9 Ibid. blurb on back cover

10 Ibid. Comment by Steve Scott, p6

11 Ibid. p30

12 Gary Smalley, *For Better or For Best*, p55

13 Ibid. p107

14 Ibid. p115

15 Ibid. p124

16 Ibid. p125

17 Ibid. p95

18 Ibid. pp96-97

19 Cited from article 'Gary Smalley – the Psychology of Matriarchy' by Albert James Dager, 1989 Media Spotlight: http://www.mediaspotlight.org/pdfs/Gary Smalley.pdf

20 Ibid.

21 Ibid.

22 Amazon customer review, *If Only He Knew*, http://www.amazon.de/review/R21G679IYS7GQ3

23 Amazon customer review, *If Only He Knew*, 'If I could I would give this a zero', September 18, 2005: http://www.amazon.com/If-Only-He-Knew-Resist/product-reviews/B000OHGO22?pageNumber=8

24 Gary Smalley & John Trent, *The Language of Love*, 1988, published by Focus on the Family, p35

25 Ibid. p42

26 Ibid. pp52-54

27 *The Berean Call*, 'Science Falsely So-Called', Dave Hunt, February 1, 1989: http://www.thebereancall.org/content/science-falsely-so-called

28 Ibid.

29 Ibid.

30 Cited from *Good News Magazine*, 'Gary Smalley on Love and Marriage', article by Jerry Aust, May/June 1997

31 Gary Smalley, *Making Love Last Forever*, Thomas Nelson, 1996, acknowledgements, page x: http://books.google.co.uk/books?id=7C-IVQV8JKsC&printsec=frontcover&source=gbs_atb#v=onepage&q&f=false

32 Gary Smalley, *Secrets to Lasting Love*, Fireside, Simon & Schuster, 2001, p31

33 Ibid. p21

34 Ibid. p16

35 Ibid. p27

36 Ibid. p29

37 Ibid. p31

38 Ibid. p31

39 Carl Rogers, *On Becoming a Person*, Houghton Mifflin Company, 1961, pp323-24

40 Gary Smalley, *The DNA of Relationships*, Smalley Publishing Group, 2004, p4

41 Ibid. p13

42 Ibid. p14

43 Ibid. p14

44 Ibid. p41

45 Ibid. p42

46 Ibid. p60
47 Ibid. p12
48 Ibid. p12
49 Ibid. p115
50 Ibid. p129
51 Ibid. p12
52 Ibid. pp135-136
53 Ibid. p12
54 Cited from *People Magazine*, 'Kathie Lee's Crisis' by Tom Gliatto, 2 June 1997, Vol. 47, No.21
55 Gary Smalley, *Your Relationship with God*, Tyndale House Publishers, 2006, p8
56 Website, Smart Marriages, Smalley taping in Boise/Witcher on Divorce/ Mon April 12, 1999:
http://lists101.his.com/pipermail/smartmarriages/1999-April/002113.html
57 Gary Smalley, *Your Relationship with God*, p9
58 Ibid. p14
59 Ibid. p152
60 Ibid. p141
61 Ibid. p143

13

Gary Chapman's languages of love

Humanist psychotherapist Carl Rogers envisaged a new version of marriage that was free of the old restraints imposed by biblical Christianity. He repudiated out of hand the idea that husband and wife have different roles in marriage. He said couples needed new ways of relating, new kinds of partnership where they learn from their mistakes and profit from their successes. He advocated the need for more research that would help men and women find new ways of getting the best from their sexual relationships.

A number of psychologists took up Rogers' challenge, setting up research protocols to investigate marriage and human relationships to find out what works. Gary Smalley was one of the first Christian marriage educators to join the search, as we saw in the last chapter. And where Gary Smalley led, others have been keen to follow. The result is a thriving Christian marriage education movement as many marriage educators, among them Dr Gary Chapman and Dr Emerson Eggerichs (see chapter 14) in the USA, and Rob Parsons in the UK, have joined the search to find the secret of marital happiness.

In this chapter we examine the contribution of Dr Gary Chapman, an internationally respected marriage and family life expert. He is a Senior Associate Pastor of Calvary Baptist Church in Winston-Salem, North Carolina. Dr Chapman is a graduate of Moody Bible Institute and holds a degree in anthropology from Wake Forest University. He also received a degree in religious education from Southwestern Baptist Theological Seminary. He has thirty years' experience as a marriage counsellor, and speaks extensively throughout the USA and internationally on marriage, family, and relationships. He is a favourite keynote speaker at the annual Smart Marriages Conference. Sales of his book, *The 5 Love Languages* (1992), have exceeded 5 million copies and earned him the Platinum Book Award from the Evangelical Publishers Association. This book has been translated into over thirty-six languages. Twenty-seven other books and five video series are among his publications. His popular radio programme, 'A Love Language Minute,' is heard on more than 100 radio stations across the USA.

The Marriage You've Always Wanted Conference, led by Gary Chapman, is advertised by Moody Conferences, a department of Moody Bible Institute, Chicago, as 'a time of fun and discovery that can help you build the love relationship of your dreams. Whether you're getting married in six months—or have been married 60 years—you'll get solutions you can use. With biblical advice and a healthy dose of laughter, Dr Chapman gives valuable tips on breaking unhealthy patterns and choosing to develop a God-honouring, happy marriage.'[1]

There is no doubt that Gary Chapman is one of the most respected figures in the Christian marriage education field. Many marriage education courses promote his philosophy of the 'five love languages'.

Chapman's languages of love

In *The 5 Love Languages*, reprinted for the third time in 2010, Chapman claims to reveal the secret to love that lasts. He says that he is indebted to a host of professionals who have influenced his concepts of love, among whom are psychiatrists Ross Campbell and Judson Swihart.[2] He believes that 'the desire for romantic love in marriage is deeply rooted in our psychological makeup... With all the help available from media experts, why is it that so few couples seem to have found the secret to keeping love alive after the wedding?'[3] But Chapman has found the answer to this question. 'The problem is that we have overlooked one fundamental truth: People speak different love languages... Your emotional love language and the language of your spouse may be as different as Chinese from English.'[4] He says that the important thing is to speak the love language of your spouse. 'Once you identify and learn to speak your spouse's primary love language, I believe that you will have discovered the key to a long-lasting loving marriage.'[5] So if we want our spouse 'to feel the love we are trying to communicate, we must express it in his or her primary love language'.[6]

The emotional love tank

Chapman says that while philosophical and theological systems have made a prominent place for love, 'psychologists have concluded that the need to feel loved is a primary human emotional need'.[7] The purpose of his book is to focus on 'the kind of love that is essential to our emotional health'.[8] Chapman's basic premise is that deep inside every individual there exists an invisible emotional 'love tank', and an empty tank is the cause of most marital problems. 'Could it be that deep inside hurting couples exists an invisible "emotional love tank" with its gauge on empty? Could the misbehavior, withdrawal, harsh words, and critical spirit occur because of the empty tank?'[9] And so he poses the question: 'If we could find a way to fill it, could the marriage be reborn?' He then states his philosophy of marriage: 'I am convinced that keeping the emotional love tank full is as important to a marriage as maintaining the proper oil level is to an automobile. Running your marriage on an empty "love tank" may cost you even more than trying to drive your car without oil.'[10] So the proposition is that a husband and wife each have a love tank that needs to be constantly replenished to keep their marriage happy and successful.

From the above it is clear that Chapman follows the psychological view that love is a feeling—and hence a need that must be met. A husband must make his wife *feel* that she is loved in order to meet this need. Moreover, Chapman claims that this feeling is a basic human need; in effect, psychology has turned a subjective feeling into an emotional need.

Five Languages of Love

From his extensive experience as a marriage counsellor, Chapman claims he has discovered that there are five love languages, namely: words of affirmation; quality time; receiving gifts; acts of service; and physical touch. The challenge is for a husband and wife to first discover, and then to learn to speak the primary love language of their spouse, for to do so will radically alter their own and their spouse's behaviour. Speaking their primary love language will fill their spouse's love tank. 'When your spouse's emotional love tank is full and he feels secure in your love, the whole world looks bright and your spouse will move out to reach his highest potential in life. But when the love tank is empty and he feels used but not loved, the whole world looks dark and he will likely never reach his potential for good in the world.'[11]

1) Words of affirmation

Chapman says that one way to express love emotionally is to use words that build up. He tells us that 'psychologist William James said that possibly the deepest human need is the need to feel appreciated. Words of affirmation will meet that need in many individuals.'[12] If you decide that your spouse's love language is words of affirmation then you should keep a notebook, and 'when you hear a lecture on love or you overhear a friend saying something positive about another person write it down. In time, you will collect quite a list of words to use in communicating love to your spouse.'[13] You can say positive things about your wife when she is not present, and you can even 'tell your wife's mother how great your wife is. When her mother tells her what you said, your remarks will be amplified, and you will get even more credit.'[14]

And Chapman provides a number of suggestions on how to use words of affirmation. You can 'set a goal to give your spouse a different compliment each day for one month', or 'write a love letter'.[15] He says that verbal compliments, such as, 'Do you ever look hot in that dress! Wow!' or 'You look sharp in that suit,'[16] are powerful communicators of love. Words of affirmation can help our feelings of insecurity. 'We lack courage, and that lack of courage often hinders us from accomplishing the positive things that we would like to do. The latent potential within your spouse in his or her areas of insecurity may await your encouraging words.'[17]

He says that to develop an intimate relationship we need to know each other's desires. 'If we wish to love each other, we need to know what the other person wants.'[18] And we must 'make our needs and desires known in the form of a request'.[19] So in Chapman's eyes, love is giving our spouse what they want.

The problem with this approach is that it is so completely contrived. Does a wife really want to be complimented with a phrase that her husband overheard at a party? Scripture warns, 'let us not love in word or in tongue, but in deed and in truth' (1 John 3.18). But there is a much more disturbing problem. The positive affirmation concept, as we saw

151

in chapter 9, is a tool of positive psychology. This is not the way of the Christian faith; it is wrong to use flattery, for 'a flattering mouth works ruin' (Proverbs 26.28). Christians do not find their security in words of affirmation, but in Christ: 'for I know whom I have believed and am persuaded that He is able to keep that which I have committed to Him until that Day' (2 Timothy 1.12).

2) Quality time

Quality time means doing something together and giving our full attention to the other person. We must seek to discover the thoughts and feelings of our spouse by talking to them. 'Quality conversation requires not only sympathetic listening but also self-revelation.' But self-revelation does not come easy for some of us. 'Many grew up in homes where the expression of thoughts and feelings was not encouraged but condemned... By the time we reached adulthood, many of us have learned to deny our feelings.'[20]

Chapman says that in order for a wife to feel loved, her husband must learn to reveal himself. If her primary love language is quality time, her emotional love tank will never be filled until he tells her his thoughts and feelings.[21] So when a husband decides to learn the language of quality conversation it will be like learning a foreign language. 'The place to begin is by getting in touch with his feelings, becoming aware that he is an emotional creature in spite of the fact that he has denied that part of this life.'[22] Here Chapman is simply promoting the teaching of Carl Rogers, who said that husband and wife learn a great deal about the other when they continue to share their own feelings. Rogers says that your attitude should be, 'I want to share myself and my feelings with you, even when they are not all positive.'[23]

And if your spouse's love language is quality time then 'take a walk together through the old neighbourhood where one of you grew up. Ask questions about your spouse's childhood', or 'ask your spouse for a list of five activities that he would enjoy doing with you', or 'camp out in the living room. Spread your blankets and pillows on the floor'.[24] The trivial nature of the advice from Chapman is sure evidence of the intellectual poverty of his much-acclaimed *5 Love Languages*. It is difficult to believe that Christian people, who read God's Word, can be taken in by such trivia.

3) Receiving gifts

If you discover that your spouse's primary love language is receiving gifts, then you must learn to become a proficient gift giver. Start by making a list of all the gifts your spouse has expressed excitement about receiving through the years. You will understand that purchasing gifts for your spouse is investing in your relationship and filling his or her emotional love tank; 'and with a full love tank, he or she will likely reciprocate emotional love to you in a language you will understand'.[25] So if your spouse's love language is receiving gifts, 'try a parade of gifts: leave a box of candy for your spouse in the morning; have flowers delivered in the afternoon; give him a gift in the evening', or 'give your spouse a gift every day for one week' and 'keep a gift idea notebook'.[26]

Here Chapman is encouraging a heart of materialism and covetousness in marriage by encouraging a husband to pander to his wife's selfishness. Does a Christian wife really need a gift every day to be convinced of her husband's love? This advice is deeply contrary to the mind of Christ. Our Lord warns us not to lay up treasures on earth, 'For where your treasure is, there your heart will be also' (Matthew 6.21). Scripture teaches that it is more blessed to give than to receive. Flooding a wife with gifts is not a sign of love, but of foolishness.

4) Acts of service

Chapman warns us that 'learning the love language of acts of service will require some of us to re-examine our stereotypes of the roles of husbands and wives'.[27] He says that because of the sociological changes in society we can no longer cling to the male and female role models that we inherited from our parents. 'A willingness to examine and change stereotypes is necessary in order to express love more effectively.'[28] Men, in particular, need to work hard at tearing down the old stereotypes. Chapman suggests that you print note cards with the following: 'Today I will show my love for you by… picking up the clutter, paying the bills, fixing something that's been broken a long time, weeding the garden.'[29] And you must 'give your spouse a love note accompanied by the act of service every three days for a month'.[30]

Scripture teaches that young wives are to be taught to be homemakers who are obedient to their own husbands (Titus 2.5). The virtuous wife is a godly woman, who willingly works with her hands night and day as 'she watches over the ways of her household' (Proverbs 31.27). 'Her husband is known in the gates, when he sits among the elders of the land' (Proverbs 31.23). Her children call her blessed and her husband praises her excellence (Proverbs 31.28). Chapman is again denying the teaching of Scripture by not recognising the headship role of the husband (Ephesians 5.22-24). He is encouraging the equal-regard view of marriage that is dear to the heart of the marriage psycho-education movement. He is actually denying and denigrating what God has ordained.

5) *Physical touch*

Chapman tells us that physical touch is a powerful vehicle for communicating marital love. 'For some individuals, physical touch is their primary love language. Without it, they feel unloved. With it, their emotional tank is filled, and they feel secure in the love of their spouse.'[31] He provides a number of tips about how we should touch our spouse. For example, 'as you walk from the car to go shopping, reach out and hold your spouse's hand'; or, 'While your spouse is seated, walk up behind her and give her a shoulder massage.'[32]

Scripture teaches that a sexual relationship is an essential part of marriage. 'Let the husband render to his wife the affection due her, and likewise also the wife to her husband. The wife does not have authority over her own body, but the husband does. And likewise the husband does not have authority over his own body, but the wife does. Do not deprive one another except with consent for a time...' (1 Corinthians 7.3-5). So we already know the importance of physical touch from Scripture, without Chapman having to pontificate—for touch is obviously part of the sacred intimacy of marriage, which is a one flesh union. Why do we need a 'Christian psychologist' to reveal the obvious?

Chapman's philosophy of life

Having explained the five languages of love, Chapman now turns to his philosophy of life. And this helps us to understand what he actually believes. He tells us that 'psychologists have observed that among our basic needs are the need for security, self-worth, and significance... my sense of self-worth is fed by the fact that my spouse loves me... her love builds my self-esteem.'[33] He says that the need for significance is the emotional force behind much of our behaviour. 'Life is driven by the desire for success. We want our lives to count for something. We have our own idea of what it means to be significant, and we work hard to reach our goals. Feeling loved by a wife or husband enhances our sense of significance.'[34] He continues with his philosophy: 'I am significant. Life has meaning. There is a higher purpose. I want to believe it, but I may not feel significant until someone expresses love for me... Without love, I may spend a lifetime in search of significance, self-worth, and security. When I experience love, it influences all of those needs positively. I am now freed to develop my potential.'[35]

Chapman's self-centred worldview is shaped by his belief in the teachings of positive psychology. His life is driven by the desire for success. He demands his wife's love to build his self-esteem, for only then does he feel significant. And only when he feels loved does he respond positively and feel free to develop his full potential. This is nothing but a sophisticated expression of our sinful nature. How different was the worldview of the apostle Paul: 'But what things were gain to me, these I have counted loss for Christ. Yet indeed I also count all things loss for the excellence of the knowledge of Christ Jesus my Lord, for whom I have suffered the loss of all things, and count them as rubbish that I may gain Christ' (Philippians 3.7-8).

No distinction between believers and unbelievers

In his writing, Chapman makes no distinction between believers and unbelievers. In his discussion of emotional needs, he makes no distinction between believers, redeemed by the blood of Christ, who have been transferred from the power of darkness into the kingdom of Christ, and unbelievers, who are dead in their trespasses and sins, ruled by the spirit of the age and slaves to the lusts of the flesh. Indeed, in Chapman's thinking the Christian faith is irrelevant to what he calls the emotional needs of a couple. Therefore all his advice is based on the premise that the needs of believers and unbelievers are the same. But Scripture makes clear the distinction between the kingdom of light and the kingdom of darkness (Ephesians 5.8-11). Clearly the 'needs' of believers and unbelievers are fundamentally different. The prime need of unbelievers is the forgiveness of sin. The prime need of believers is the grace and help of God to deny themselves daily, take up their cross, and follow Christ. A believer, indwelt by the Holy Spirit, is commanded to live a life worthy of the Gospel of Christ. The fact that Chapman makes no distinction suggests that he does not recognise the power of the Gospel to transform the life of a believer.

Emotional needs

The concept of emotional needs is at the centre of Chapman's thinking. He says that our emotional health depends on having our emotional needs met, and claims that the most basic emotional need is to 'feel' loved. His emotional love tank metaphor helps us to measure the degree to which our need to feel loved is being met. He explains that our need for emotional love must be met by other people, usually our spouse. When this need is not met, we feel deprived, dissatisfied and unwell.

So to be emotionally healthy a couple must meet each other's need to 'feel' loved. Failure to do so results in what Chapman refers to as 'misbehavior'. He illustrates this 'truth' by relating the story of a husband, Brent, who was leaving his wife, Becky, because his love tank was empty.[36] When Brent confided that he had formed a loving relationship with another woman, Chapman sympathised because he understood that Brent was being pushed by his emotional need to seek love outside the marriage. 'Thousands of husbands and wives have been there—emotionally empty, wanting to do the right thing, not wanting to hurt anyone, but being pushed by their emotional need to seek love outside the marriage.'[37] So poor Brent, to meet his emotional need and so fill his emotional love tank, had little option but to commit adultery because he felt that his wife had not loved him in the right way. Chapman's theory implies that adultery is an understandable response to an empty love tank. His thinking is consistent with the humanistic concept of situation ethics, and far from the divine moral absolutes taught in the Bible. Chapman's model of felt need panders to our sinful nature and denies God's moral law.

Another difficulty with the concept of emotional need is that it can only be met by our spouse 'feeling' loved. Yet the 'feeling' of love is a highly subjective and notoriously unreliable emotion. We all know from our own experience that feelings are liable to change all the time. This means that a wife who is deeply loved by her husband, at some point in time might not 'feel' that she is loved. Equally, an unfaithful husband can deceive his wife into feeling loved by his smooth, flattering words, but have no love for her in his heart. This is called hypocrisy, for his love is only lip-deep—he is only pretending to love her, when in reality he is deceiving her to achieve his own ends. How many men in clandestine relationships make their wives 'feel' loved by the use of deceptive words?

Biblical understanding of need

In a general sense God, in his providence, supplies the needs of all creation (Genesis 8.22), for he makes the sun to shine on the righteous and the unrighteous, and rain to fall on all mankind. He makes the grass grow and ripens the harvest. He provides food for the birds and beasts. Therefore our Lord said in his Sermon on the Mount, 'For your Father knows the things you have need of before you ask Him' (Matthew 6.8). The God who feeds the birds of the air and clothes the grass of the field knows that we need food and clothing. But the priority is not to seek after *things*, but to seek first the Kingdom of God. And the promise of God is that he will supply all the needs of his people. The apostle Paul could say: 'And my God shall supply all your need according to His riches in glory by Christ Jesus' (Philippians 4.19).

Believers have a great High Priest, Jesus the Son of God, who knows and sympathises with our weaknesses and struggles, for in his human nature he was in all points tempted as we are, yet without sin. Our Saviour suffers with us, and he understands our real needs. Therefore, in our time of deepest need, we can confidently come to the throne of grace through our Lord Jesus Christ—to our Heavenly Father, that we may obtain mercy and grace to help us overcome our weaknesses and to meet our needs (Hebrews 4.14-16). The message is clear—in our time of need we must come to the throne of grace to find help.

King David, that man of many trials, who knew only too well his own sinful corruption, could say, 'The LORD is my shepherd; I shall not want... He restores my soul' (Psalm 23.1, 3). So the promise of our Lord is that he supplies all the needs of his people. He will restore our soul;

he will meet our deepest spiritual need in Christ. He has blessed us with all spiritual blessings in the heavenly realm in Christ (Ephesians 1.3). Therefore the hymn-writers could pen these words: 'All I have needed Thy hand has provided. Great is Thy faithfulness, Lord unto me', and 'My Shepherd will supply my need, Jehovah is His name'.

What then, in the light of Scripture, are we to make of the 'emotional needs' construct of psychology? Chapman's theory teaches me that I must seek to have my emotional needs satisfied or I will be emotionally unwell. I must look to other people, especially my spouse, to meet my emotional needs. Yet Scripture, which does not mention emotional needs, teaches that all my needs are met in Christ—I am complete in Christ (Colossians 2.10). As a follower of Christ, I must look to the needs of other people, not to my own needs. This is the true strength of the Christian life and the practical remedy for our tendency to self-centredness.

All fallen human beings have sinful desires, wants and lusts. How do we distinguish between emotional needs, selfish desires and the lusts of the flesh which war against the soul? How easy it is for us to be deceived by the deceitfulness of sin. A real danger of the emotional need concept is that it redefines sinful desires as emotional needs. It allows a husband to justify his adultery as meeting his emotional need to feel loved.

Counterfeit love

The idea that Christian believers have an emotional love tank that others need to fill is pure psychological speculation that demeans the meaning of love. Scripture warns, 'Let love be without hypocrisy' (Romans 12.9). What Chapman has imparted to us are lessons in the hypocrisy of love.

The 5 Languages of Love is based on a caricature of love that comes from the mindset of positive psychology. According to Chapman, if my love language is words of affirmation, I feel loved when my wife praises me by telling me how wonderful I am. If my love language is quality time, I feel loved when my wife spends time listening empathetically to my deepest feelings. If my love language is receiving gifts, I feel loved when my wife gives me things that really amuse me. If my love language is acts of service, I feel loved when my wife waits on me hand and foot while I watch my favourite TV programme. If my love language is physical touch, I feel loved when my wife touches me in a way that gives me physical pleasure. The problem with Chapman's flawed theory of love is that it turns a wife into a robot who meets all her husband's needs, desires and lusts, and does so without a murmur of dissent. Can such a wife say she loves her husband? Yes, in five languages! But does she mean it, or has she been programmed to gratify the needs of her selfish husband?

But this is counterfeit love, a contrived version that panders to my selfishness. It is a concept of love that focuses on me and my sinful desires and passions. It is an emotional feeling that is lip-deep and self-serving. It is a feeling that lasts only as long as there is something to be gained by me. It is based in hypocrisy, pretence, dishonesty and cynicism.

So from where did Chapman get his flawed understanding of love? He freely concedes that a host of professionals and psychiatrists helped him shape his concept of love. Why did he find it necessary to turn to psychiatry to learn about love? Is the God of Scripture not the God of love? Does Scripture not teach the true meaning of love? It must surely be plain to every Christian that there is a vast difference between the version of love promoted by the psychological mind of Gary Chapman and the teaching of Scripture.

Genuine love

The biblical view of love is completely different. Christian believers, having been justified by faith, have access by faith into the grace of God in which they stand and 'the love of God has been poured out in our hearts by the Holy Spirit who was given us' (Romans 5.5). The fruit of the Spirit includes love, longsuffering, kindness and gentleness (Galatians 5.22). Love is manifest in the life and atoning work of Christ. While we were yet sinners Christ died for us. Nothing in all creation is able to separate us from the love of Christ. We love Christ because he first loved us. The command of Christ is that we should love one another. Husbands are commanded to love their wives as Christ loves the Church (Ephesians 5.25), and wives should love their husbands (Titus 2.4). We should love not in word or in tongue, but in deed and in truth (1 John 3.18).

Love is not primarily a 'feeling'. First and foremost it is an attitude, a commitment, and an act of obedience to God's commands—something that surpasses mere feelings and survives our passing moods.

The way of genuine love is revealed in the life of Christ, who sacrificed his life for the Church. The characteristics of genuine love are described in 1 Corinthians 13. Love is kind and patient; it rejoices in truth; it bears all things and endures all things. Love does not envy, is not rude, is not puffed up, does not seek its own, is not provoked, and thinks no evil. Notice that love is characterised by kind, selfless behaviour and by a love for the truth. We are to speak the truth in love. Love always puts the interests of others first, and my interests last. Love suffers and endures all things for other people. It is the mark of a true disciple of Jesus Christ. A Christian husband and wife love each other because Christ first loved them, and has commanded them to love one another.

Chapman's heresy – humanistic psychology in Christian clothes

The humanist psychology movement of the 1950s and 1960s, following the teachings of Abraham Maslow (discussed in chapter 14) and Carl Rogers (discussed in chapter 6), succeeded in popularising the concept of emotional needs. The heresy of Gary Chapman is that he teaches the godless concepts of humanistic psychology in the name of Christ. He follows Maslow's so-called 'hierarchy of needs', and Roger's teaching around self-worth and self-esteem. He even goes down the human potential pathway, claiming that the man who feels deeply loved is free to develop his full human potential. There is nothing in his writings to suggest that he understands or cares about the true Gospel of Christ.

Is the Church being edified by the teachings of Gary Chapman? The answer must surely be a resounding no! The above analysis demonstrates the heretical nature of Gary Chapman's teachings—his languages of love have no place in the true Church of Jesus Christ.

(Endnotes)

1 Moody Conferences website, http://www.moodyconferences.com/con_conferencemain
2 Gary Chapman, *The 5 Love Languages – The secret to love that lasts*, Northfield Publishing, reprinted 2010, p9
3 Ibid. p13

4 Ibid. pp14-15
5 Ibid. p16
6 Ibid. p16
7 Ibid. p19
8 Ibid. p20
9 Ibid. p23
10 Ibid. p23
11 Ibid. p34
12 Ibid. p46
13 Ibid. p47
14 Ibid. p47
15 Ibid. pp51-52
16 Ibid. p37
17 Ibid. p40
18 Ibid. p45
19 Ibid. p45
20 Ibid. p64
21 Ibid. p64
22 Ibid. p65
23 Carl Rogers, *Becoming partners – Marriage and its Alternatives* (first published 1972), Constable and Company, reprint 1988, p209
24 Gary Chapman, *The 5 Love Languages*, pp71-72
25 Ibid. pp79-80
26 Ibid. p87
27 Ibid. p101
28 Ibid. pp101-102
29 Ibid. p105
30 Ibid. p105
31 Ibid. p109
32 Ibid. p120
33 Ibid. p143
34 Ibid. p143
35 Ibid. p144
36 Ibid. p134
37 Ibid. p135

14

Emerson Eggerichs – Maslow's disciple

Emerson Eggerichs is another big name in the Christian marriage education industry. As a young man he received degrees in biblical studies and communications from Wheaton College, Chicago, and was later awarded a Masters in Divinity from Dubuque Seminary, Iowa. From the 1980s he was senior pastor of East Lansing Trinity Church, Michigan, for almost twenty years. During that time he claims to have discovered the secret of communication between husbands and wives. He left the pastorate to launch Love and Respect Ministries in August 1999, and to devote his time to helping couples build healthy lasting marriages. He and his wife, Sarah, present Love and Respect Marriage conferences to eager audiences across the USA.

He claims that his popular 'love and respect' theory is based on wisdom gleaned from three decades of marriage counselling, as well as scientific and biblical research. His best-seller, *Love & Respect: The Love She Most Desires; The Respect He Desperately Needs* (2004), was a Book of the Year award winner, and has sold over 1.3 million copies. In a later book, *The Language of Love and Respect: Cracking the Communication Code with Your Mate* (2007), Eggerichs claims to present 'a practical, step-by-step approach for how husbands and wives can learn to speak each other's distinctly different language—respect for him, love for her. The result is mutual understanding and a successful, happy marriage.'[1]

Eggerichs explains his theory: 'Women, you will learn how to communicate your need for love in a way that sounds respectful to your husband, without losing your identity and influence. Learning the Language of Respect enables your husband to hear you, resulting in deeper connection. Men, you will learn to use the Language of Love in ways you haven't heard before, meeting your wife's deepest need without sacrificing your uniqueness as a man. This will enable her to hear your deepest need for respect.'[2] Your goal in reading the book 'is to gain greater self-understanding so you can respond to your spouse more lovingly or respectfully'.[3]

Not without truth

As we shall see, Eggerichs' approach to marriage education is truly syncretised, for he combines Scripture with his psychological theories. Some of what he teaches does contain truth. He says that 'we don't have a marriage crisis in the church; we have a faith crisis. After all, no one can really practice Love and Respect unless he or she does it unto Jesus Christ'.[4] He says that when you love or respect unconditionally regardless of the outcome you are following God and his will for you. Husbands and wives should be practising Love and Respect principles first and foremost out of obedience to God and his command in Ephesians 5.33. 'Remember: in the ultimate sense, your marriage has nothing to do with your spouse. It has everything to do with your relationship to Jesus Christ.'[5] And to this we can all agree. Yet throughout the book he mixes Scripture with his psychological ideas. The impression is always that Scripture is not sufficient; it needs to be enhanced by the wisdom that comes from psychology. And herein we see the real danger of Eggerichs' teaching, for he has cleverly combined truth with error, and the difficulty is to disentangle the two.

Eggerichs' theory of motivation

Eggerichs' love and respect approach is based on the idea that a couple are always in one of three 'cycles'—the Crazy Cycle; the Energizing Cycle; the Rewarded Cycle. 'When a wife feels unloved she tends to react in ways that feel disrespectful to her husband. When a husband feels disrespected, he tends to react in ways that feel unloving to his wife.'[6] This is the Crazy Cycle—without love a wife reacts without respect; without respect, a husband reacts without love. The Energizing Cycle is where a wife's respect motivates his love and his love motivates her respect. 'But to motivate, you must understand your spouse's need. The key to motivating another person is meeting that person's deepest need—love for her and respect for him.'[7] The Rewarded Cycle teaches that 'his love blesses regardless of her respect, and her respect blesses regardless of his love'. This Cycle 'is not primarily about you and your marriage; it is about you and Jesus Christ'.[8]

Eggerichs explains how he discovered the Energizing Cycle. He was sitting in his study when it dawned on him to ask, 'What does the Bible say about how to motivate a husband to be more loving?'[9] He writes: 'As I was reading Ephesians 5.33, I believe God prompted me to ask: "What would happen if a wife met her husband's need for respect?" The answer seemed obvious: "He would be energized. That is, he would be *motivated* to love her in return." As I pondered that, another question arose, and its answer became obvious: "What would happen if a husband met his wife's need for love?" Of course, "She would be energized and *motivated* to respect him in return."[10] [my italics] Notice Eggerichs' assumption—love and respect are basic human *needs*.

Eggerichs continues: 'Having seen this positive energizing connection between Love and Respect as stated in Ephesians 5.33, I decided it was like a cycle—an Energizing Cycle: His love *motivates* her respect. Her respect *motivates* his love.'[11] And so Eggerichs was able to state, 'the key to *motivating* another person is meeting that person's deepest need'[12] [my italics]. But Scripture does not say that. Scripture does not use the word motivate when referring to love and respect. God commands a husband to love his wife, whether or not she respects him. Likewise God commands a wife to respect her husband, whether or not he loves her.

Maslow's theory of motivation

Here we must make the point that Eggerichs' theory of motivation is consistent with Abraham Maslow's psychological theory, which holds that human beings are motivated when their basic needs are gratified, and that they suffer psychopathology when their needs are thwarted.

Abraham Maslow (1908 – 1970) is one of the founders of humanistic psychology. He became recognised as the leader of the humanistic school of psychology that emerged in the 1950s and 1960s, which he referred to as the 'third force'—a force beyond Freudian psychotherapy and Skinner's behaviourism. Humanistic psychology was based on the idea that people possess the inner resources for growth and healing, and that the aim of therapy is to help remove obstacles to achieving this. Maslow was openly hostile to traditional biblical Christianity.

Maslow's theory of motivation was based on the idea that human beings have a set of basic needs—the famous Maslow Hierarchy of Needs. Stated briefly, these basic needs are: physiological (hunger), safety, love, esteem, and self-actualization. The lowest need in the hierarchy must be met before the person is motivated to meet the second need and so on up the hierarchy. Gratification and deprivation are important concepts in Maslow's theory.[13] Gratifying a need motivates a person to move up the hierarchy, while deprivation of a need leads to psychopathology. Maslow argues that a man who is thwarted in any of his basic needs may fairly be seen as a sick man, just as the man who lacks vitamins or minerals. Maslow is propagating the 'man is a victim' syndrome. All people have needs that demand to be satisfied. The reason a person behaves badly is because a basic need has not been gratified, so it's not really his fault. He is a 'victim' of society or of other people who have failed to satisfy his basic needs. In this way of thinking, there is no recognition that human needs and desires might be evil.

In Maslow's worldview the problem of man, who is intrinsically good, is that all his needs have not been satisfied. This causes people to become maladjusted or even mentally ill.

In *A Theory of Human Motivation* (1943), Maslow said that human beings have a deep need for love. 'If both the physiological and the safety needs are fairly well gratified, there will emerge the love and affection and belongingness needs… In our society the thwarting of these needs is the most commonly found core in cases of maladjustment and more severe psychopathology… Practically all theorists of psychopathology have stressed thwarting of the love needs as basic in the picture of maladjustment.'[14] Maslow continued: 'Who will say that a lack of love is less important than a lack of vitamins? Since we know the pathogenic effects of love starvation…'[15] According to Maslow a lack of love is a major cause of maladjusted behaviour.

Eggerichs has applied Maslow's theory to the marital situation, as he places the emotional needs of husband and wife at the centre of the marriage relationship. He says that God's command in Ephesians 5.33 is 'because obviously He [God] knows a wife needs love and a husband needs respect'.[16] Eggerichs says he asked himself what happens when a wife meets her husband's need for respect. 'The answer came to me: he is energized… It seemed to me that he would be *motivated* to meet his wife's need for love.'[17] So the purpose of God's command, according to Eggerichs, is to meet the emotional needs of husband and wife. Eggerichs goes on to claim that when a wife's need for love is thwarted, she responds by treating her husband with disrespect—and that is his own fault, because he failed to gratify her need for love. Likewise a husband, who does not have his basic need for respect gratified, reacts by treating his wife badly— and she is then at fault, because she failed to show him the respect that he so desperately needs.

Eggerichs' theory of motivation implies that a wife must look to her husband to meet her emotional need for love. The definition of idolatry, according to Webster, is 'the worship of idols or excessive devotion to, or reverence for some person or thing'. By this definition the wife who sees her husband as the only one who can meet her deepest needs is an idolater. Likewise the idolatry of the husband is his excessive dependency on his wife to meet his desperate need to feel respected. Both look to each other to satisfy their needs, when they should be looking to the Lord who has promised to supply all their needs according to his riches in glory by Christ Jesus (Philippians 4.19).

A problem inherent in a theory that encourages a married couple to speak to each other in a manner contrived to fulfil the other's emotional needs, is that it produces an entirely self-centred view of marriage in which husband and wife look to each other for the gratification of their selfish desires. This is most certainly not what Paul is advocating in Ephesians 5. Eggerichs has taken one verse from Ephesians (5.33) and interpreted it outside of the context of the book in general or the chapter on marriage in particular. This is not the correct way to understand Scripture.

The real message of Ephesians

The love and respect commanded by God in Ephesians 5 is entirely different from that envisaged by Eggerichs, and must be seen and interpreted in the context of the whole book and of other Scripture. A Christian husband, made spiritually alive by the grace and mercy of God, has the love of Christ shed abroad in his heart through the mighty working of the Holy Spirit. He daily seeks to put off the old, selfish, sinful nature with its deceitful lusts, and to put on the new spiritual nature, which is created in true righteousness and holiness (Ephesians 4.24). A Christian husband loves his wife because he is commanded by God to love his wife as Christ loves the Church. And he loves his wife because he has promised to love and cherish her until separated by death. He seeks to love his wife with the love Christ has poured into his heart. This love is not expressed mainly in words, but in action, sacrifice and truth. He does not need to be 'energized' (*motivated*) by his wife's 'respect-tool' to love her; he loves her because she is his wife, his one flesh helper in Christ.

Likewise, a Christian wife understands that marriage is a symbol of the relationship between Christ and the Church. She knows that God commands her to submit herself to her husband with an attitude of respect. She respects her husband because it is the right thing to do in the governance of the family; because he is the God-given head of the family and the father of their children. The thought that she is motivating her husband to love her does not enter her mind. She does not need to be 'energized' (*motivated*) by her husband's 'love-tool' to be obedient to the command of God. Note that there is no mention or inference in Ephesians 5 that love and respect have anything to do with feelings or emotions.

Emotional need for love and respect

Eggerichs explains how his theory works in practice. When a husband comes home late for dinner and the wife erupts in criticism and tears, the real issue is 'that she feels unloved, and when she angrily attacks his character, he feels disrespected'.[18] So the real issue is that a 'wife needs love as she needs air to breathe. Picture, if you will, that the wife has an air hose leading to a love tank'.[19] When her husband steps on her air hose with unloving behaviour, he will see her deflate before his eyes. In a similar way, the husband has his own air hose leading to his respect tank. If she steps on his 'air hose with sharp, critical remarks, his supply of respect will be cut off, and he will react negatively because his deepest need in not being met'.[20]

The implication of this example is that women have a fundamental emotional need for love, and men a fundamental emotional need for respect. In marriage this need must be met by their spouse. Failure to meet these needs results in a wife feeling unloved and a husband feeling disrespected—each feels deep hurt. If a wife's basic need is not met she becomes deflated and angry, causing her to act disrespectfully, and a husband then reacts negatively and becomes unloving and even nasty to his wife. It follows that husband and wife must be constantly meeting the emotional needs of their partner, must be constantly filling their love and respect tanks. And both must be very careful how they tread, lest they tread on their spouse's air hose, even by mistake, for that can have disastrous consequences for their relationship.

Communication is the biggest problem

Eggerichs is convinced that the major problem for the typical couple is communication.[21] He knows this because surveys conducted by Focus on the Family and by Love and Respect Ministries both show that 'for men and women the biggest problem was lack of communication'.[22] And we must not assume that both spouses speak the same language, for, according to Eggerichs, they don't. He tells us that after more than three decades of counselling married couples, and conducting numerous marriage conferences, he has learned that, in fact, the wife speaks a 'love language' and the husband speaks a 'respect language'.[23] Because men and women are speaking a different kind of language there is little or no communication. The implication is that before Eggerichs made his remarkable discovery, men and women, speaking different languages, have been unable to communicate.

God supposedly revealed this great truth to Eggerichs from a single verse of Scripture, Ephesians 5.33. As he paraphrases it, 'I am commanded to love Sarah [his wife] because she needs love; in fact, she speaks love. Love is the language she understands... Sarah is commanded to respect me because I need respect; in fact, I speak respect. Respect is the language I understand.'[24] Therefore the key to communicating in marriage is to have a mutual understanding of each other's language.

Pink and blue glasses

Eggerichs insists that because men and women are different in their biology and their marital roles, they interpret the world differently and therefore have difficulty in communicating with each other. Based on this assumption, he has developed his theory of blue and pink sunglasses. He refers to communication between men and women as 'blue' and 'pink', and asserts that 'being aware that men see and hear in blue and women see and hear in pink (very differently) is extremely important. Working at decoding each other's messages is essential.'[25] He says that 'women look at the world through pink sunglasses, while men look at the same world through blue sunglasses—and believe me, they do not necessarily see the same thing... My work with husbands and wives tells me that women hear with pink hearing aids and men hear with blue hearing aids.'[26]

This theory implies that men and women need a special understanding in order to communicate. That is, they need to be able to decode what the other is saying. Failure to decode leads to misunderstanding and problems in the relationship. But this theory is contrary to Scripture, for Scripture teaches that believers 'are all sons [both men and women] of God through faith in Christ Jesus. For as many of you as were baptized into Christ have put on Christ. There is neither Jew nor Greek, there is neither slave not free, there is neither male nor female; for you are all one in Christ Jesus' (Galatians 3.26-28). As brothers and sisters in Christ, we have the mind of Christ and the Spirit of Truth, and as husband and wife walk in the light of Christ, they have fellowship with one another. Christian couples interpret the world through the light of Scripture, not through pink and blue sunglasses and hearing aids. Eggerichs' clinical experience (always an unreliable guide, depending as it does on taking sinful human behaviour at face value) has been elevated above the plain teaching of Scripture.

Decoding

Having declared that men and women cannot communicate properly because they see the world through different sunglasses, Eggerichs develops his theory of 'decoding'. Men and women can only understand each other when they learn the skill of decoding. He gives an example—when he and his wife arrived early at the airport on their way to a marriage conference, she said to him, 'I am really hungry. I was thinking about getting something to eat. Is that okay?' He responded that he was not really hungry and his wife said, 'Well, I thought the two of us could sit down and be together for a nice meal. Okay, then, I'm going to get something to eat', and steamed off, clearly upset. She felt unloved because her husband had not decoded her language. He should have known that when she said she was hungry what she actually meant was that she wanted them to have a cosy, romantic meal. Eggerichs explains his failure: 'Sarah was expecting Love—my willingness to grab a bite to eat with her—and didn't get it because I was too preoccupied to decode her invitation properly.'[27]

The key message from this episode is this: to communicate, you must learn to decode. Eggerichs says that 'from my own experience married to Sarah and from working with thousands of other couples, I am convinced that men and women actually speak to each other in code.'[28] He then draws his conclusion: 'In the typical marriage the woman will be the sensitive, intuitive one while the man will be more matter-of-fact and, at times, insensitive without meaning to be. This is why *every* husband should know how to decode his wife—and vice versa'[29] [my italics]. Eggerichs says that he and his wife 'decode each other and step gingerly around each other's air hose practically on a daily basis'.[30] What kind of marriage is this? Does Sarah always 'steam off' when she doesn't get her way?

Eggerichs is telling us that to have a proper relationship with our spouse and to really understand them, we need to learn to decode their language. Without this skill we are lost, and our marriage is doomed. But how do we learn to decode? The answer is through attending Eggerichs' marriage conferences, watching his DVDs and reading his books. The clear inference is that Scripture is not enough. We can spend our life studying Scripture and still not be able to decode what our wife actually means. So Eggerichs' theory places us in bondage to marriage psycho-education.

Love is a feeling

Eggerichs, like Gary Chapman, says a wife must 'feel' loved to satisfy her deepest emotional need. When a wife 'feels' unloved, she experiences a deep hurt and is not energised in her marriage. 'She is prone to react in ways that are critical and disrespectful when she feels unloved!'[31] Therefore 'a husband must go the extra mile and meet his wife's deepest need for love'.[32] Eggerichs' teaching, that a Christian wife who does not 'feel' loved by her husband has an unmet emotional need, shows a complete misunderstanding of the work of Christ in the heart of a believer. 'Behold what manner of love the Father has bestowed on us, that we should be called children of God' (1 John 3.1). For who or what shall separate us from the love of Christ? Not tribulation, not distress, not persecution, not even an unloving spouse and an unmet emotional need.

We saw in the last chapter that the idea of emotional needs and achieving emotional healing is a construct of humanistic psychology. Carl Rogers (see chapter 6) placed great importance on emotional needs. But Scripture does not speak of emotional needs. A believer does not live by reference to his emotional needs, but by every word that proceeds from the Word of God. So do believers have an 'emotional need' to feel loved and to feel respected by other people? Not according to Scripture. There is nothing in the Bible that tells us to depend on our emotions, but there is much that warns us not to follow our sinful desires and lusts. 'Therefore do not let sin reign in your mortal body, that you should obey it in its lusts' (Romans 6.12). The danger of 'emotional needs' theory is that it encourages a person to see their sinful passions, desires and lusts as legitimate needs. The tendency of the sinful heart, if given the chance, will be to define selfish desires as emotional needs, legitimise them and seek ways to satisfy them.

Tools for developing love and respect

Eggerichs says, 'Every couple needs to realize they must consciously make the effort to get on what we call the Energizing Cycle and apply its principles, which provide tools they can use to communicate better and more effectively.'[33] As we have seen above, the Energizing Cycle is based on the idea that if a wife meets her husband's need for respect, he would be energised to love her in return. Similarly, if a husband meets his wife's need for love, she would be energised and motivated to respect him in return.[34] He builds her up with love and she builds him up with respect.

To help a husband remember how he is to love his wife, Eggerichs developed the acronym COUPLE—closeness, openness, understanding, peacemaking, loyalty, and esteem. The acronym to help wives respect their husband is CHAIRS—conquest, hierarchy, authority, insight, relationship, and sexuality. Concerned that the words 'hierarchy' and 'authority' might be offensive to women, Eggerichs checked out with a group of feminist wives that the words were acceptable to them. He says that the two acronyms 'provide a framework of six loving principles a husband can practice and six respectful principles a wife can practice to make Love and Respect happen between them'.[35]

Eggerichs wants us to recognise the 'typical negative remarks that need decoding and then offer positive suggestions for what to say in response that will keep the energizing cycle going. Whatever offensive words might have been spoken, always listen for your spouse's basic need.'[36] The purpose of the cycle is always to meet your spouse's basic needs. When a husband makes an unloving comment, a wife must realise it is 'really a cry for respect that needs decoding'.[37] When a wife senses that her husband is feeling less than respected and supported, she could try some energising remark like: 'Honey, you're right. I get too preoccupied with the children. Will you forgive me?'[38]

A wife who figures out that her husband feels his position as head of the family is being threatened or ignored may say: 'Honey, I'm sorry for coming across in a way that belittles you. This has nothing to do with you. These are my fears rooted in my childhood. Will you forgive me?'[39]

Critique of Love and Respect

A perceptive reviewer of Eggerichs' *Love and Respect* (2004) made the following comments: '*Love and Respect* is not Christian. By adding, "need/s" to the treatise (page 15, paperback), which implies a "need state" and by trying to integrate communication theory with God's word, Eggerichs takes his work out of the Bible and out of orthodox Christianity (and into popular psychology). On page 17, he talks about "primary needs." There is not one word on one page of the entire Bible which affirms that man has a "need state" other than for God, His Son, Jesus Christ, and His redemption …

'The section in Ephesians for wives and husbands… is about a fulfilled state of having received Grace, which enables one to act upon this Divine gift and put on the new self. The issues of submission for wives and sacrificial love for husbands flow from the new, true and hidden self in Christ. The entire point is that we no longer have needs only (lusts, idols and active sin) based in the (sinful) flesh. Putting needs back into the equation is a subtly false teaching and work of the anti-Christ to lead Christians away from renouncing sin, receiving and putting on new life in Christ and relying on His redemptive power. While a false palaver may appease sin (flesh-based needs) for a while, sooner or later this will wear off; sin will return and one will be resentful, angry and bitter that one's "needs" (for love or respect) were not met by one's spouse. The door is then open for Satan to tempt a break in relationship. It is important to note that Eggerichs never mentions sin and the need for repentance. He barely mentions Jesus and spends most of the time weaving a mix of secular psychology and biblical references, which are presented out of context.'[40]

The real message of Ephesians

Eggerichs has cleverly mixed Scripture with the humanistic psychology of Abraham Maslow. He has turned Christian husbands and wives into inadequate and emotionally needy people who desperately need to feel loved and respected. He uses Maslow's hierarchy of needs to identify 'love' and 'respect' as basic human needs, and Maslow's motivational theory to claim that husbands and wives need to be motivated to 'love' and 'respect' each other. Eggerichs has reduced love and respect to a psychological 'need' for one spouse and a psychological 'tool' for the other. He has encouraged husbands and wives to become idolaters who look to each other, not the God of Scripture, to supply all their deepest needs.

As stated at the beginning of the chapter, there is some truth in what Eggerichs says about love and respect in Christian marriage. Ephesians 5.22-33 provides God's plan for marriage that clearly lays out the distinctive roles of husband and wife, and not some psychological theory of human motivation, as Eggerichs claims.

Men and women are fallen sinners who require God's guidance to maintain relationships, especially in marriage. Each has their own characteristic temptations in the marital union that cause disharmony and unhappiness. The husband is liable to stop loving his wife and to start lording it over her. The wife is liable to ignore her role as helper and resent her husband's headship role, thus setting off a power struggle. The message of Scripture is that love and respect should always be mutual and sincere. The husband's burden of headship is to be recognised by the wife showing him genuine respect because he is the head of the family, and father of her children; the woman's subordinate, and therefore more vulnerable position of obedience, is to be supported by the sacrificial and self-giving love of her husband. There is hardly a more dismal picture than a Christian marriage where the husband feels ruled by his wife, or the woman feels unsupported and unloved by her husband. God's wisdom in Ephesians is to be accepted and obeyed, and not turned into a psychological theory, as Eggerichs has done.

Eggerichs' heretical teaching has created caricatures of love and respect. Those who follow his teachings are placing their faith in the false dogma of humanistic psychology. Eggerichs and his ilk—other false teachers like Gary Smalley and Gary Chapman—cling to the forlorn hope that fallen human beings can improve their relationships with the help of a few psychological tips.

(Endnotes)

1 Emerson Eggerichs, *The Language of Love and Respect: Cracking the Communication Code with Your Mate*, Thomas Nelson, 2007, cited from blurb on back cover
2 Ibid. preface x
3 Ibid. xii
4 Ibid. p29
5 Ibid. p29
6 Ibid. p11
7 Ibid. p134
8 Ibid. p230
9 Ibid. p40
10 Ibid. p139
11 Ibid. p139
12 Ibid. p134
13 Cited from *Motivation and Personality*, Abraham Maslow, third edition, Harper & Row, 1987, chapter 2, 'A Theory of Human Motivation', p17
14 Ibid. pp20-21
15 Ibid. pp30-31
16 Eggerichs, *The Language of Love and Respect*, p40
17 Ibid. p40
18 Ibid. p15
19 Ibid. p15
20 Ibid. p15
21 Ibid. p4

22 Ibid. p4
23 Ibid. p4
24 Ibid. p5
25 Ibid. pp15-16
26 Ibid. pp54-55
27 Ibid. pp89-91
28 Ibid. pp92-93
29 Ibid. p97
30 Ibid. p116
31 Ibid. p41
32 Ibid. p43
33 Ibid. p138
34 Ibid. p139
35 Ibid. p146
36 Ibid. p167
37 Ibid. p168
38 Ibid. p170
39 Ibid. p171
40 Cited from Amazon.com, Customer reviews of *Love & Respect*, 'Christian?', May 12, 2006, by Richard Day, Old Greenwich, CT USA

15

Focus on the Family – Essentials of Marriage

James Dobson, founder of Focus on the Family, is the man who has done more than any other to bring the dogma of self-esteem into the Church. He has had a long-term close working relationship with Gary Smalley, the trailblazer of Christian marriage psycho-education, and together these two men share the distinction of being regarded as the twin pillars of the Christian psychology movement. One of their most significant collaborations is the marriage education programme, 'Essentials of Marriage'. Focus on the Family is now focusing on marriage psycho-education in a big way.

Essentials of Marriage

Essentials of Marriage is a programme that provides advice from top Christian relationship experts, such as Dr Gary Smalley, Dr John Trent, Dr Gary Chapman, Dr Gary and Barb Rosberg, and Drs Les and Leslie Parrott. These men and women, with their deep knowledge of psychology and vast experience in marriage counselling, are portrayed by the Essentials programme as experts in the field of relationships, experts who are able to help us deal with our marriage problems and build strong families.

Focus on the Family's marriage education course is delivered through three packages that each consist of a DVD, a participant's guide and a leader's guide. The three packages are entitled: 'Who did you really marry?', which deals with personality types, communication and love languages; 'Handle with Care', which deals with emotions, finance and sexuality; and 'Higher Love', which deals with God's design for marriage. A marketing DVD, with posters, invitation cards, sermon starters and PowerPoint slides, is designed to help churches publicise an Essentials of Marriage event. The programme, faithful to the ethos of Focus on the Family, is deeply immersed in psycho-education.

In this chapter we examine the Essentials of Marriage course, which claims to help us see marriage through God's eyes, in the light of biblical truth.

Using psychology to identify your needs

The first session, taken from 'Who did you really marry?' aims to help a couple appreciate rather than lament their personality differences, and to concentrate on combining their complementary strengths. Psychologist and best-selling author Dr John Trent helps a couple look at their personality differences. This is considered to be important because 'couples often tell therapists that one of their toughest challenges is adjusting to a spouse's personality. Many of those people are ready to give up and resign themselves to a miserable state of existence. Others fear their situations will worsen to a point where the spouse's personality turns repulsive—and divorce will be inevitable'.[1] We are asked to complete a survey that helps us to think about how we are already handling our spouse's personality. And then the crunch question: 'Did you and your spouse take a personality test before marriage, and if not why not?'[2] The implication is that not to have taken a personality test before marriage is foolish or careless or both. So right from the start of the course we are led to believe that psychology and personality testing have a lot to offer.

The DVD for this session looks at differences between spouses and shows how concentrating on strengths can make those differences an asset instead of a liability. We are reassured, 'You'll have fun deciding what types you and your spouse are, and how to make the most of it.'[3] According to Dr Trent there are four personality types—lions, golden retrievers, otters and beavers (see page 130). Lions tend to approach problems aggressively, while golden retrievers tend to step away from problems. Otters tend to be laid back, and beavers are industrious. The good news is that any combination can learn to get along. We are asked to describe our personality type and that of our spouse, and then answer the question: 'What conflicts do you think John Trent would expect you to have?'[4] The implication is that conflict in marriage is generated by our personality type. But Scripture teaches that we fight because we give way to the works of the flesh that include hatred, outbursts of wrath, selfish ambition and dissensions (Galatians 5.20).

Genesis 25 is read to describe the personalities of Jacob and Esau and how they might interact. To help, we are told that Jacob may have been an introvert and Esau an extrovert.[5] These are personality traits described and popularised by the famous psychologist Carl Jung, also well known for his fascination with the occult.[6] But Scripture does not comment on the so-called personality types of Jacob and Esau, for it is showing us something far more important, namely that Esau treated with contempt the spiritual aspect of his birthright. In other words, Esau despised the things of God (Hebrews 12.16-17).

Here we have a typical example of the way the Essentials programme misuses Scripture to support a psychological interpretation of life. The session ends with the leader commenting: 'If you tend to see your spouse's personality in the worst possible light, make a list of your spouse's traits – maybe the top 12 or so – and circle all the negative ones. Then come up with a more positive term for each of those traits.'[7] We are told that 'most of us can stand negative behavior for a while. But everyone has a limit!'[8] If this is the case in your marriage, 'you may need help from a counselor to express your frustration and find a healthy tolerance level'.[9] The group leader encourages any struggling couples to contact a Christian counsellor recommended by their church.

This session on personality traits is typical of the whole Essentials programme. It is steeped in psychological theory and jargon. The idea that the complexity of the human personality can be described by four animals is ludicrous—some would even call it 'psychobabble'. It is unbelievably patronising to reduce human personalities to animal categories, especially in the context of Christian marriage. And while Scripture is quoted, there is no attempt to accurately interpret and understand the message of Scripture. Instead, Scripture is twisted to support the psychological theories of Focus on the Family, not to understand the will of God. The Lord says: 'Inasmuch as these people draw near with their mouths and honour Me with their lips, but have removed their hearts far from me...' (Isaiah 29.13). Focus and its marriage educators seem to have no interest in the biblical view of marriage described in chapter 5.

Learning to communicate

The next two sessions deal with communication. DVD host Dr Greg Smalley (son of Gary Smalley) says ineffective communication is one of the greatest problems facing couples today. To the rescue come Drs Les and Leslie Parrott, 'popular authors and speakers on all things marital. Instead of telling us to talk, they show us how.'[10] They share two principles that can help every couple stay connected: clarifying content and reflecting feelings. We are told to make sure that our messages are getting through, and especially the emotions behind them.

In the second session on communication we are taught four things couples need in order to feel safe enough to communicate (time, approval, loyalty and quality), and author and speaker Gary Smalley (his ministry is described in chapter 12), 'explains the deepening levels of communication that couples can experience as they feel safer with each other'.[11] Gary suggests using 'the fast-food drive-thru as a communication model – asking a series of questions to find out what your spouse thinks, feels and believes'.[12] For example, what three questions would you ask if your wife poses the question: 'Does this dress make me look fat?'[13] The course leader is told to let volunteers call out suggestions, and to 'affirm any that show a caring attitude and would be likely to reveal the other spouse's thoughts, feelings, or beliefs'.[14] It is difficult to believe the Christian people, who read God's Word, can actually participate in such a facile exercise.

Learning to deal with conflict

In sessions four and five we are taught how to navigate safely through conflicts. Dr Gary Rosberg and wife Barbara, co-founders of the international ministry America's Family Coaches, give advice on how to face friction. We are told that 'failing to resolve conflict is the number-one predictor of divorce'.[15] Here we have a statement of the obvious! We are told we must initiate forgiveness, treat our spouse as our best friend, be a safe person, and stop trying to change our partner. We are provided with conflict-resolving tools.[16] We are shown how to use 'I' statements when we are angry with our spouse. For example the statement, 'You never stand up for me when your dad calls me a loser', could be better expressed as follows: 'When your dad calls me a loser, I feel angry—and when you don't disagree with him, I feel angrier.'[17] When both partners lack the skills to deal with conflict, we are told that it is crucial to get outside help from a good family therapist or a pastor who has time and expertise to work with us on an ongoing basis.[18] So in the eyes of Focus, the answer to marital conflict when both partners lack skills, is to seek help from the profession of family therapy, the profession that has consistently demonstrated its ideological opposition to the biblical view of marriage, as we saw in chapter 2.

The second session on conflict management helps you 'figure out what works best for you'.[19] This session, hosted by Dr Greg Smalley, includes a DVD segment based on the findings of marriage researcher Dr John Gottman: 'First, couples need to accent the positive—because it takes five positive experiences to counteract one negative one. That's five compliments to every criticism. In fact, simply listing each other's positive traits can change spouses' attitudes in as little as a week.'[20] Dr Juli Slattery, a clinical psychologist and author, then shares the rest of Gottman's prescription: 'Avoid criticism, contempt, defensiveness, and stonewalling, and develop a real friendship with your mate.'[21] Dr Greg Smalley enthusiastically endorses Gottman's theory that we need five positive experiences to counteract each negative one. 'Have a two-minute contest with your spouse to see who can list the most positive thing about the other.'[22] We are told that 'seeing your spouse in a positive light and giving him or her positive reinforcement is one of the most important things you can do for your relationship'.[23] We are told to think positive and to reject negative thoughts. 'Identify the negative thought and question its validity. Replace it with a positive, accurate thought or belief.'[24] So Focus encourages participants to live by the positive psychology theories of John Gottman. A Christian couple attending the Essentials programme need to understand that they are being taught to base their relationship on the godless ideas of the positive psychology movement.

Learning the languages of love

In session six we deal with the languages of love. In a DVD, Dr Gary Chapman explains that 'there are five ways to express and perceive love: words of affirmation, quality time, gifts, acts of service and physical touch', as we saw in chapter 13. The aim of this session is to help 'spouses grow closer by identifying and appreciating each other's preferred ways of expressing and recognizing love'.[25] To apply the principles you are given ten expressions of love based on the five love languages, and you must come up with specific examples to express your love. Suggestions include: eight words of affirmation that do not include the word love; eight words of affirmation to the tune of 'She'll be coming round the mountain'; quality time that involves a can opener; quality time that doesn't involve food or drink; an act of service that requires wearing gloves; an act of service that starts with the letter d; and so on.[26]

If, after hearing about the languages of love, you feel stuck, then here's what you should do—make a date with each other once a week and try a communication exercise. 'For example, the wife talks for 10 minutes about feelings or issues she has; the husband does nothing but listen. He may respond only with, "I don't understand; could you restate that" or "What I hear you saying is…" Then he talks for 10 minutes and she listens.'[27] The idea that a wife and husband should talk for 10 minutes about their feelings comes from the theories of Carl Rogers.

It is difficult not to discern the superficial understanding of love and the trite nature of the activities that are being promoted by this course. How Christians who have the Word of God can listen to this diet of puerile nonsense is hard to understand.

Learning about great sex in marriage

The booklet, 'Handle with Care', has two sessions on great sex in marriage. The icebreaker of the first session emphasises that most churches do not teach from the Song of Solomon. And the reason – according to Focus – is because some people find it too sensual for the sanctuary. We are encouraged to read the Song of Solomon, for 'it celebrates the kind of relationship God meant husbands and wives to enjoy'.[28] However, many reliable Christian commentators interpret the Song of Songs as a picture of the Church as the Bride of Christ. The love affair is between Christ and his Church. It seems that Focus would like to turn the Song of Solomon into a sex manual. For a more edifying and spiritual view of this book, see *The Mutual love of Christ and His People*, Peter Masters, Wakeman Trust, 2004.

Learning to deal with anger

A session on expressing anger the right way aims 'to help spouses express their anger in ways that bring them together instead of driving them apart'.[29] A DVD features Dr Gary Rosberg and Barb Rosberg, who team up with psychologist Dr Archibald Hart, a former dean of the School of Psychology at Fuller Theological Seminary, to explain how 'to keep this powerful emotion from turning into rage or revenge'.[30] According to Dr Hart, 'anger is like a smoke alarm; it tells you that something's wrong and you need to figure out what it is'.[31]

Learning about depression

Dealing with depression is the subject of the next session. The aim is 'to help group members identify signs of depression in a spouse if such signs exist, to help them urge a depressed spouse to get professional counseling, or to help them prepare for the possibility that they or a spouse will become depressed in the future'.[32] In the DVD, three counsellors, Mitch Temple, Gary Rosberg and Juli Slattery, tell the unvarnished truth about their own battles with depression.[33] The session starts by making the point that 'when sadness lasts, it may be depression—and it can turn a relationship upside down'.[34]

The experiences of Elijah and Job are used as examples of depression in the Bible. The principles learnt in this session, it is suggested, will help you 'find out whether your spouse is depressed', and prepare you for 'a future time when your spouse might be depressed'. And perhaps you need to 'let your spouse know that you're depressed', or even to 'help your spouse get treatment for depression'.[35] Participants are helped to prepare for the possibility that they or their spouse, or both, could someday become depressed. The advice is to learn all we can about depression and to contact a counsellor in case of need. The session leader must 'remind spouses that if they need guidance on depression or living with a depressed mate and would like to speak with a therapist, Focus on the Family maintains a referral network of Christian counselors.'[36]

The whole tone of this session is to inculcate the psycho-secular version of depression into the minds of the participants. (This subject is discussed in some detail in my book, *Christ or Therapy?*, Wakeman Trust and Belmont House Publishing, 2010). We are led to believe that the 'disease' of depression is extremely common. It is hard to avoid the conclusion that Focus is using its marriage education as a recruiting ground for its Christian counselling services. Focus follows the psycho-secular view that all depression is a disease and needs treatment, rather than recognising that much of what gets diagnosed as depression is part and parcel of the ups and downs of life that we all experience. Downcast Christians need the wisdom and help of Scripture, not the psychotherapy of a counsellor.

Questioning the role of husband and wife

The session, 'It's not about you', aims to show what the inventor of marriage (God) has to say about it. The plan is to 'help spouses grow closer by working to reflect the oneness of the Trinity, rather than pursuing their own interests'.[37] Participants watch a DVD which explains how God's view of marriage counts the most, and are then asked a few questions to help them think through what they have heard. One question asks how they would compare the biblical view of marriage to the perspective offered by a number of TV shows, such as the Simpsons and Desperate Housewives. Ephesians 5.21-33, which deals with the marriage union, the headship of husband and submission of wife, is read and participants are asked: 'Are there are any words in this passage that bother you?' The course leader is warned that 'some participants may have misgivings about submit and head, questioning what the roles of men and women should be... Don't try to resolve these issues now; simply acknowledge them.'[38] However, the leader is given a clear instruction: 'As needed, you may want to point out that submission is a yielding of one's rights, not a debasing of oneself to placate or impress another, and is for all Christians (verse 21)'. In other words, make sure that participants understand that submission is *mutual*. The message of verse 22, namely, that wives are to submit to their husbands as the Church submits to Christ, is conveniently downplayed.

So we see that Focus on the Family is in practice distorting Scripture to teach equal-regard marriage. Clearly the message of the headship of the husband and submission of the wife, as taught in the Bible, does not fit with the psycho-education message that is being delivered by Focus.

Merging psychological theory with Scripture

Focus's approach to marriage education is based on syncretism, in that it merges the teachings of Scripture and psychology. Every session starts with a psychological theory, and then Scripture is quoted to support the psychological theory. In this way Focus can claim that it is integrating the best ideas from psychology and Scripture in order to get the best of both worlds. After all, why should Christians be deprived of the benefits that come from psychological tools and skills? Our examination, however, demonstrates that Focus is devoted to the way of psychology, not the way of Scripture, for Scripture is twisted to make it appear to support the theories of positive psychology. And so there is little difference between the marriage education offered by Focus and that offered by any of the secular marriage education programmes. The only real difference is that Focus has bolted on a number of Scripture quotes. But Scripture is always secondary – it is hauled out as an after thought to support the views of the psychologists.

Essentials brings the full force of psychological thinking to bear on marriage. It teaches the personality traits developed by Gary Smalley and John Trent, and the psychological theories of Gary Chapman. It promotes the positive psychology of John Gottman and accepts his research as revealing the truth about marriage. Like positive psychology, Essentials tell us to think positive thoughts and to reject negative ones; we are told to replace negative thoughts with positive thoughts. Following Carl Rogers' advice that to communicate properly we must learn to share our feelings, Essentials encourages the wife to talk for 10 minutes about her feelings, while her husband listens patiently. And then it's the husband's turn.

Because the messages of psychology are primary, it is no surprise that Essentials of Marriage is presented by experts who are highly experienced in psychology and marriage and family therapy. In the eyes of Focus, only experts trained in psychological theories understand the deep problems of marriage, for only they have the special knowledge and skill to teach about marriage.

A significant point about Focus's band of psychological experts is that most of them have participated in the conferences of the secular Coalition for Marriage, Family and Couples Education—Dr Gary Chapman, Dr Gary Smalley, Les and Leslie Parrot have all made presentations at the annual Smart Marriages Conference. They have felt at home in the citadel of marriage psycho-education, and have eagerly grasped the opportunity to be associated with the psycho-education ideology promoted by Diane Sollee and her colleagues. It appears they have had no difficulty in leaving their Christian beliefs at the door of Smart Marriages conferences. So we must understand that those who present the Essentials of Marriage course are part of the Smart Marriages movement discussed in chapter 3—a movement that is ideologically opposed to biblical marriage and which actively promotes equal-regard marriage.

We must conclude that Essentials of Marriage is a dismal failure, for by combining Scripture with psychological theories, it has fallen into the great sin of syncretism, and is leading thousands upon thousands of people along a road that leads to compromise and despair. Christians who would be faithful to Scripture should avoid Essentials of Marriage like the plague, and warn others of its dangers. In reality, Essentials of Marriage is actually Essentials of Psychology.

(Endnotes)

1 Focus on the Family, *Essentials of Marriage*, 'Who did you really marry?', Participant's guide, Tyndale House Publishers, 2009, p1

2 Ibid. p3

3 Ibid. p3

4 Ibid. p5

5 Focus on the Family, *Essentials of Marriage*, 'Who did you really marry?', Tyndale House Publishers, 2009, Leader's guide, p9

6 Richard Noll, *The Jung Cult*, Princeton University Press, 1994, pp76-80

7 'Who did you really marry?' Leader's guide, p11

8 'Who did you really marry?' Participant's guide, p10

9 Ibid. p11

10 Ibid. p15

11 'Who did you really marry?' Leader's guide, p23

12 'Who did you really marry?' Participant's guide, p27

13 Ibid. p28

14 'Who did you really marry?' Leader's guide, p28

15 'Who did you really marry?' Participant's guide, p40

16 'Who did you really marry?' Leader's guide, p35

17 Ibid. p40

18 'Who did you really marry?' Participant's guide, pp45-46

19 Ibid. p47

20 Ibid. p49

21 Ibid. p49

22 Ibid. p50

23 Ibid. p53

24 Ibid. p56

25 'Who did you really marry?' Leader's guide, p57

26 Ibid. pp66-67

27 'Who did you really marry?' Participant's guide, p67

28 Focus on the Family, *Essentials of Marriage*, 'Handle with Care', Tyndale House Publishers, 2009, Leader's guide, p21

29 Ibid. p33

30 Focus on the Family, *Essentials of Marriage*, 'Handle with Care', Tyndale House Publishers, 2009, Participant's guide, p39

31 Ibid. p41

32 'Handle with Care', Leader's guide, p45

33 Ibid. p45

34 Ibid. p47

35 'Handle with Care', Participant's guide, p56

36 'Handle with Care', Leader's guide, pp55-56

37 Focus on the Family, *Essentials of Marriage*, 'Higher Love', Tyndale House Publishers, 2009, Leader's guide, p13

38 Ibid. p19

16

Sixty minute wisdom of Rob Parsons

In the UK Christian marriage education is being actively promoted by The National Couple Support Network, a partnership between Care for the Family and the Family Life Department of Anglican church, Holy Trinity Brompton, London, the creators of The Marriage Course, considered in the next chapter. The purpose of the network is to offer marriage preparation education to engaged couples throughout the country.[1] The ambitious plan of these two organisations is to deliver Christian marriage education across the UK.

Care for the Family

In 1988 Rob Parsons, a trained lawyer, left legal practice to start Care for the Family as a department of Christian Action, Research and Education (CARE) Trust, a charity of which he was a board member. Care for the Family, which has become an independent charity, claims that its work is motivated by Christian compassion. It has been involved in marriage and family education since the early 1990s, running events and courses across the UK, and creating resources that are used all over the world. In 1998, the charity moved to the current National Family Centre on the outskirts of Cardiff.

Rob Parsons is an international speaker on relationships and the family, and the author of numerous best-selling books. He claims to have spoken to hundreds of thousands of people about marriage in different cultures across the world. He believes that 'marriages can be revolutionised by somebody speaking plainly about the traumas which hit many of us, and breaking through the sense of isolation that makes us feel "this is just us".'[2]

Care for the Family produces books and reports on family life, and organises seminars, counselling and a confidential phone line for church leaders. It also provides accredited training courses for those who want to support parents and families. 'Our training events stand alone for those who want to develop their skills and knowledge, but are also essential elements for anyone wanting to become a Licensed Facilitator of our courses.'[3] It believes that research provides the answer to marriage and family problems. We are reassured that 'research tells us that marriage is good for us – we're more likely to live longer, and be happier and healthier, if we're married'.[4] In *The Sixty Minute Family*, Parsons emphasises the importance of psychological research. He writes: 'Some research has suggested that to flourish as human beings – to experience a sense of well-being – we need more positive comments than negative ones in our lives – to a factor of three to one.'[5] To equip people for working with parents, Care has developed a training module that is 'both practical and interactive, looking at key evidence based theories, research and also their practical application when working with adults'.[6]

A key message of Care for the Family is that to have a good marriage we must learn to communicate properly. 'You need to develop honesty in your communication and learn to talk together about how you feel... This includes resolving to have no secrets and to share your thoughts and feelings, your hopes and your dreams. In doing this you make yourselves vulnerable.'[7]

The 21ˢᵗ Century Marriage Seminar

In this DVD-based marriage education programme, Rob Parsons shares insights into the big issues that most couples face. The DVD blurb says that 'despite the pressure of living in a century of constant change, you can still forge a relationship that will last a lifetime... So take time together, sit back and enjoy as Rob encourages you and helps you to nurture a marriage that will blossom in the 21ˢᵗ Century.'[8]

The first session begins with Parsons telling us that 'love begins to die when we believe that we don't matter anymore'. Three ways to let your partner know that they matter are: to show that you appreciate them; to praise them; and to often be affectionate toward them. We are told to discover the power of praise. 'How often do you praise your partner – every day, once a week or never? How does that make them feel?'[9] We should find something positive to say about our partner. Parsons has written: 'The power of praise is awesome. There is hardly a person on the face of the earth who does not respond to it… Praise does so many things at once. It tells us that what we are doing is right.'[10] As we have already heard, this is a well-worn technique of positive psychology.

In the next session we are told a number of things about acceptance. We must accept what we can't change and therefore stop looking for perfection; we must talk about change, and we must change ourselves.[11] The claim that we can change ourselves for the better is consistent with the self-improvement ideas propagated by the human potential movement. This is the philosophy that lies behind *21st Century Marriage*.

The session entitled 'January love' explains that every marriage goes through difficult times. We then have the usual session on communication – 'talk about what's bothering you'; tips for being a good listener are to listen with your eyes and look at each other when you are talking and listening.[12]

The session, 'When the sparks fly', deals with conflict resolution. Let your partner know how you are feeling, but do not insult your partner or call them names or describe them with negative words. Tell your partner the little things that have hurt you and wait for a suitable time to discuss things that make you angry. In the discussion that follows start with, 'I feel', not 'you always', or, 'you never'.

Two sessions deal with handling debt and the 'affair'. Parsons is careful not to use the word adultery, and never says that an affair is morally wrong. He says, 'Most people who have an affair say that they didn't go looking for it. It is so easy to slip into an affair.'[13] The final session deals with sex. The message is that lots of couples have problems with sex, but your sex life can improve. You are told to 'list ways you can make your love life fun. Start to do some of them as soon as possible. If you feel really stuck, read a suitable book or find a relationship counsellor to help you both.'[14]

What we have received from Parsons is little more than a series of lessons in the skills and tools of positive psychology. We are told to learn the power of praise and affirmation, we must learn to communicate our feelings, we must think positively and avoid negative thoughts and words. There is no biblical teaching. We learn a great deal about Parsons when he is asked to respond to the important question: 'What advice would you give to a young couple about to be married?' This is surely an opportunity to point a young couple to the biblical understanding of marriage. But Parsons does not use Scripture to answer this question; rather he imparts to his listeners his own 'timeless' wisdom. He says that he has often thought about how to answer this question.

Here is his answer: 'I think that I would say to them that tough times will come and you will have to fight to keep love alive. When that time comes believe that it's normal. Second, I would say that the time will come when you think that you should have married someone else—that the person I should have married is somewhere out there. But all I would say to you is that that person turns out to be an illusion; and so often working through these tough times with this person that you've committed to will be the best thing; it's not always possible I understand that, but see if you can do that… Believe that things can change; time and time again they find life again. Finally, laugh together. Diane and I often laugh a lot; we often laugh as we go to sleep. But we often laugh together. Laugh as much as you can. You will know pain, kids may break your heart, you may know times of sickness and illness, but that needs to be alongside times of helpless laughter. And surprise each other. Always keep that element no matter how old you get together, see if you can surprise each other, even shock each other occasionally. It's not a bad thing to keep your love alive.'[15]

It appears not to have entered Parsons' mind to give a young couple biblical advice on marriage. Because Parsons does not use Scripture in his teaching, he is unable to help a couple understand the meaning and purpose of marriage from the Bible. So he has nothing to say to a young couple on what the Bible teaches about marriage; he does not tell them that God ordained marriage between a man and his wife at the time of creation; he says nothing about marriage being a 'one flesh', life-long union of which God is the author; he does not say that marriage forms a new family; he does not tell a young couple to read Ephesians chapter 5 in order to understand the roles of husband and wife.

Parsons' Sixty Minute books

Parsons' version of marriage and family education is presented in the *Sixty Minute* series of books—*The Sixty Minute Father* (1995), *Marriage* (1997), *Mother* (2000) and *Family* (2010). The first point that strikes the reader is that these books give virtually no biblical teaching. It is immediately apparent that Parsons' view of marriage and the family is built on what others have told him and around the power of his stories and his grasp of psychology, not the power of Scripture.

The Sixty Minute Marriage

The Sixty Minute Marriage (1997) is Parsons' definitive statement on marriage. His aim is to present 'an action plan to revolutionise every relationship'.[16] The amazing claim is that your relationship will be transformed in one hour. Scattered throughout the book are 'action pages'. He explains, 'I asked various people to share simple lessons they had learned in their marriages; choose those that may help you.'[17] He provides the following snippets of advice: 'Listen with your eyes'; 'Take walks together more often'; 'Don't confuse your partner's need for space with rejection'; 'Give your partner flowers when it's not their birthday'; 'Have a television-free evening occasionally'; 'Hold hands more often'; 'Try not to be completely predictable'; 'Try to laugh together'; 'Revisit some of the places that were favourites when you first met'; and so on. The advice is simple common sense with a few psychological tips thrown in.

The reader is fed a rich diet of stories from which Parsons draws profound truths about marriage and the way people should relate to each other. Here is an example of one of his stories. He tells of the time he and his wife were invited for a meal to the home of a young couple just returning from honeymoon. The evening was perfect until the dessert arrived, which was a sponge that had an endearing Frisbee-like look. And the husband made a little joke about the sponge. The wife was so upset that she threw the dessert at her husband, burst into tears and ran out. Parsons interprets the event: 'I began to tell him what I thought had happened. We talked about his father-in-law, a man whom I knew well.' According to Parsons the father-in-law had constantly brought his wife down in public. 'The young woman now crying upstairs had watched

191

her father break every ounce of self-esteem his wife might have had, and finally he had killed her love for him.' Parsons told the husband that his new wife had seen her father in him. 'He is still alive – but it is as if a ghost came.' The husband said very little but his life was completely changed. And then Parsons imparts his words of wisdom: 'We can learn to recognise the old characteristics, the painful memories, the petty opinions – the things from yesterday long gone that conspire to rob us of love today. And if we acknowledged them, so much of our behaviour and reactions can be understood and – as important – changed.'[18]

Parsons has used a Freudian interpretation of the event that suggests behaviour is determined by our past, especially the action of our parents. He explains that the reason the young wife threw a dessert at her husband, in front of her guests, is because her father treated her mother badly. In other words, the wife's behaviour is determined by the way her father treated her mother—she is a victim of her cruel father. There was no suggestion that this conduct was immature, self-centred and shameful in a Christian wife.

The Sixty Minute Father

The Sixty Minute Father (1995) is a classic self-help book that is devoid of biblical teaching. Rather than looking to Scripture to understand the role and responsibility of fatherhood, Parsons says he 'asked a number of fathers to tell me things they had done with their children that were simple yet proved to be significant in their relationship'.[19] Once again Parsons' advice is based on human wisdom. He provides ten goals and says that 'each of them is a powerful tool in the work of a father and each has the potential to change your life and the lives of your children – forever'.[20] So readers are led to believe that Parsons' self-help advice, not Scripture, will change their lives forever, which when you think about it, is an absurd claim.

What is this powerful, life-changing advice? 'Children love receiving letters. If you have to be away from home, drop them a line.'[21] 'Kneel to talk to toddlers and listen with your eyes'.[22] 'Go with your teenager to listen to his or her favourite band. Listen to some of the group's music the week before – it will help you through the pain barrier'.[23] 'Develop family traditions. These could be as simple as cooking hamburgers every

Saturday night – your children look forward to them and remember them when they are grown.'[24] 'Make a list of values that are important to you. Ask yourself whether you are effectively passing those on to your child.'[25] 'Discover LEGO – it seems to work with children from 0 – 100!'[26] Well, this is hardly world shattering stuff. And surely a wise Christian father should not condone the godless, worldly rock music scene of their teenage children.

The Sixty Minute Family

The Sixty Minute Family (2010) is Parsons' latest offering that also promises to transform your relationships forever. Much of the advice has appeared in the other *Sixty Minute* books. But we learn a great deal about what Parsons really stands for by the company he keeps. As Scripture asks, 'Can two walk together unless they be agreed?' (Amos 3.3). Two examples illustrate the point.

The amoral sex education of Suzie Hayman

On the first page of Parsons' book we read a list of endorsements. The longest and most enthusiastic is written by Suzie Hayman, a BBC agony aunt and Relate-trained counsellor. She likes the book very much: 'With wit and insight Rob Parsons gets to the heart of what makes families work – time, attention and encouragement… too many families are destroyed by parents simply not making their children and their partners their main priority. Parsons shows you how to do so by listening, communicating and having fun.'[27] This glowing endorsement from a BBC agony aunt is meant to encourage people to read the book.

But what we are not told is that Hayman worked for the Family Planning Association and Brook Advisory Centres for many years, or that she is the author of a number of highly controversial sex manuals. Her sex education booklet, *Say yes? Say no? Say maybe?* (1999), published by Brook, is aimed at under-age children and provides them with advice on how to obtain and use condoms. The amoral nature of this booklet is discussed in my book *Lessons in Depravity* (2003). Yet Care for the Family is prepared to use a woman who has been in the forefront of promoting amoral sex education in the UK to endorse its products. This says much about the moral standing of Care for the Family—it is so indifferent to biblical standards of conduct among young people that it has publicly associated itself with the amoral ideology of the Family Planning Association and Brook.

The positive psychology of Barbara Fredrickson

Parsons refers to the work of positive psychologist Dr Barbara Fredrickson, regarded by some as the 'genius' of the positive psychology movement, who has a strong personal commitment to New Age and Buddhist practices, as discussed in chapter 9. Parsons quotes her research that to flourish as human beings, and to experience a sense of well-being, 'we need more positive comments than negative ones in our lives – to a factor of three to one'.[28] There is no doubt that Parsons is completely given over to the positive psychology bandwagon.

Teenagers – What every parent has to know

In this book, *Teenagers! What every parent has to know* (2007), Parsons gives advice to parents on how they should nurture and care for their teenage children. The book claims to help parents understand what is going on in their teenager's brain, and deals with the big issues: sex, drugs and self-esteem. What is surprising is that a book from an organisation that claims to be based on Christian principles does not use Scripture.

The source and bedrock of Parsons' guidance is humanistic psychology. Scattered throughout the book are over a dozen mentions of psychologists and numerous psychological opinions. We are told that one psychologist likened the teenage experience to the launch of a spacecraft.[29] Parsons says that he talked with a psychologist who told him that the problem was 'that many parents don't really love their kids'.[30] He quotes psychologist Anna Freud, who said that 'adolescents are excessively egoistic, regarding themselves as the centre of the universe and the sole object of interest'.[31] He mentions psychologist Dr John White, who said, 'There is no pain like parental pain.'[32] He mentions that 'psychologist Dr Madeline Levine talks of the tragedy that she sees daily in her counselling rooms as she talks with children whose parents love them, but will not give them the space to develop in their own way and at their own pace'.[33]

Parsons explains the reason for bad behaviour among teenagers. He says that we used to think that the hormonal changes that occur in puberty were the cause of teenagers' bad behaviour, but recent research has changed the scene as neuroscientists have been able to track the development of the teenage brain. MRI scans show that in the early teenage years the brain undergoes another previously unrecognised growth spurt.[34] 'The reason that being around some teenagers is similar to sitting at the base of an emotional Mount Etna is that their brains have not yet developed the full ability to control their emotions. The fact is that sometimes they can't help it very much when they are at their most infuriating… this means that not only the ability to control emotions, but the ability to make sound judgements to take a longer view and to postpone immediate gratification for the sake of longer-term gains – is limited.'[35] The point that Parsons is making is that teenagers, with their as yet not fully developed brains, are not really responsible for their actions.

Parsons concludes that it helps us deal with bad teenager behaviours 'if we believe that not only are they not our fault, but in some ways they are not their fault either'.[36] So nobody is to blame for the bad behaviour of teenagers, for they just can't help themselves because their brain is not yet fully developed. All that parents can do is to try and understand the reason for the bad behaviour of their teenager, and put up with it in the hope that in time the behaviour may improve. This is, of course, a highly deterministic view of life that denies the most basic doctrines of Scripture. The Lord said, 'the imagination of man's heart is evil from his youth' (Genesis 8.21). Yet parents are being asked to believe that the behaviour of a young person is determined by their immature brain, over which they have no control, and therefore they are not responsible for their actions. The purpose of this flawed advice is to encourage parents to condone the unruly behaviour of their teenagers.

But this is not the way of the Christian faith. God commands his people to diligently teach their children his moral law (Deuteronomy 6.7). And children are commanded to honour and obey their parents in the Lord, for this is right (Ephesians 6.1-3). Wisdom literature gives this instruction: 'Train up a child in the way he should go, and when he is old he will not depart from it' (Proverbs 22.6). And to a young person:

'My son, if you receive my words, and treasure my commands within you, so that you incline your ear to wisdom… then you will understand the fear of the LORD and find the knowledge of God' (Proverbs 2.1-2, 5). Therefore 'a wise son heeds his father's instruction, but a scoffer does not listen to rebuke' (Proverbs 13.1).

This is the infallible instruction of God's Word. Scripture is clear that the sinful nature of teenagers needs curbing and training. We note that the advice in Ephesians is balanced by a warning to the father, who is responsible for discipline in the family, not to provoke his children to wrath and discouragement as he trains and admonishes them in the Lord. Yet Parsons wants parents to follow the 'wisdom' of modern research rather than biblical instruction. For parents to follow Parsons' advice and abandon God's wisdom is to fail in their Christian duty to love and discipline their children.

When it comes to sex, Parsons says, 'try to talk about sex without embarrassment. You want your teenagers to have a positive view of sex and if possible a healthy future sex life… Be careful about the way you talk about people who have different values to you. If you use derogatory language about celebrities, or even friends of your teenager who have chosen a lifestyle you don't agree with, she will remember. Perhaps one day she'll make a decision she knows you wouldn't approve of. The last thing you want her to feel is, "I couldn't tell my mother – she'd call me a slag".'[37] What Parsons is saying is that a parent should be careful not to let their teenage daughter know that they believe certain types of sexual conduct are wrong. Parents must be careful not to condemn the promiscuous lifestyle of celebrities, so that should their daughter decide to sleep around she will be able to tell her parents and still feel sure of their approval. But this advice is amoral, for it suggests to parents that they should not teach their daughter that sleeping around is wrong. Surely the last thing that a parent wants is for their daughter to behave like a 'slag'. Here we see the fruit of an arrogant mind that has rejected God's Word. What Parsons is teaching parents is pure folly.

Self-esteem

The really big issue, according to Parsons, is self-esteem. We are told that 'people with low self-esteem (or, if you like, negative feelings about themselves) may be badly treated by others and are quite likely to treat themselves badly. This could manifest itself in eating disorders, teenage pregnancy or even suicidal thoughts.'[38] Parsons explains his theory of self-esteem. 'A healthy self-esteem is about valuing yourself for who you are, not what you can do. It's what psychologists call "intrinsic self-worth" – a belief that we have value irrespective of what we achieve or how others regard us.'[39] Parsons' total acceptance of the benefit of self-esteem dogma is further evidence of his commitment to the psychological way. He eagerly accepts the self-esteem ideology of humanistic psychology, but almost entirely avoids the teaching of Scripture.

Self-esteem dogma has gained enormous influence over the last three decades in both the secular and Christian worlds. It lies at the heart of the Christian counselling movement. There are literally hundreds of Christian self-help books, such as *Teenagers!*, that point to the importance of 'healthy' self-esteem as a necessary ingredient for a successful life, and teach parents techniques for enhancing their children's self-esteem. The popular American Christian psychologist, Dr James Dobson, has probably done more than any other person to promote the dogma of self-esteem in the Church at large.

But we must understand that self-esteem dogma is, root and branch, the construct of humanistic psychology—it has emerged from the mind of Abraham Maslow, Eric Fromm and Carl Rogers. The humanists, who believe in the inherent goodness of human nature and reject the concept of sin, have sought a plausible explanation for the problem of human misery and unhappiness. In an attempt to explain away the effects of sin on the human condition, they have developed the psychological construct of 'low self-esteem'. The great fallacy of self-esteem dogma is that it does not acknowledge the effect that sin has on human beings; it does not recognise that unregenerate man is a slave to sin. It is no surprise that both humanist psychologists and the flawed Christian counselling movement have chosen to replace the spiritual problem of sin with the psychological problem of low self-esteem. The issue of self-esteem is dealt with in more detail in my book, *The Dark Side of Christian Counselling*, Wakeman Trust, 2009.

What does Rob Parsons stand for?

Two things are clear from our analysis of Rob Parsons' teaching. First, his teaching on marriage and the family is not based on God's Word. When asked to give a young couple advice about marriage, he does not refer to Scripture but to the trivial thoughts of his own mind—he tells them to laugh as much as they can. We will search in vain for meaningful biblical instruction in the reports and seminars of Care for the Family. Why do Parsons and his organisation avoid Scripture? Is such an approach honouring to God? While Care for the Family claims to be a Christian organisation, all the evidence suggests otherwise.

Second, Parsons is totally committed to the way of humanistic psychology. His thinking is shaped by the latest psychological research. His books are replete with references to psychological ideas, and he makes numerous quotes from psychologists. His belief in of the power of praise, his promotion of positive feelings, his commitment to unconditional acceptance, his teaching on self-esteem, are all ideas that come from the school of positive psychology.

Let us be clear that the teaching of Rob Parsons is not based in biblical truth. So what we get from Care for the Family is a strong dose of positive psychology that masquerades as Christian teaching.

(Endnotes)

1 Engage website of Care for the Family, National Couple Support Network: http://www.engagetoday.org.uk/engaging-couples/national-couple-support-network

2 Rob Parsons, *The Sixty Minute Marriage*, Hodder & Stoughton, 1997, p17.

3 Care for the Family website, 'Training with Care for the Family': http://www.careforthefamily.org.uk/training/

4 Care for the Family website, 'Welcome to marriage matters'

5 Rob Parsons, *The Sixty Minute Family*, Lion Hudson, 2010, p37

6 Care for the Family website, 'Working with parents': http://www.careforthefamily.org.uk/working-with-parents/

7 Care for the Family website, 'Improving communications': http://www.careforthefamily.org.uk/article/?article=690

8 Cited from DVD cover of *21ˢᵗ Century Marriage*, short talks by Rob Parsons, Care for the Family, 2009

9 *21ˢᵗ Century Marriage* Booklet, Care for the Family, Session One

10 Rob Parsons, *The Sixty Minute Father*, Hodder & Stoughton, 1995, p72

11 *21ˢᵗ Century Marriage* Booklet, Session Two

12 *21st Century Marriage* Booklet, Session Four

13 *21st Century Marriage* Booklet, Session Seven

14 *21st Century Marriage* Booklet, Session Eight

15 Cited from *21st Century Marriage* DVD, short talks by Rob Parsons, Session 9, Q&A, Care for the Family, 2009, catalogue no. DVD 11

16 Rob Parsons, *The Sixty Minute Marriage*, Hodder & Stoughton, 1997, back cover

17 Ibid. p13

18 Ibid. pp55-56

19 Rob Parsons, *The Sixty Minute Father*, p14

20 Ibid. p16

21 Ibid. p28

22 Ibid. p45

23 Ibid. p45

24 Ibid. p60

25 Ibid. p95

26 Ibid. p95

27 Rob Parsons, *The Sixty Minute Family*, cited from first page

28 Ibid. p37

29 Rob Parsons, *Teenagers! What every parent has to know*, Hodder & Stoughton, 2007, p9

30 Ibid. p53

31 Ibid. p29

32 Ibid. p56

33 Ibid. p187

34 Ibid. p26

35 Ibid. p27

36 Ibid. p30

37 Ibid. p97

38 Ibid. p135

39 Ibid. pp141-142

17

The Marriage Book – lessons in positive psychology

The Marriage Course, a well-known Christian self-help course that aims to improve marriages by focusing on a psychological understanding of relationships, is massively popular in the UK. Because of apparent concern about the breakdown of Christian marriages, it is being embraced with open arms by churches across the doctrinal spectrum. The Course, which originated from Holy Trinity Brompton, London, (a charismatic church within the Church of England), shares the same doctrinal position as the Alpha Course, also originating at Holy Trinity Brompton. So we can think of the Alpha Course and The Marriage Course as two sides of the ministry of this famous church. Latest estimates suggest The Marriage Course is being taught in around 70 countries worldwide.

The Course is promoted as being for couples who are married or in a long-term cohabiting relationship, who have been together for at least one year, and who would like their relationship to be the best it can be. A happy couple gives the following endorsement. The wife says: 'The Marriage Course saved our marriage. Pete had no hope beforehand and the turnaround was dramatic. However, the impact of The Course was much more than that. The Course provided a window through which love's incredible healing and renewing power streamed in. Bathing in that light, we were brought not just closer together, we were brought closer to the presence of love's source; really close: the deep intimacy that comes from knowing and being known, by one another and by God who is love.'

The husband comments: 'The Course gave me the ability to see our relationship in a completely new way. It challenged me to ask myself, did I want the bad things in our life to have the final word on our relationship? A glimmer of hope came back, which over The Course grew to a real desire and commitment to rescue our relationship and make that our number one goal. Our marriage is now such fun and so very exciting. Who wouldn't want to see that sort of thing spread around a bit more?'[1]

We are invited to a Marriage Course party hosted by the Rev Nicky Lee and wife Sila. 'Come as a couple or why not consider inviting some friends to come along too? You do not have to be married to bring your friends along! Individuals can enjoy the party with their friends who they would like to introduce to the course. It will be a great evening out with tables for two to eight people. Enjoy a delicious two course meal, and be entertained by a magician and live music. The evening will be hosted by Nicky and Sila Lee, who will give a short talk on what makes a marriage grow.'[2]

In *Christ or Therapy* (2010), I analyse The Marriage Course in some detail. This chapter deals with the philosophy of the Reverend Nicky Lee, an Anglican minister, and his wife Sila, the founders and promoters of The Marriage Course.

The Marriage Book

The Marriage Book (2000), written by Nicky and Sila Lee, describes the dogma that lies behind The Marriage Course. The book starts by describing what it calls the 'marriage wheel', with God in the centre and commitment in the outer circle. Around God are the seven spokes that are 'needed if the marriage wheel is not to bump and jar, especially when the road gets rough'.[3] The seven spokes are: The art of communication; love in action; resolving conflict; the power of forgiveness; parents and in-laws; good sex; and building strong foundations. We are told that 'the marriage relationship is designed by God to be an adventure of love that lasts a lifetime. The Bible contains much practical advice about how to make such an intimate relationship work.'[4]

At the heart of *The Marriage Book* is the idea that marriage is an equal-regard relationship between husband and wife. We are told that Christ's teaching on marriage was given in an age when the wife was considered inferior and a husband expected to impose his will on her. The authors then selectively quote two verses from Ephesians 5—verse 25 and part of verse 28 from the NIV: 'Husbands, love your wives, just as Christ loved the church and gave himself up for her'; and, '...husbands ought to love their wives as their own bodies'. They then give their interpretation: 'Paul's instruction reflected the extraordinary respect and concern that Jesus himself showed towards women... Jesus gave equal value to men and women. This affected the marriage relationship profoundly as Christian belief and teaching spread through Europe. To follow the example of Jesus means to respect each other and to value each other's opinions. It rules out the possibility of either husband or wife expecting to impose their will in decisions that affect them both.'[5]

The Lees are clearly attempting to create the impression that the Bible teaches that marriage is an equal-regard relationship between husband and wife. But almost every well-taught Christian will see immediately that the Lees are misusing Scripture, for they have left out a significant part of the text, and in doing so have fundamentally altered the meaning to suit their false teaching. They have deliberately left out what Scripture says about the roles of husband and wife. So we see that verses 22 to 24, which deal with the roles of husband and wife, have been totally omitted from the text of *The Marriage Book*. What is it that the Lees are trying to hide from the unsuspecting reader? 'Wives, submit to your husband as to the Lord. For the husband is the head of the wife as Christ is the head of the church, his body, of which he is the Saviour. Now as the church submits to Christ, so also wives should submit to their own husbands in everything' (Ephesians 5:22-24, NIV). Here we have the central thesis of The Marriage Course. It does not teach about the roles of husband and wife as taught in the Bible—rather it teaches the humanistic view of equality in the roles of husband and wife as taught by Carl Rogers, Virginia Satir and John Gottman. Scripture has been selected and misused to support the ideology of equal-regard marriage; the verses that teach that wives should submit to their husbands in everything have simply been excluded.

This is an extremely important issue, for it shows that both *The Marriage Book* and The Marriage Course blatantly twist Scripture in order to promote a heretical view of marriage. Here we must note the warnings of Deuteronomy, 'You shall not add to the word which I command you, nor take from it, that you may keep the commandments of the

LORD your God which I command you' (Deuteronomy 4.2). 'Whatever I command you, be careful to observe it; you shall not add to it nor take away from it' (Deuteronomy 12.32).

And the apostle John gives his warning: 'For I testify to everyone who hears the words of the prophecy of this book: If anyone adds to these things, God will add to him the plagues that are written in this book; and if anyone takes away from the words of the book of this prophecy, God shall take away his part from the Book of Life, from the holy city, and from the things which are written in this book' (Revelation 22.18-19). The book of Proverbs warns: 'Do not add to His words, lest He rebuke you, and you be found a liar' (Proverbs 30.6).

The art of communication

The Marriage Book says that we must talk about our feelings. 'But emotions are a fundamental part of being human and we must learn to talk about our feelings if we are to communicate effectively in our marriage... Deep communication requires us to be open about our inner selves and to make ourselves vulnerable to each other. If we fail to communicate painful and complex emotions and try to cope on our own, we drift apart. For those of us who feel unable to *recognise*, let alone *talk about*, our feelings, change is possible'[6] [Lees' italics].

We must also learn to listen. 'Listening is a powerful way of showing that we value each other, but it is also costly. It takes effort to listen to our husband or wife as they pour out their feelings or express their opinions.'[7] We are to acknowledge our partner's feelings and repeat back in our own words what our partner has been telling us. This is very helpful, 'particularly when deep feelings are being expressed... Acknowledging feelings in this way may seem unnatural and contrived at first but it is a powerful tool in learning to listen and in building emotional intimacy.'[8]

Nicky Lee illustrates the importance of communication from his personal experience. When a group leader dropped out unexpectedly he decided to lead the group for four evenings. When he told his wife of his decision she was angry with him. 'A few weeks later she started to tell me how upset she was that I had given away some of our free evenings without discussing it with her. Feeling full of self-pity, I immediately defended my decision. I realised later that the real need was to listen to Sila and understand her feelings. She was hurt. She felt that the people on the course were more important to me than our family.'[9] How sad that the Lee's marriage appears to be so inward looking that Sila seems to be more concerned about her own needs than the people to whom her husband, a minister of the Gospel, should be ministering.

We have already seen in previous chapters, that the above advice is the bread and butter of every secular and Christian psycho-education programme. It was the humanistic psychology of Carl Rogers that developed the techniques of deep communication and taught that relationships should be based on our feelings—the Lees are, in practice, promoting the theories of Carl Rogers.

Positive affirmation

Following the advice of Gary Chapman, *The Marriage Book* says that paying compliments is an excellent way of cherishing each other and all of us can learn to do it. Try something as simple and direct as: 'You look really great in that suit'; 'You handled that meeting brilliantly'; 'I love the way you always think of the right thing to say'.[10] We are told that gratitude confers value and worth upon someone, and so we must practise offering thanks. For example, 'Thank you for taking out the rubbish', or, 'Thank you for taking my trousers to the cleaners', or, 'I'm so grateful you remembered my mother's birthday.'[11]

We are told to use words positively to inspire courage in each other. 'It is within our power to give the encouragement which will enable our husband or wife to reach their potential. Conversely, if we criticise, our words have the power gradually to rob our partner of their self-worth and self-confidence. When we encourage, we are saying to each other, "I believe in you".'[12]

If verbal affirmation is deeply important to our husband or wife 'and they have not received any for some time, they will probably be feeling low. To hear positive words from you again will be like reaching an oasis in the desert. As we learn to build our partner up with words, we will reach a new level of love and intimacy in our marriage.'[13]

Here we are being given a heavy dose of positive psychology. The insincerity is overwhelming; it is all so superficial, so transparent, so contrived. In effect, a husband is being asked to act like a con man. He must just learn to say the right positive words, not what is truly in his heart; just say the words, however untrue, and his wife's self-worth will be built up. This advice creates a marriage that is a charade, filled with words that have been learned, but that have no substance.

By now it must be obvious that The Marriage Course is built on the shaky foundation of positive psychology, discussed in chapter 9, with its emphasis on positive thoughts, positive affirmations and deep feelings. How tragic that having forsaken Scripture, The Marriage Course has little more to offer than the tools and skills of positive psychology and other secular theories.

Therapeutic forgiveness

We are told that we must learn to forgive all who offend against us so that we feel better. 'But if we choose to forgive by an act of our will the feelings of forgiveness will follow... When we forgive, that forgiveness may benefit our husband or wife, but ultimately we are the ones who benefit most by being free.'[14] Here *The Marriage Book* provides us with a heart-rending story to make sure we understand forgiveness. A young woman, Irene, meets Roger, an older man who sweeps her off her feet, so she moves in with him, becomes pregnant and marries him. When a middle-aged woman from the village turns up on her doorstep, Irene discovers that her husband is having an affair. 'She [the middle-aged woman] was holding a love letter which Roger had written to her sixteen-year-old daughter. He and the girl were lovers. The mother was particularly upset because she too was having an affair with Roger.'[15] After counselling, Roger eventually leaves his wife, Irene, and goes to live with his secretary, who was pregnant with his child. Understandably, Irene was very upset and angry with Roger. Indeed, as she thought of the way she and her child had been wronged she felt bitterness towards him.

Then Irene realised that her unforgiveness was like a parasite, feeding upon her and growing stronger as it was allowed to thrive. 'She determined, by a decision of her will, to forgive... She would begin to pray for Roger and his new family... She began to feel a wonderful lightness and peace, and finally freedom – the freedom to start afresh.'[16]

This view of forgiveness is unbiblical, for there is no thought of repentance and reconciliation. It is an entirely selfish enterprise – we are told to forgive so that we feel better. But what is the point of such forgiveness? What does it accomplish? It is a meaningless gesture that completely submerges the biblical view of repentance and the forgiveness of sin.

The authors interpret their parable for us. 'Choosing to forgive enables us to move forward without being weighed down by the "chains of bitterness and handcuffs of hatred". At first we may still feel acute pain, but forgiveness allows the recovery to start. It is like being stung by a bee. When the sting is taken out, the skin is not instantly restored but it opens the way for healing to take place.'[17] We are told that only forgiveness can heal our emotional wounds. 'We often seem to forgive layer by layer, like the process of peeling an onion. We may find that we need to go on choosing to forgive for the same hurts on a daily basis in order to be set free. The less we forgive, the harder it is to do so. But if we forgive once, it becomes easier to do so the next time. And as we forgive, the emotional bruising gradually heals and our marriage moves on.'[18]

So *The Marriage Book* promotes a therapeutic version of forgiveness that has nothing to do with the Christian faith. The last two decades have seen a massive increase in the idea of therapeutic forgiveness. This renewed interest has been driven to a large degree by the positive psychology movement and New Age thinking, with generous funding from the vast resources of the John Templeton Foundation.

Childhood pain

The Marriage Book has a chapter entitled, 'How to address the effects of childhood pain'. The chapter is written 'for those whose childhood and upbringing are casting a shadow over their own marriage'.[19] We are told that 'the failure of parents to show unconditional love is likely to leave deep wounds. The key is whether our memories of our childhood are happy or painful. For some, these memories are so painful that amnesia has set in and they cannot easily recall anything of what they felt during their upbringing. As a result of experiences from childhood, we may find that at times we react irrationally towards our partner or another third party. These reactions can be very disturbing for our husband or wife.'[20] There are two dangers. The first is a sense of hopelessness in the person who has been hurt, who must be careful not take on the role of a victim. The second danger is 'a lack of understanding by their partner, who may blame them rather than seek to help... those who have been deeply hurt, may need the help of an experienced counsellor'.[21]

We are invited to ask ourselves if our parents met our needs in childhood. 'It is important to take an honest look at what was lacking and the consequences this is having on our relationships now. We should not be surprised if, as we do so, we encounter a strong sense of anger, or other emotions such as sadness, rejection, fear and shame. These emotions will have been suppressed over a long period.'[22] Husband and wife must learn to grieve with each other over their unmet childhood needs, which constitute a type of bereavement. 'If a husband or wife can talk about what was lacking in the past, their partner can seek to provide emotional support through their willingness to listen, without trying to explain away the feelings or minimalise the effect.'[23]

We must learn to forgive our parents for causing our childhood pain. 'Where we have been deeply hurt we will need to keep on deciding to forgive... our forgiveness is not to be conditional either upon our parents' (or step-parents') understanding of where they have failed us or upon a change of attitude in them... it will not always be advisable or indeed possible to express our forgiveness directly to those who have hurt us.'[24] The reader is told: 'Dare to believe God's unconditional love for you. As you do, so God will gradually replace the pain of unmet childhood needs with a sense of security and comfort.'[25] And as we forgive our parents, 'we may become aware that, because of the unseen motive to satisfy childhood needs, we have acted irrationally and upset others, especially those we love most.'[26]

Here we are being given a Freudian interpretation of childhood pain. The assertion is that our parents, because they did not meet all our childhood needs, are the cause of many of our problems. We are told we must forgive them for the way they failed in their task as parents. And we must do this without necessarily letting our parents know that we have forgiven them. This attitude towards parents is completely against the fifth commandment to honour our father and mother. It panders to the disastrous and now discredited 'recovered memory therapy' of the 1990s, when adult children were persuaded by clever psychotherapists to delve into their unconscious mind to recover (false) memories of parental abuse and then accuse their parents. Families were torn apart by false accusations of abuse, and many fathers and some mothers actually went to prison solely on the basis of these false memories. This is simply another example of the unbiblical approach of *The Marriage Book*. The psychological concepts of therapeutic forgiveness and unconditional love are discussed in detail in my book, *Christ or Therapy?* (2010).

The false teaching of The Marriage Course

The Marriage Book forms the ideological foundation of The Marriage Course, so energetically promoted by Holy Trinity Brompton. The seven sessions of The Course focus on the skills of positive psychology, and tens of thousands of unwary Christians are being misled into believing that positive thinking and positive emotions are part of the Christian faith. We have seen how The Marriage Course cynically selects and twists Scripture in order to promote the humanistic concept of equivalence of roles in marriage (so-called equal-regard marriage), entirely ignoring the biblical concepts of headship and submission. So the essential biblical message about the role of husband and wife, and the governance of the family, as described in Scripture, is simply disregarded. At this point we see the absolute conflict between two opposing views of marriage – a *psychological* view of marriage created by the theories of The Marriage Course, and *biblical marriage* revealed by God's Word.

What is so appalling about The Marriage Course is that it teaches its heretical doctrine of marriage in the name of the Christian faith. It uses the flawed thinking of marriage psycho-education, which it parades as Christian, to inculcate the ideas of humanistic psychology and the human potential movement into the heart of the Church. The false teaching of The Marriage Course has traduced the meaning and purpose of marriage. And because many churches no longer teach the biblical view of marriage, their congregations are easy prey to the alluring promises offered by the psychological model of marriage.

(Endnotes)

1 The Marriage Course website. Stories, Pete and Gill, http://relationshipcentral.org/marriage-course/stories
2 Holy Trinity Brompton website, The Marriage Party
3 Nicky and Sila Lee, *The Marriage Book*, Alpha International, first published 2000, reprint 2009, p12
4 Ibid. p15
5 Ibid. pp160-61
6 Ibid. pp61-62
7 Ibid. p67
8 Ibid. pp77-78
9 Ibid. pp78-79
10 Ibid. pp98-99
11 Ibid. p99
12 Ibid. p99
13 Ibid. p102
14 Ibid. p201
15 Ibid. p202
16 Ibid. pp202-203
17 Ibid. p203
18 Ibid. p204
19 Ibid. p249
20 Ibid. p251
21 Ibid. p252
22 Ibid. p253
23 Ibid. pp253-254
24 Ibid. p256
25 Ibid. p257
26 Ibid. p258

18

Syncretism of marriage psycho-education

The evidence presented in this book can only be correctly interpreted within the context of the spiritual war of the two 'seeds' described in Genesis 3. The conflict over marriage, discussed in the first four chapters, is part of the perpetual battle between the seed of Satan, the enemy of God, and the Seed of the Woman, who is Christ and his Church (discussed in chapter 5). The seed of Satan, who are the children of disobedience (Ephesians 2.2), are deeply hostile to God's good plan for marriage and the family. In his rebellion against God and his hatred of mankind, Satan has sought to destroy God's creation and all that is holy, good and true. A major target in Satan's war is the divine plan of marriage outlined in chapter 5.

War on marriage

The marriage psycho-education movement, with its roots in the godless philosophy of humanistic psychology and the human potential movement, is an important front in the spiritual war against the Church of Jesus Christ our Lord.

A fierce warrior in the attack on marriage was humanist psychologist Carl Rogers (chapter 6), the man who, together with Abraham Maslow, laid the foundation for the human potential movement. The cry was that human beings without God and his moral law could improve themselves and achieve a life of happiness with successful relationships. Rogers taught that to build a relationship we needed to reveal ourselves by sharing our deepest feelings. He created a caricature of traditional marriage as oppressive and demeaning to women. He said freedom lay in experimentation and sexual liberation, and so his alternatives to marriage included a variety of open sexual relationships. Putting into practice what he preached, Rogers had an adulterous relationship with a woman colleague that caused great offence and deep suffering to his faithful wife. Rogers said we must live by our own sexual choices and not allow ourselves to be shaped by the rules and the roles thrust upon us by the Church. He outlined the syllabus for marriage education— communication skills, learning to express real feelings, conflict resolution and positive affirmation.

Where the humanist psychologists had led, Virginia Satir (chapter 7), widely regarded as the mother of marriage and family therapy, was keen to follow. Like the humanist psychologists, she rejected the Christian faith, believing rather that human beings are unique manifestations of the 'Universal Life Force'. But she was more than a family therapist—she was a revolutionary in the struggle for a new utopian way of living, a new moral order in which people achieve self-worth, in which relationships are positive, loving and happy. She openly set herself against the Christian faith and its teachings on marriage and the family. 'Let us remember that old, traditional, entrenched, familiar attitudes die hard... I am working on the side of nurturing the new ways, and I invite you to join me.'[1]

Satir's vision was to empower people to reach their full potential. Her approach to therapy was based on the idea of personal growth. She believed that all human beings have an innate drive to grow and evolve a positive energy that moves them towards becoming, as she put it, more fully human. Her commitment to the human potential movement had a large influence on the profession of marriage and family therapy. As a firm advocate of what she called 'positive pairing', she challenged the headship/submission model of Scripture. Despite her profound antipathy towards the biblical view of marriage and the traditional family, she was accepted and venerated as the pioneer of marriage and family therapy.

Dr John Gottman (chapter 8) is widely accepted as the foremost world authority on what makes relationships work. In the field of positive psychology he is well known for his 5-to-1 ratio of positive to negative language, and how this ratio predicts the success of relationships. Gottman stated the purpose of his research programme in bold terms.

'My goal has been nothing more ambitious than to uncover the truth about marriage.'[2] He asks us to accept that his research, not Scripture, will establish the truth about marriage and relationships.

Gottman developed the idea of the 'emotionally intelligent husband', and paints a dismal picture of the husband who still believes in the concept of male headship. The new husband must be taught to share marital power with his wife, for if marriage is to succeed it must be an equal-regard relationship. The emotionally intelligent husband must willingly relinquish headship of the family, cede power to his wife and do more housework.

The three giants of marriage psycho-education, Carl Rogers, Virginia Satir and John Gottman, have all launched attacks on the biblical model of marriage. The advent of positive psychology in the late 1990s simply enhanced and strengthened the marriage psycho-education movement. The aims of marriage psycho-education and positive psychology are virtually the same, namely, to build skills and to teach techniques and provide tools that enable people to achieve the best things in life and marriage. A feature of the new psychology is that all negative thoughts must be rejected, and positive thoughts and positive emotions must be cultivated by positive affirmations. Behind positive psychology is the mindset and influence of New Age spirituality.

Secular marriage education

The marriage psycho-education movement developed as a bid to save the tarnished, pro-divorce reputation of the profession of marriage and family therapy. Diane Sollee (chapter 3), a prominent marriage therapist, had the presence of mind to realise that her profession's anti-marriage sentiments were becoming odious to the general public. She readily made the transition from marriage *psychotherapy* to marriage *psycho-education*, and the Coalition for Marriage, Family and Couples Education was born. Her ambition was to use marriage psycho-education to change the culture of marriage. This cultural change meant replacing traditional beliefs about marriage in two ways. The first was to recognise that all sexual relationships, such as cohabitation and same-sex partnerships, have an equal moral standing; and the second was to promote the concept of equal-regard marriage.

The PAIRS programme (chapter 11) is a classic example of secular marriage psycho-education. Built on the ideas of the human potential movement and the techniques of positive psychology, it is the best programme the human mind is capable of devising. Indeed, PAIRS teaches over 60 skills that they say are necessary for maintaining successful relationships. The most important skills are the ability to listen empathetically, to communicate our deepest feelings, to reject negative thoughts, to praise and affirm our partner, to resolve conflicts and to forgive.

The PAIRS programme is a way that seems right to man, but that has entirely excluded the God of Scripture. At its heart is a utopian view of human nature that comes from Virginia Satir's claim that human intentions are positive and good, and that with the right education we are capable of almost unlimited self-improvement, and therefore the ability to live flourishing and successful lives without God.

Christian marriage education

Christian marriage psycho-education is a huge industry in the USA and the UK, and many other countries. As we have already noted, The Marriage Course is available in around 70 countries worldwide. We have looked at a sample of the key personalities who helped to develop the Christian version of marriage education.

Dr Gary Smalley (chapter 12) can be seen as a trailblazer of Christian marriage psycho-education. He worked so closely with Diane Sollee of the Coalition for Marriage, Family and Couples Education, that he was able to use her network to generate an audience for his infomercial, 'Love is a Decision'. He fully supported the secular psycho-education programmes of John Gottman, Harvel Hendriks, and Sherod Miller. He said that if couples received instruction using these programmes, 'America could see the divorce rate significantly lowered within 10 years'.[3] When Smalley taught that true and lasting love is based on sharing our deepest feelings, he was propagating the teaching of Carl Rogers.

The effect of Smalley's ministry has been to trivialise the meaning and purpose of marriage in the eyes of society, and to promote the idea that Christians need a range of psychological tools and techniques to have a successful marriage. He has singularly failed to teach a biblical view of marriage; in fact, it is doubtful that he even understands what

Scripture teaches about marriage and the family. Throughout his long career he has claimed the ability to uncover hidden keys for the Church. Using psychological theories, he has discovered hidden keys to successful parenting, to loving relationships and to lasting marriages. Every few years he has come out with a new secret that will improve our life forever. Smalley's new paradigm for relationships, unveiled in *The DNA of Relationships*, is supposed to change our lives and have a profound impact on our culture. Assessed in the light of Scripture, Smalley is a modern-day Gnostic who teaches that Scripture is not enough—we all need his special hidden knowledge to enjoy long-lasting, successful relationships.

We have seen that Gary Chapman's teaching on the 'languages of love' (chapter 13) is based on the humanistic psychological theories of Abraham Maslow and Carl Rogers. He passionately follows Maslow's hierarchy of needs, and eagerly promotes Roger's teaching around self-esteem. He is committed to the concepts of secular psychology and even follows the human potential pathway, claiming that a man who is deeply loved is free to develop his full human potential.

According to Emerson Eggerichs (chapter 14), 'the key to motivating another person is meeting that person's deepest need—love for her and respect for him!'.[4] This statement is consistent with Maslow's theory of motivation, which holds that human beings are motivated when their basic needs are gratified. Eggerichs has applied Maslow's theory to the marital situation, as he places the needs of husband and wife at the centre of the marriage relationship. His theory of love and respect has turned 'love' into an emotional need for the wife, and a psychological tool for the husband. Likewise, he has made 'respect' an emotional need for the husband, and a psychological tool in the hands of the wife. The implication is that a wife must look to her husband to meet her emotional needs, and vice versa.

Essentials of Marriage (chapter 15), the psycho-education programme of Focus on the Family, is steeped in positive psychology. It is dominated by experts trained in psychological theories. In the eyes of Focus, only psychologists have the knowledge and ability to understand the deep problems of marriage and therefore only they are able to teach about marriage. Essentials is a dismal failure, for by combining

Scripture with psychological theories, it has fallen into the great sin of syncretism and is leading many Christian couples along a road that ends in compromise and despair.

Care for the Family claims that its work is motivated by Christian compassion. However, Rob Parsons (chapter 16), the head of Care for the Family, does not base his teaching about marriage and the family on God's Word. He prefers the wisdom and stories that come from the counselling room. He is committed to the way of psychology, and his books are replete with references to psychological ideas. His belief in the power of praise, his promotion of positive feelings, his commitment to unconditional acceptance, his teaching on the importance of self-esteem, are all ideas that come from the school of positive psychology. So what we get from Rob Parsons and Care for the Family is a strong dose of positive psychology that masquerades as Christian teaching on marriage and the family.

Nicky and Sila Lee (chapter 17), in *The Marriage Book*, create the impression by quoting from Scripture that the Bible actually teaches marriage is an equal-regard relationship between husband and wife. But the Lees have twisted Scripture by leaving out the verses that teach about the roles of husband and wife, and in doing so they have fundamentally altered the meaning of Scripture to justify their false teaching. The Lees enthusiastically promote the doctrines of positive psychology. They encourage their readers to talk about their feelings and to follow a therapeutic version of forgiveness that has nothing to do with the Christian faith.

Our study leaves little doubt that marriage education is a major route through which psychological theories enter the Church, hence the term 'marriage psycho-education'. Because the programmes revolve around marriage and relationships, and include an element of truth and a certain amount of common sense, it is easy to miss the amount of psychological theory that is being propagated. Indeed, many who attend a marriage education course have no idea that they are going to be taught the skills and tools of positive psychology.

The intellectual poverty of the 'Christian' marriage educators has been laid bear for all to see. Much of the advice is trite, trivial and utopian, for they are simply repackaging the concepts of humanistic psychology, and presenting them as some new discovery or profound secret. Placed alongside the wisdom of Scripture, the foolishness of their humanistic advice is obvious. The intense marketing efforts to promote their conferences, and sell their vast range of books and DVDs, suggests that the Christian marriage educators are making a great deal of money. Indeed, Smalley was open about the large amount of money that he has made through his 'ministry'. And so the obvious question: Is Christian marriage education a ministry or a business?

The Christian marriage educators are so closely aligned to the thinking of their secular colleagues that they are enthusiastically welcomed at the annual Smart Marriages conferences organised by Diane Sollee. We have seen that the 'Christian' marriage educators have joined themselves to the secular marriage education movement. What is the significance of this collaboration? The answer comes from Scripture.

Sin of syncretism

Israel was guilty of the great sin of syncretism, which is the merging of two religious systems. During Old Testament times God's people were frequently tempted to join themselves to the gods of the surrounding pagan nations, whilst still claiming to worship the LORD. The warning of Scripture is clear—those who worship other gods inevitably have their hearts turned away from the true God. It is not possible to truly worship the God of Scripture and the gods of the nations at the same time, for no man can serve two masters. Syncretism always results in separation from God—it was the great sin that fuelled Israel's idolatry and led to her eventual destruction.

The syncretism of the Christian marriage education movement is that it has turned away from the God of Scripture to the 'foreign gods' of humanistic psychology. It claims to honour the Bible, while interpreting it in the light of man-made psychological theories, which fundamentally distort biblical truth. Throughout this book we have seen clear evidence that the Christian marriage education movement is founded on a spirit of syncretism, whereby Christian marriage educators, such as Gary Smalley, Gary Chapman, Emerson Eggerichs, Rob Parsons, and Nicky and Sila Lee, have turned to the ideas of humanistic psychology and the techniques, tools and skills of positive psychology, and have brought these pernicious ideas into the Christian Church. Just as Israel attempted to worship *both* the LORD and foreign gods, so the Christian marriage education movement attempts to bring together two fundamentally opposed views of marriage.

The great sin of the Christian marriage education movement is syncretism. It has purposely and deliberately joined itself with the godless secular marriage education movement. It has purposely and deliberately brought together the holy with the profane, and in doing so has sinned against the character and holiness of God. By turning to the teachings of humanistic psychology, it has declared to the world that the teachings of Scripture are insufficient. By bringing the tools and skills of positive psychology into the Church, it is teaching that Christian believers need more than Christ for a life of holiness.

It is saying loud and clear to the unbelieving world that Christian couples need the tools and skills of positive psychology to achieve marital happiness.

But the message of Scripture is that we are complete in Christ. Scripture is sufficient, and all that a Christian couple need for a blessed married life is contained in Scripture. Scripture gives clear instruction for husband and wife, father and mother. Moreover, God gives the strongest warning that his people are not to join together with the works of darkness (2 Corinthians 6.14-18). Come out and be separate is the message of God, for believers are a holy nation, God's own special people (1 Peter 2.9). We do not need any man (*psychologist*) to teach us, for we have the Holy Spirit of God in our hearts (1 John 2.20). He will teach us all things and enlighten us with the wisdom of God (John 16.13). Therefore we must not follow the wisdom of man, which is puffed up and proud (1 Corinthians 3.18-19). We must beware the wisdom of the world – in this case, humanistic psychology – which is enmity against God (Romans 8.7).

How has the Church been so deceived?

We have seen the foolish, silly theories of the so-called 'Christian' marriage educators. The obvious question is this: How is it possible for Christian believers, in whom the Word of God dwells richly, who are indwelt by the Spirit of Truth, to sit and listen to the false wisdom that comes from the marriage education industry? How is it possible that Bible-believing churches, in both the UK and the USA, and also elsewhere, are promoting marriage psycho-education programmes like The Marriage Course of Holy Trinity Brompton and Essentials of Marriage of Focus on the Family? How is it possible that the writings of men like Gary Smalley, Gary Chapman, Emerson Eggerichs and Rob Parsons have become best-sellers among Christian people?

Itching ears

The apostle Paul answers these questions. He tells us that a time will come when many church-going men and women 'will not endure sound doctrine, but according to their own desires, because they have itching ears, they will heap up for themselves teachers; and they will turn their ears away from the truth, and be turned aside to fables' (2 Timothy 4.3-4). Today we live in such a time, a time when those in the Church who are nominal believers cannot get enough of the fables that come from the imposters of the Christian marriage education movement.

Failure to teach the biblical view of marriage

A major reason that true Christian believers are deceived by the marriage educators is that they no longer understand what the Bible teaches about marriage. And this is because many pulpits no longer teach the biblical view of marriage. Many pastors are reluctant to teach about marriage because they have long since themselves deserted the biblical view; and many are embarrassed by the issues of divorce and remarriage. As a consequence, teaching about marriage has passed from the pastor into the hands of the psychologist. The so-called marriage experts, both Christian and secular, are now virtually all psychologists, and it is widely accepted by Christian leaders that psychological research provides the answer to the secret of marital success. The shepherds of Christ's flock have left their sheep to be ravaged by the wolves (Acts 20.28-31).

The Church's silence on the doctrine of marriage means that the divine plan for marriage is not being taught. As a consequence most people, both believers and unbelievers, have little knowledge of what Scripture says about marriage. And it is into this vacuum in biblical teaching that the marriage education movement has so successfully moved with its psycho-education messages.

What needs to be done?

The Church needs to respond to the false teaching of the marriage education movement by actively doing four things.

Let us identify and expose false teaching

Scripture warns that Christians should expect false teachers to appear in their midst and many will follow their pernicious and deceitful teachings (2 Peter 2.1-2). Believers are instructed to 'Beware lest anyone cheat you through philosophy and empty deceit, according to the tradition of men, according to the basic principles of the world, and not according to Christ' (Colossians 2.8). Today the apostle Paul would undoubtedly warn against the empty deceit and false teaching of the marriage psycho-education movement. We should not be like children, 'tossed to and fro and carried about with every wind of doctrine, by the trickery of men, in the cunning craftiness of deceitful plotting' (Ephesians 4.14). With wisdom and discernment the elders and pastor of the local church, with their flock, should look carefully at what is being taught around the issue of marriage. Like the Bereans, all teaching should be examined against the Word of God to test its truthfulness (Acts 17.10-12). Any use of psychological terminology should arouse concern. Any programme that promotes self-improvement through the learning of man-made skills and tools must be condemned. Books and DVDs that claim to promote marriage education should be carefully reviewed, and a careful note made of those that promote the psychological way to self-improvement. Marriage seminars should be scrutinised and the congregation actively warned not to follow false teachers. Indeed, the pulpit should be bold enough to name false teachers and to warn against their books and seminars. A feature of false teachers is their interest in money, and also the slick marketing techniques they use to sell their goods. They must be actively exposed and opposed. The flock must be protected against wolves in sheep's clothing that promote the seductive theories of marriage psycho-education.

Let us avoid all contact

The Word of God is emphatic that false teachers and their teaching are not only to be exposed, but they and their teaching are to be strictly avoided. Members of the congregation should be taught to avoid all contact with the false teaching of the marriage psycho-educators. Let us avoid their books, together with their seminars and conferences. One effective means of reducing their impact is to deprive false teachers of monetary gain and celebrity status. We must also advise others of the biblical reasons for this strict avoidance. To do so will alert yet others to the falseness of what is being taught. Christian believers must separate themselves from false teaching as an active behaviour. This is a biblical duty clearly commanded in such texts as Matthew 7.15-20; Romans 16.17-18; 1 Timothy 6.3-5; 2 Timothy 3.5; 2 John 10-11.

Let pastors preach expository sermons

Pastors, who are the shepherds of God's flock, must feed the flock with sound doctrine and expository preaching, for the Holy Scriptures are 'profitable for doctrine, for reproof, for correction, for instruction in righteousness' (2 Timothy 3.16). Such teaching gives believers everything they need for life and godliness (2 Peter 1.3). The Church, which is the pillar and ground of the truth (1 Timothy 3.15), must reject the false teachings of the Christian marriage educators and teach the whole counsel of God (Acts 20.27), and this includes teaching about marriage from Scripture. The reason believers are taken in by false teaching is that they are not properly grounded in Scripture. Paul was astonished that the Galatians were so quickly thrown into confusion by false teachers, but it was because they deserted the truth and turned back to the weak and miserable principles of man-made wisdom. What did Paul do? He correctly taught them, warning that they should not be deceived (Galatians 1.6-7, 4.9, 6.7). So the role of the pastor, as the shepherd of the flock, is to teach the sheep the truths of Scripture, and to do so in a consistent and systematic manner. In this way he truly shepherds his flock, that they might not be led astray by the sweet-sounding call of a false teacher.

Let us provide everything needed

If not psychotherapy, marital counselling, or even marriage education, then what has the Church to offer to those who experience marital disharmony? What seems to have been forgotten in the takeover of the

Church by the psychotherapy industry, and its spin-off, marriage psycho-education, is the fact that God promises that he has provided *all things* that we need for life and godliness (2 Peter 1.3), including for marriage. All things mean just that, *all things*. The Christian counselling world and the Christian marriage educators, on the other hand, insist that we need more than the promises of God. We are asked to accept that the theories of modern psychology provide just what God is unable to supply. Marriage psychological counselling and its offshoot, marriage psycho-education, must therefore be recognised as a false Gospel.

What then are the 'all things' promised in 2 Peter 1.3 that we need for life and godliness? The 'all things' includes hearing God's Word preached; daily reading of Scripture and prayer, with personal confession of sin; Bible study; regular church attendance and worship; fellowship with other believers; avenues of service; pastoral discipline; discipleship; and witness. Through these God-given means of grace the Holy Spirit works to conform believers to the image of Christ and to build up the body of Christ on earth, the Church. Through obedience to God's Word, and the work of the Holy Spirit, the life of a believer is progressively conformed to the image of Christ. It is not always comfortable or easy; but it is God's way. Compared with the complexities of the psychological way, God's way is simple and spiritual—it has kept and blessed generations of godly believers long before the advent of modern psychology.

So, when a troubled married couple approach a pastor for help, he should say, 'Let this church, this faith, provide everything you need.' The troubled couple might be introduced to another married couple, who are godly, mature and experienced. They would come alongside the troubled couple and spend time with them, addressing not so much their 'problem' but most importantly their spiritual growth. The biblical meaning and purpose of marriage as a one-flesh union created by God would be explained. They would be told that as husband and wife, they are to work together to build the Church, and not to focus on themselves. By conversation, admonition and encouragement centred on the Word of God, by speaking the truth in love (Ephesians 4.15-16), and by relying upon the effectual work of the Holy Spirit, the couple can be provoked to love and good works (Hebrews 10.24). In this way their focus moves from themselves and their 'problem' to the Lord and his redemption.

Conclusion

We live in a day when a spiritual war is being waged within the Church. False teachers, who claim to be Christians, have infiltrated the Church and are teaching heretical doctrines. The contention of this book is that much of what passes for 'Christian' marriage education is, in fact, heresy. The current easy acceptance of the seductive theories of marriage psycho-education by the Church is surely a sign of God's judgement. By acquiescing in the godless teaching of the marriage education movement, the Church is putting its trust in the 'false gods' of secular humanism and modern psychology.

We live in perilous times when many have a form of godliness but deny the power and sufficiency of Scripture. The Church must again accept the sufficiency of Scripture as it teaches about marriage. The Church must remember again that God has indeed provided 'all things' that we need for life and godliness, for we are complete in Christ. Christian couples do not need marriage education, they need to study and live by God's Word. And finally, the Church must reject the false and heretical teachings of the Christian marriage educators and teach the whole counsel of God as it pertains to marriage.

(Endnotes)

1 Virginia Satir, *The New Peoplemaking*, Science and Behavior Books, 1988, p385
2 John Gottman and Nan Silver, *The Seven Principles for Making Marriage Work*, (first published 1999), paperback edition published by Orion Books, 2000, p2
3 Gary Smalley, *Secrets to Lasting Love*, Fireside, Simon & Schuster, 2001, p21
4 Emerson Eggerichs, *The Language of Love and Respect: Cracking the Communication Code with Your Mate*, Thomas Nelson, 2007, p 134

**For other books in Dr Williams'
trilogy on the influence of psychology
on the Christian faith see next pages**

The Dark Side of Christian Counselling

Published in 2009 by Wakeman and Belmont House Publishing

It is amazing how rapidly the Christian counselling movement has spread through churches in the UK, teaching that hurts and depressions once considered part of normal life are illnesses to be treated. It implies that for 1900 years the Bible has been insufficient for the woes of God's people, or for their sanctification, but that now we have the 'insights' of anti-Christian psychologists to make good the deficit.

In this book medical doctor Ted Williams challenges these claims, giving the most clear-cut and interesting overview of the counselling movement and of the giants of secular psychology who are pillars of its 'faith'.

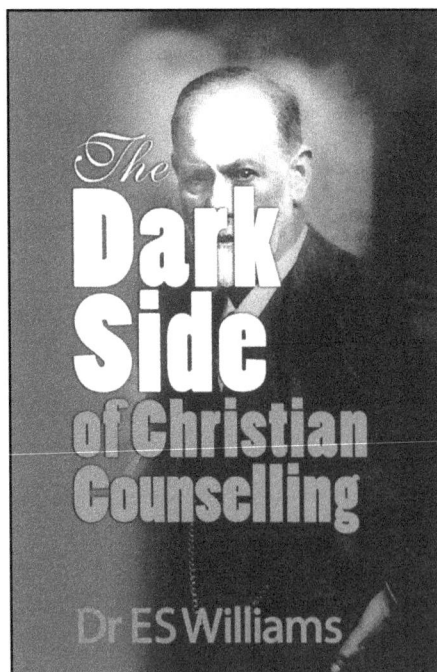

Christ or Therapy?

For Depression and Life's Troubles

Published in 2010 by Wakeman and Belmont House Publishing

It is not widely realised that there is an irreconcilable difference between the remedies for sadness and grief set out in the Bible, and those put forward by the world of psychotherapy. A gulf also exists between the biblical policy for marriage, and that proposed by secular marriage guidance psychologists. Many well-known evangelical authors and churches, however, have turned entirely to the secular remedies and policies in these matters. This book shows what the differences are, including a remarkable review of depression in the Bible, and its relief. This is the keenly awaited sequel to an earlier book – *The Dark Side of Christian Counselling* – by medical doctor Ted Williams.

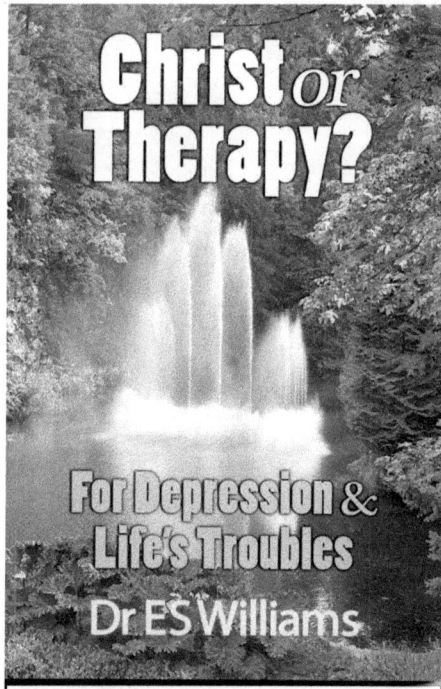

www.ingramcontent.com/pod-product-compliance
Lightning Source LLC
Chambersburg PA
CBHW060621070426
42447CB00040B/1360